The Symbolist Movement in Literature

Arthur Symons (1865–1945) was one of the most active editors, poets, critics and translators of the Victorian *fin de siècle*. He contributed to the *Yellow Book*, edited the *Savoy*, and translated works by Paul Verlaine, Stéphane Mallarmé and Emile Zola among others, as well as publishing several collections of his own poetry, including *Silhouettes* (1892) and *London Nights* (1895). His work is central to understanding the impact of Decadence and Symbolism on English literature. He was particularly influential on the early modernist writers, helping to introduce poets such as T.S. Eliot to nineteenth-century French literature. Although he lived until 1945, his later career was overshadowed by a mental breakdown he experienced in 1908.

Matthew Creasy is a lecturer in English literature at the University of Glasgow. He has published essays and articles on the work of James Joyce, William Empson and Virginia Woolf.

FyfieldBooks aim to make available some of the great classics of British and European literature in clear, affordable formats, and to restore often neglected writers to their place in literary tradition.

FyfieldBooks take their name from the Fyfield elm in Matthew Arnold's 'Scholar Gypsy' and 'Thyrsis'. The tree stood not far from the village where the series was originally devised in 1971.

> Roam on! The light we sought is shining still.
> Dost thou ask proof? Our tree yet crowns the hill,
> Our Scholar travels yet the loved hill-side

from 'Thyrsis'

Arthur Symons

The Symbolist Movement in Literature

Edited with an introduction by
Matthew Creasy

Fyfield*Books*

CARCANET

First published in Great Britain in 2014 by
Carcanet Press Limited
Alliance House
Cross Street
Manchester M2 7AQ

www.carcanet.co.uk

A CIP catalogue record for this book is available from the British Library

ISBN 978 1 84777 125 4

The publisher acknowledges financial assistance from Arts Council England

Typeset by XL Publishing Services, Exmouth
Printed and bound in England by SRP Ltd, Exeter

Contents

The Symbolist Movement in Literature

Acknowledgements

For permission to reproduce Symons' writings, thanks are due to Brian Read on behalf of the Literary Estate of Arthur Symons. Thanks for help and assistance are also due to staff at Glasgow University Library, the National Library of Scotland, the Moody and Jones Libraries at Baylor University and the British Library. I'm grateful to the School of Critical Studies at the University of Glasgow for a period of research leave in 2012 to complete this project. Gratitude is also due to Helen Tookey at Carcanet for editorial support and tolerance. Thanks also go to my wife and children for their love and patience while I was working on this volume.

Introduction

Some books change your life. In December 1908, while still an undergraduate in his junior year at Harvard, T.S. Eliot took down a new volume from the shelves of the Harvard Union. *The Symbolist Movement in Literature* by Arthur Symons contained eight essays on individual nineteenth-century French writers, from Gérard de Nerval to the Belgian dramatist Maurice Maeterlinck. Although Eliot was already studying French literature under Irving Babbitt, Symons' book was, he later recalled, 'a revelation':

> But if we can recall the time when we were ignorant of the French symbolists, and met with *The Symbolist Movement in Literature*, we remember that book as an introduction to wholly new feelings, as a revelation. After we have read Verlaine and Laforgue and Rimbaud and return to Mr. Symons' book, we may find that our own impressions dissent from his. The book has not, perhaps, a permanent value for the one reader, but it has led to results of permanent importance for him.[1]

Eliot's use of 'we' here is most likely editorial, but he was speaking for his peers too. For *The Symbolist Movement* was Symons' most popular book: Mary Colum describes how undergraduates in Dublin 'devoured' it,[2] amongst them James Joyce, whose biographer suggests that it set him reading and translating Paul Verlaine and packed him off to Paris at the end of 1902 in search of literary exile.[3] Mallarmé too was to prove a lifelong interest for Joyce because of *The Symbolist Movement*, and Ezra Pound would describe Symons as one of his 'gods' (along with Plato, Dante, Longinus and others) in 1911.[4]

1 T.S. Eliot, 'The Perfect Critic', in *The Sacred Wood* (London: Faber, 1920), p. 5.
2 Mary Colum, *Life and the Dream* (Dublin: Dolmen Press, 1966), p. 52.
3 Richard Ellmann, *James Joyce* (Oxford: Oxford University Press, 2nd edn, 1982), p. 76.
4 See David Hayman, *Joyce et Mallarmé: Stylistique de la suggestion*, 2 vols. (Paris: Lettres Modernes, 1956), pp. 28–32; G. Thomas Tanselle, 'Two Early Letters of Ezra Pound', *American Literature* 34:1 (1962), p. 118.

Eliot's criticisms of Symons, however, may also be representative. Although Joyce became indebted to Symons for aid
in publishing his first collection of poems, *Chamber Music*, he
expressed doubts about him privately. Eliot's sense of obligation
was strong enough for him to credit Symons on a number of
occasions, both in public and privately: he even made a point
of expressing his 'his peculiar debt of gratitude' directly, while
corresponding with Symons as editor of the *Criterion*.[5] But on each
occasion that he acknowledged Symons' influence in print, Eliot
qualified his praise, noting that 'it was a very good book for its
time', but expressing the hope that Peter Quennel's *Baudelaire and
the Symbolists* would render it obsolete;[6] remarking subsequently:
'as criticism I cannot say that Symons' book stands the test of time'.[7]
Eliot was scrupulous on these occasions to credit Symons with
stimulating his desire to read more about the writers discussed in
The Symbolist Movement ('it did make the reader want to read the
poets Mr. Symons wrote about'), but also to point out the limits
of Symons' study, observing the absence of Tristan Corbière from
the book and querying the inclusion of Villiers de l'Isle Adam and
Maeterlinck.[8]

Eliot's critical response to *The Symbolist Movement* both confirms
its importance and sheds some light on the relative neglect of
Symons' work in the twentieth century. While scholars are aware
of his work, Symons' writings have generally languished after their
brief period of popularity at the start of the twentieth century.
His prose has found a small amount of space in anthologies, but
otherwise remained out of print: this volume is the first new print
edition of *The Symbolist Movement* in over 50 years and the only
version to pay much attention to the accuracy of the text since
Symons first published it. This may be attributed to the kinds of
fault identified by Eliot: it may stem from the adverse effects upon

---

5 T.S. Eliot to Arthur Symons, 14 November 1923, in *The Letters of T.S. Eliot:
Volume 2. 1923–1925*, ed. Valerie Eliot and Hugh Haughton (Yale: Yale
University Press, 2009), p. 275. The first part of the letter rejects two short
stories by Symons for publication in the *Criterion*.

6 T.S. Eliot, 'Review of Peter Quennell *Baudelaire and the Symbolists*', *Criterion*
9 (January 1930), p. 357.

7 T.S. Eliot, 'Foreword', in Joseph Chiari, *Contemporary French Poetry* (1952),
quoted in *Inventions of the March Hare*, ed. Christopher Ricks (London: Faber,
1997), p. 402.

8 Eliot, '*Baudelaire and the Symbolists*', p. 357.

Symons' reputation after the mental breakdown he experienced in 1908, or it may be because Symons' status as a critic and poet of the *fin de siècle* fits poorly with some critical models of Modernist writing as a decisive break with its immediate precursors – models which are now being scrutinised and questioned.[9]

Dwelling retrospectively on his reservations, Eliot gives only limited credit to the intensity of his response to Symons' book when he first read it.[10] As they are preserved in the notebook known as *Inventions of the March Hare*, Eliot's early poems bristle with allusions to Jules Laforgue, the strongest immediate poetic influence upon Eliot at the time. But other poets discussed by Symons stimulated allusions, echoes and poetic re-workings too. And these allusions and influences converge: written in November 1909 and first published in the *Harvard Advocate* on 12 January 1910, the opening line of Eliot's early poem 'Humouresque' ('One of my marionettes is dead') borrows directly from the first line of the second stanza of 'Locutions des Pierrots' ('encore un de mes pierrots morts'), which Symons had quoted in full in *The Symbolist Movement*. But, as Christopher Ricks observes, Eliot's substitution of 'marionettes' for 'pierrots' is also indebted to Symons' discussion of Maeterlinck's use of masks and puppets in his Symbolist plays.[11] The confluence suggests the way in which Symons lies behind Eliot's encounter with both writers.

'Humouresque' is subtitled 'After J. Laforgue' and Eliot remained clear throughout his life about Laforgue's role in his discovery of a poetic voice at this formative period in his artistic career, noting that he 'was the first to teach me how to speak, to teach me the poetic possibilities of my own idiom of speech'.[12] But

---

9   See, for example, the brisk treatment Meredith Martin gives to clichéd accounts of Modernism's break with the nineteenth century in *The Rise and Fall of Meter: Poetry and English National Culture, 1860–1930* (Princeton: Princeton University Press, 2012), esp. pp. 2–5.

10 He took immediate action, travelling into Boston in search of a bookshop selling foreign texts, obtaining a copy of Adolphe van Bever and Paul Léautaud's anthology *Les Poètes d'aujourd'hui* (1908) and ordering the complete works of Jules Laforgue (he was, he reckoned afterwards, the first person in America to import them).

11 See Ricks' note to 'Conversation Galante', another of Eliot's poems invoking 'marionettes': *Inventions of the March Hare*, p. 103.

12 T.S. Eliot, 'What Dante Means to Me', in *To Criticise the Critic* (London: Faber, 1965), p. 126.

he gives little credit to Symons for shaping his understanding of Laforgue's distinctive poetic vocabulary, which Symons described as

> a kind of travesty, making subtle use of colloquialism, slang, neologism, technical terms for their allusive, their factitious, their reflected meanings, with which one can play, very seriously. The verse is alert, troubled, swaying, deliberately uncertain, hating rhetoric so piously that it prefers, and finds its piquancy in, the ridiculously obvious. It is really *vers libre*, but at the same time correct verse, before *vers libre* had been invented. (p. 54)

This might also be a description of 'The Love Song of J. Alfred Prufrock', with its shifting registers and vocabulary and the varying rhythms and line-lengths that embody the tortured self-consciousness of the speaker. Even the terms of Eliot's sense of 'revelation' at his first encounter with Laforgue through *The Symbolist Movement* may owe something to Symons, who describes Laforgue's prose as a 'discovery' (p. 56).

The influence runs deep: Symons' description of 'this art of Laforgue' as 'an art of the nerves [...] it is what all art would tend towards if we followed our nerves on all their journeys' (p. 57) helps provide Prufrock with a memorable image ('as if a magic lantern threw the nerves in patterns on a screen'), but also suggests a fragile sensibility that would echo in Eliot's other mature verse ('my nerves are bad tonight. Yes, bad') and sketches a restless urban impulse that informs the opening to 'Prufrock' ('Let us go then, you and I') and beyond. As Barry Faulk has argued, in teaching Eliot to read Laforgue, Symons may also have taught him how to read life in the modern metropolis.[13]

Eliot is undoubtedly right that Symons' book has its weaknesses: even Frank Kermode describes it as 'scrappy' and 'often disagreeably imprecise', while crediting Symons with a key role in the development of the Symbolist 'Image' in modern poetry.[14] *The Symbolist Movement* has a resonance within the twentieth century that includes Symons' role in prompting major figures such as

---

13 Barry Faulk, 'T.S. Eliot and the Symbolist City', in *A Companion to T.S. Eliot*, ed. David E. Chinitz (Oxford: Blackwell, 2009), pp. 31–32.
14 Frank Kermode, *Romantic Image* (London: Routledge and Kegan Paul, 1957; repr. 2002), pp. 127; 128–29.

Joyce and Eliot to read nineteenth-century poetry and form their own judgements, but its significance also extends beyond this. Murray Pittock, for example, has claimed that Symons' influence is not to be found in 'explicit endorsements, but in the amount of critical writing which agrees with its theoretic assumptions'.[15] *The Symbolist Movement*, then, does not simply mediate between French literature and English speakers; it mediates between the *fin de siècle* and Modernism.

★★★

Eliot is unlikely to have been ignorant of *The Symbolist Movement* before he read it. Although it was the first version published in the United States, the copy he picked up in the Harvard Union was not the first edition, which had been published in London eight years earlier. What's more, by the end of the nineteenth century, its author had a reputation as a Decadent poet as well as a critic. In 1895, reviewing Symons' second collection of poems, *London Nights*, an anonymous critic in the *Pall Mall Gazette* had dismissed him as 'a very dirty-minded man' who recorded his 'squalid and inexpensive amours' in verse.[16] His poem 'Stella Amaris', which purports to recall a one-night stand with a prostitute in terms invoking comparisons with the Virgin Mary, came in for particular censure.

His reputation in the 1890s as a Decadent writer may seem a long way from Symons' roots as the son of a dissenting Wesleyan minister and his first literary obsession with the works of Robert Browning. Encouraged in his literary pursuits early by a young schoolteacher, Charles Churchill Osbourne, Symons joined the Browning Society aged 16 and published an essay on 'Robert Browning as a Religious Poet' in the *Wesleyan-Methodist Magazine* aged 18. Through his new connections to the scholarly founder of the Browning Society, Frederick J. Furnivall, Symons then found editorial work, writing introductions to Shakespeare's plays and longer poems. This led to further editorial work with Havelock

---

15 Murray G.H. Pittock, *Spectrum of Decadence: The Literature of the 1890s* (London: Routledge, 1993), p. 70.

16 Quoted in Karl Beckson, *Arthur Symons: A Life* (Oxford: Clarendon Press, 1987), p. 118.

Ellis on the Mermaid Series of Elizabethan plays and a slow but steady succession of commissions to write reviews for literary periodicals in London then followed.

Although Symons' first book of published criticism was a study of Browning, a crucial and formative influence upon him at this time was the Oxford aesthete, Walter Pater, whose style was a conscious 'model' for Symons' own.[17] As he found increasing amounts of work writing for publications such as the *National Review*, so he obtained increasing access to literary circles. In June 1887 Symons reviewed Pater's *Imaginary Portraits* for the *Athenaeum*; the next year they began corresponding and met in person. Having read his review of Pater, Oscar Wilde contacted Symons, suggesting he contribute to *Woman's World*; Symons sent in poems and published his first essay on French literature there in 1889, an enthusiastic profile of Villiers de l'Isle-Adam (although Wilde was no longer editor by that point). Pater played an important role here too, as an exponent of European literature. Having written about eighteenth-century French art in *Imaginary Portraits*, Pater took an increasing interest in more recent French writers, encouraging Symons' own interests, and telling him that 'the present age' was 'an unfavourable one to poets, at least in England'.[18]

The year after he met Pater, in September 1889, Symons made his first journey to Paris in the company of Havelock Ellis. This short trip was followed by a longer visit the next year from March to June 1890, during which the two men met with major French writers including Stéphane Mallarmé, Paul Verlaine and J.-K. Huysmans, who were all to feature prominently in Symons' critical writings.

At about this time, Symons was encouraged to join the Rhymers' Club, a group of contemporary poets including W.B. Yeats, Ernest Dowson, and Lionel Johnson that met at the Cheshire

---

17 Symons to Churchill Osborne, 7 May 1885, in *Selected Letters*, ed. Karl Beckson and John M. Munro (London: Macmillan, 1989), p. 16.

18 Arthur Symons, 'Walter Pater', in *Figures from Several Centuries* (London: Constable, 1916), p. 327. This essay was originally published in the *Monthly Review* in 1906 and subsequently reprinted as an introduction to Pater's *Studies in the History of the Renaissance* in 1919. See also John J. Conlon, *Walter Pater and the French Tradition* (East Brunswick: Associated University Press, 1982), which describes how Pater's objectives as 'a public critic' included 'the propagation of knowledge about French thought and culture' (p. 10).

Cheese pub in London. Having published his first collection of poetry, *Days and Nights*, in 1889, he published *Silhouettes* in 1892, revising it in 1896 to add a selection of his own translations from Verlaine. Through such social and literary connections and his ongoing journalistic activities Symons began to make a name for himself, alongside George Moore and Edmund Gosse, as an exponent of French literary styles and influences in his own right. As French *décadence* caught the imagination of English writers, Symons contributed to the *Yellow Book*, and published his essay 'The Decadent Movement in Literature' in an American periodical, *Harper's New Monthly Magazine* during June 1893.[19] When the publishers of the *Yellow Book* fired Aubrey Beardsley for his risqué illustrations, in the wake of Wilde's prosecution for 'gross indecency' in 1895, Symons contrived with Beardsley and his publisher, Leonard Smithers, to start their own periodical, the *Savoy*. Although short-lived (only six issues appeared between January and December 1896), Symons managed to pack the *Savoy* with work by Ellis, Yeats, George Bernard Shaw, Max Beerbohm and Joseph Conrad (among others), as well as publishing his own essays, poetry and translations from Verlaine and Mallarmé. The final issue included an advertisement for a book-length critical study by Symons, *The Decadent Movement in Literature*. Scheduled for publication in 1897, this would not appear for three years and under a different title: although the title page says 1899, *The Symbolist Movement in Literature* was actually published on 5 March 1900, alongside another collection of poetry, *Images of Good and Evil*.

★★★

Symons' change of title is remarkable given that he had explicitly argued at the start of 'The Decadent Movement in Literature' that both Impressionism and Symbolism were subordinate to 'that new kind of literature which is perhaps more broadly characterised by the word Decadence' (p. 169). In contrast, *The Symbolist Movement* begins with a disparaging reference to 'something which is vaguely called Decadence' (p. 7) and the observation that 'no doubt perversity of form and perversity of matter are often found

19 Reproduced here in Appendix 1.

together' (p. 7). Symons does not merely fail to acknowledge his previous essay, he reverses his position. When the anonymous reviewer attacked *London Nights* four years previously in the *Pall Mall Gazette*, Symons had considered legal redress, then opted to answer his critic by writing a preface to the second edition in which he defended his right to depict any subject matter he chose. He attacked critics who had condemned the 'bad morality' of his poems, asserting 'the liberty of art':

> I deny that morals have any right of jurisdiction over it. Art may be served by morality, it can never be its servant. For the principles of art are eternal, while the principles of morality fluctuate with the spiritual ebb and flow of the ages.[20]

Although lacking Wilde's poise and wit, this defence of aesthetic over moral considerations recalls the preface to *The Picture of Dorian Gray* (1890) ('there is no such thing as a moral or an immoral book'), offering a hint of paradox in the insistence that it is morality that is relative and fluctuating rather than the 'principles of art'.

This was not a simple appeal for artistic freedom. In *The Symbolist Movement* he remarks dismissively that the term 'Decadence' is 'rarely used with any precise meaning' and is 'usually either hurled as a reproach or hurled back as a defiance' (p. 7). He might have been describing his own earlier self: as Denis Denisoff remarks, publishing 'The Decadent Movement in Literature' in 1893 had established Symons as 'the individual most devoted to explaining the workings of decadence to the English audience'.[21] In this context, his famous description of Decadence as 'a new and beautiful and interesting disease' may itself be construed as an act of 'defiance' in response to Richard Le Gallienne's dismissal of decadence as 'limited thinking, often insane thinking'.[22] Symons' rhythm and syntax suggest a conscious attempt to shock here, trotting out the word 'disease' as a kind of punch-line.

---

20 Arthur Symons, *London Nights* (London: Leonard Smithers, 2nd edn, 1897), pp. xiii–xiv.

21 Dennis Denisoff, 'Decadence and Aestheticism', in *The Cambridge Companion to the Fin de Siècle*, ed. Gail Marshall (Cambridge: Cambridge University Press, 2007), p. 38.

22 Quoted in Karl Beckson, *Arthur Symons: A Life* (Oxford: Clarendon Press, 1987), p. 95.

Even the adoption of the term 'Decadence' itself implies a reaction of some kind – a determination to turn a negative trait (decline) into an affirmation. This is clear from the immediate context of Symons' claim:

> [...] it has all the qualities that mark the end of great periods, the qualities that we find in the Greek, the Latin, decadence: an intense self-consciousness, a restless curiosity in research, an over-subtilising refinement upon refinement, a spiritual and moral perversity. If what we call the classic is indeed the supreme art – those qualities of perfect simplicity, perfect sanity, perfect proportion, the supreme qualities – then this representative literature of to-day, interesting, beautiful, novel as it is, is really a new and beautiful and interesting disease. (p. 169)

Having alluded to the formal characteristics of Decadence ('refinement'), Symons evokes a debate about the relative merits of classicism against romanticism, one that Modernists such as T.E. Hulme would revive twenty years later. His description of Decadence as a disease is offered, then, as an affirmation of its positive qualities *against* the model of 'the classic' as he describes it, indicating that his essay was reactive and defensive in precisely the manner he would later disparage.

This reactive quality is, however, part of the importance of Symons' earlier essay, which should not simply be seen as superseded by *The Symbolist Movement*. For behind a debate about literary terms, Symons is attempting what Nietzsche would call a transvaluation of values. Nietzsche's assault on what he perceived as the tyranny of false values imposed on society by Christianity is strongly rooted in an understanding that language and customary forms of speech play a significant role in imposing those values. This is clear from his famous description of 'truth' as 'a mobile army of metaphors, metonymies, anthropomorphisms':

> [...] truths are illusions of which we have forgotten that they are illusions, metaphors which have become worn by frequent use and have lost all sensuous vigour, coins which, having lost their stamp, are now regarded as metal and no longer as coins.[23]

23 Friedrich Nietzsche, 'On Truth and Lying in a Non-Moral Sense', in *The Birth of Tragedy and Other Writings*, trans. Ronald Speirs, ed. Raymond Geuss (Cambridge: Cambridge University Press, 1999), p. 146.

In comparison, when Symons subordinates Impressionism and Symbolism to Decadence, he argues that what they have in common is their 'revolt from ready-made impressions and conclusions, a revolt from the ready-made of language, from the bondage of traditional form, of a form become rigid' (pp. 170–71). Symons claims Impressionism achieves this through a fidelity to the immediacy of the senses and experience, whereas Symbolism accesses through symbols intuitions of those aspects of experience which escape direct expression through language. Decadence, for Nietzsche, meant cultural decline: at best, the work of French Decadents offered diagnosis of this.[24] In contrast, Symons presents it as a capacity (uniting Symbolism and Impressionism) within art to resist decline through a resistance to verbal lassitude. In this respect, he confirms Linda Dowling's argument in *Language and Decadence in the Fin de Siècle* (1986) that the shocking power of Decadence lies within language itself. The disquiet expressed by critics of Decadence about the morals of its practitioners becomes an unease about the effect of its linguistic transformations upon the 'traditional forms' of moral expression.

★★★

Had Symons sustained this robust level of argument, he might be more clearly seen as anticipating Modernist attitudes towards language and cliché in the writings of, say, Bergson and Hulme. But the reversal in *The Symbolist Movement* is complete and Decadence is relegated to an 'interlude – half a mock-interlude':

> It pleased some young men in various countries to call themselves Decadents, with all the thrill of unsatisfied virtue masquerading as uncomprehended vice. As a matter of fact, the term is in its place only when applied to style; to that ingenious defor- mation of the language, in Mallarmé for instance, which can be compared with what we are accustomed to call the Greek and Latin of the Decadence. No doubt perversity of form and perversity of matter are often found together, and, among the lesser men especially, experiment was carried far, not only in the direction of style. (p. 7)

---

24 See Friedrich Nietzsche, *The Twilight of the Gods*, trans. Duncan Large (Oxford: Oxford University Press, 1998), pp. xx–xxi.

Where Symons had previously positioned 'Decadence' as an over-arching term, its range here is severely curtailed, not simply to 'style', but to a highly specific form of style associated with Mallarméan obscurities. Symons drops any pretention that Decadence might shatter convention, falling back upon conventional moral language himself ('virtue... vice') and insinuating that departure from moral conventions might be weakness ('lesser men'). Little wonder, then, that some critics have understood Symons' rejection of Decadence in favour of Symbolism as a pragmatic response to Wilde's persecution for his sexuality in 1895 and a retreat from his previous defence of liberty in his choice of subject matter. On this reading Decadence was too dangerous to espouse, too open to censorship.[25]

There are points of continuity, though, between Symons' writings. His denunciation of 'lesser' writers for example echoes his previous disdain for 'separate cliques, noisy, brainsick young people who haunt the brasseries of the Boulevard Saint-Michel, and exhaust their ingenuities in theorising over the works they cannot write' (p. 169).[26] Accordingly, it's important to realise that Symons' critical writings have limited value as literary history. For, beyond the accounts he gives of individual authors, his reference to the existence of *le décadence* and *le symbolisme* in France are confined to disparaging remarks about 'busy little *littérateurs* who are founding new *revues* every other week in Paris':

> These people have nothing to say, but they are resolved to say something, and to say it in the newest mode. They are Impressionists because it is the fashion, Symbolists because it is the vogue, Decadents because Decadence is in the very air of the cafés. (p. 177)

Jean Moréas, author of the manifesto 'Le Symbolisme', is mentioned only to belittle his poetic vanity for pursuing excessive line lengths; Gustave Kahn features only in passing references; and

---

25 See, for example, R.K.R. Thornton, *The Decadent Dilemma* (London: Edward Arnold, 1983), p. 34; Pittock, *Spectrum of Decadence*, pp. 70–71; and Joseph Bristow, '"Sterile Ecstasies": The Perversity of the Decadent Movement', in *The Ends of Epochs: Essays and Studies 1995* (Cambridge: D.S. Brewer, 1995), pp. 65–88.

26 Symons discerns a similar resistance to 'schools' within 'Crise de vers' in his essay on Mallarmé (p. 69).

none of the contemporary journals associated with these movements receives any detailed treatment. Symons' understanding of the term 'movement', then, is ideal and largely retrospective: of the writers he discusses: only Maeterlinck and Huysmans were alive when the first edition of *The Symbolist Movement* was published and Huysmans died shortly before the second edition appeared in 1908.

In bibliographical notes at the end of the book, Symons identifies his concern with 'ideas rather than with facts'; each essay, he suggested, 'is a study of a problem, only in part a literary one, in which I have endeavoured to consider writers as personalities under the action of spiritual forces, or as themselves so many forces' (p. 218). This reference to 'spiritual forces' indicates the most significant shift between 'The Decadent Movement' and *The Symbolist Movement*. Previously, he had described Symbolism as a matter of 'intuition': 'The Symbolist, in this new, sudden way, would flash upon you the "soul" of that which can be apprehended only by the soul – the finer sense of things unseen, the deeper meanings of things evident' (p. 170). Subsequently his terms changed:

> It is all an attempt to spiritualise literature, to evade the old bondage of rhetoric, the old bondage of exteriority. Description is banished that beautiful things may be evoked, magically; the regular beat of verse is broken in order that words may fly, upon subtler wings. (p. 8)

This passage from Symons' introduction to *The Symbolist Movement* crystallises several of its central concerns and draws from the terms he uses elsewhere in the book to describe his chosen writers. The reference to 'rhetoric' in this passage preserves the vestiges of Symons' previous argument about 'the ready-made of language', but it now reverberates with his own description of Verlaine's formal revolution and mastery of *vers impairs* elsewhere in the volume. Before Verlaine, Symons observes, French verse was an admirable vehicle for 'a really fine, a really poetical, kind of rhetoric' (p. 45). The word 'exteriority' has a similar resonance, recalling Villiers de l'Isle-Adam's rejection of positivism and materialist philosophies as 'that old exteriority' in favour of idealism, quoted by Symons from *Axël*.

On this reading, Symbolism no longer 'flashes' intuitions, it 'evokes' – a curiously intransitive term at times for Symons, associated with Mallarmé, whose gift was, he suggests, 'to evoke, by some elaborate, instantaneous magic of language' (p. 68). However, where he had previously referred to 'the deeper meaning of things evident', in *The Symbolist Movement* Symons refers repeatedly to 'the spiritual world' or 'the spiritual universe'. Hence Tom Gibbons' description of Symons' appeal to these 'spiritual forces' as 'amongst others things a public declaration of conversion' to a new faith in mysticism.[27]

Symons was explicit about this new direction ('I speak often in this book of Mysticism'), in dedicating the volume to Yeats, whom he anticipates as a 'perfectly sympathetic reader' (p. 4). The two men met in 1890 through the Rhymers' Club and ended up sharing lodgings during 1895 at Symons' apartments in Fountain Court within Temple, the legal district of London. During 1896 they travelled together, to Ireland and to Paris, where they attended a performance of Alfred Jarry's controversial play, *Ubu roi*. Yeats had very poor skills in the French language and, reflecting on their friendship twenty-five years later, acknowledged his debt to Symons for reading and translating Verlaine and Mallarmé to him.[28]

In return, Yeats shared his own reading in mysticism with Symons: he had taken a keen interest in Spiritualism and Theosophy since helping to found the Dublin Hermetic Order in 1885 and in 1890 became an active member of the mystical organisation, the Order of the Golden Dawn, under the charismatic leadership of MacGregor Mathers (author of *The Kabbalah Unveiled* (1887)).[29] Indeed, on their trip to Ireland, the two men came to believe during a stay at Tillyra Castle in August 1896 that Yeats' attempts to invoke 'lunar forces' had inspired Symons with his own visionary dream of a female figure, related to the Goddess Diana.[30] Yeats' correspondence confirms his role in Symons' burgeoning interest

---

27 Tom Gibbons, *Rooms in the Darwin Hotel: Studies in English Literary Criticism and Ideas 1880–1920* (Nedlands: University of Western Australia Press, 1973), p. 68.

28 W.B. Yeats, *The Trembling of the Veil* (1922), in *Autobiographies* (London: Macmillan, 1955), pp. 319–22.

29 See Roy Foster, *W.B. Yeats: A Life. The Apprentice Mage, 1865–1914* (Oxford: Oxford University Press, 1997), pp. 89–111.

30 'Biographical and Historical Appendix', in *The Collected Letters of W.B. Yeats: Volume 2 1896–1900*, ed. Warwick Gould, John Kelly and Deidre Toomey (Oxford: Clarendon Press, 1997), pp. 658–63.

in mysticism. On 10 December 1897, he wrote to George Russell
that

> Symons is becoming more & more of a mystical writer. He is
> writing now about a French Mystic who 'lost the whole world
> & gained his own soul' or in other words went mad. He is living
> almost a strict life too.[31]

This 'French Mystic' is Gérard de Nerval, subject of the first essay
in *The Symbolist Movement*, originally published in the *Fortnightly
Review* in 1898 and quoted here. Yeats' letter is suggestive about
Symons' decision to place the essay on Nerval at the start of the
book, both establishing Nerval's historical role as a Romantic
precursor to the Symbolist Movement and providing an immediate connection with the importance of mystical concerns to the
collection as a whole.

The timing of Yeats' letter provides some perspective on
the process of Symons' interest in mysticism. But his increasing
interest in related topics is also witnessed by the particular aspects
of his chosen writers that Symons singles out. For example, where
Symons had discussed Maeterlinck's drama in 'The Decadent
Movement', his essay 'Maeterlinck as a Mystic' in *The Symbolist
Movement* addresses the Belgian author's prose writings, specifically
Le Trésor des humbles. In *The Symbolist Movement*, Symons memo-
rably describes *À Rebours* as 'the breviary of the decadence' (p. 73),
consolidating a comparison he had first made in an article from
1892, where he describes Des Esseintes, Huysmans' protagonist,
as

> [...] a type rather than a man: he is the offspring of the Decadent
> art that he adores, and this book a sort of breviary for its worship-
> pers. It has a place of its own in the literature of the day, for it
> sums up, not only a talent, but a spiritual epoch.[32]

In contrast, *The Symbolist Movement* examines those novels written
after *À Rebours* (some of which had admittedly not been published
in 1892), detailing Huysmans' return to Catholicism. Symons

---

31 Yeats, *Collected Letters 2*, p. 154.
32 Arthur Symons, 'J.K. Huysmans', *Fortnightly Review* 51:303 (March 1892),
   p. 412. Symons added this essay to *The Symbolist Movement* in 1919 and it is
   included here in Section II.

concentrates in particular upon *La Cathédrale* and Huysmans' fasci-nation with the cathedral at Chartres as place of worship, art object and symbol.

The sequence of Symons' writings confirms Yeats' under-standing of his interest in mystical questions as ongoing. This shift in perspective even affects the resonance of Walter Pater. Previously, 'The Decadent Movement' had compared Pater and W.E. Henley with their French contemporaries, but *The Symbolist Movement* does not discuss any writers in English. Pater's influence is, however, felt throughout the volume through passing allu-sions (Symons is fond of citing passages cited fondly by Pater) and within its rhythmic, repetitive prose style, particularly in Symons' conclusion to the volume, which begins:

> Our only chance, in this world, of a complete happiness, lies in the measure of our success in shutting the eyes of the mind, and deadening its sense of hearing, and dulling the keenness of its apprehension of the unknown. (p. 88)

This clearly echoes Pater's declaration in his 'Conclusion' to *Studies in the History of the Renaissance* that, given the brevity of human life, 'our one chance is in expanding that interval, in getting as many pulsations as possible into the given time'. The answer for Pater lies in 'the love of art for art's sake' which promises 'frankly to give nothing but the highest quality to your moments as they pass'.[33] As Patricia Clements points out, Symons owes a clear 'formal debt' to Pater, both in terms of style and in terms of his preoccupation with mortality and the consequences of humanity's awareness of its mortality. But, as Clements observes, these echoes also serve to emphasise the difference between their conclusions.[34] Pater advocates a sensual indulgence in 'pulsations' and values art as a means of amplifying pleasure and thus lengthening lived experi-ence. But Symons values Symbolism in art as a source of ex-stasis: instead of amplifying sensation or pleasure, it aids us to 'realise the infinite insignificance of action, its immense distance from the current of life [...] On this theory alone does all life become

33 Walter Pater, *Studies in the History of the Renaissance*, ed. Matthew Beaumont (Oxford: Oxford University Press, 2010), pp. 120–21.
34 Patricia Clements, *Baudelaire and the English Tradition* (New Haven: Princeton University Press, 1985), pp. 203–205.

worth living, all art worth making, all worship worth offering'
(p. 90). Given Symons' previous reputation as a poet and critical advocate of Decadence, the unfolding of the latter sentence
must have surprised some readers, as it moves from 'life' to 'art'
to 'worship'. The distance from Pater, his mentor and stylistic
model, is pronounced and his newfound interest in mysticism
given prominence.

★★★

The reference to Symons' essay on Nerval in Yeats' letter provides
a reminder of the volume's origins in his prolific career as a literary
journalist. During 1898, for example, he published 45 contributions to journals and periodicals, a pamphlet on Aubrey Beardsley
and a translation of *L'Aube* by Émile Verhaeren. All of the essays in
The Symbolist Movement, except for the introduction and conclusion, had been published previously in periodicals, as Symons'
changing response to Huysmans confirms. Where Symons lauds *À
Rebours* in 'The Decadent Movement', his focus on *La Cathédrale*
in *The Symbolist Movement* can partly be attributed to the fact that
considerable portions of the text derive from his review of that
novel, in the *Saturday Review* on 12 February 1898. The title of this
article, 'M. Huysmans' New Novel', betrays its responsive nature,
pointing to the role that occasion and external events may have
played in the shaping of Symons' book.

The influence of occasion upon Symons' criticism includes
the outlets available to him for journalistic publication. He wrote
another twenty articles and reviews for the *Saturday Review* in 1898
and had published three other pieces on Huysmans in previous
years, including the account of *À Rebours* in 'The Decadent
Movement' and a previous article on 'M. Huysmans as Mystic'
for the *Saturday Review* in 1895. So it is possible that the eventual
shape of his essay on Huysmans in *The Symbolist Movement* was
determined by the commissioning editor at the *Saturday Review*
who asked Symons to cover Huymans's latest book, as a regular
contributor with a reputation for writing about French topics.

The *Saturday Review* played an important role here more
generally, for the essays on Mallarmé, Rimbaud, Verlaine and
Laforgue were also first published there or contain material that

appeared there. At first glance, this may seem surprising, for the *Saturday Review* had been established in 1855 by Alexander James Beresford Beresford Hope, MP, to cover important political, social and cultural issues exclusively in reviews and leading articles. It appeared weekly in order to offer a more regular, responsive alternative to older, established monthly periodicals such as the *Edinburgh Review* and *Quarterly Review*. Remarkably successful, by 1868 its weekly circulation exceeded 10,000, becoming 'an index of leading critical opinion and [...] an influence upon literary taste', according to Merle Bevington.[35] This conservative vessel for 'the voice of the educated upper middle class' does not sound like an ideal venue for a writer, such as Symons, associated with an advanced, transgressive and foreign movement such as Decadence or Symbolism.[36]

In 1894, however, the magazine was bought by charismatic, Irish-born American editor and journalist Frank Harris for £560.[37] Prior to this, in the 1880s, the *Saturday Review* had become moribund, sustained only by the remnants of its reputation from the 1860s. The period of Walter Herries Pollock's editorship from 1883 to 1894 had been one of 'steady decline'.[38] But Symons' first contributions to the *Saturday Review* coincide exactly with the arrival of Harris: he may even have been deliberately brought in to help with the magazine's renewal, as part of a team of young, bright journalistic contributors that included H.G. Wells, George Bernard Shaw and Max Beerbohm.

Laurel Brake has described Harris's instrumental role in publishing work by Walter Pater and Oscar Wilde previously in *The Fortnightly Review*, pointing out that Wilde first published 'The Truth of Masks' and 'Pen, Pencil, and Poison' there under Harris's editorship. He was, Brake suggests, open to 'Wilde's libertine, provocative and light-hearted defence of the aesthetic perfection

---

35 Merle Mowbray Bevington, *The Saturday Review 1855–1868: Representative Educated Opinion in Victorian England* (New York: Columbia University Press, 1941), p. vii.

36 Francesca Benatti, 'The Saturday Review', in *Dictionary of Nineteenth-Century Journalism*, ed. Laurel Brake and Marysa Demoor (London: British Library, 2009), p. 558.

37 Philippa Pullar, *Frank Harris: A Biography* (New York: Simon and Schuster, 1976), p. 170.

38 Bevington, *The Saturday Review*, p. 323.

of the life of a murderer and forger'.[39] More generally, his liber-
alism as editor was amenable to French literature. The period of
his editorship at the *Saturday Review*, then, gave Symons an outlet
for his own material of this kind.

Confronted with a literary text in the singular form of a book,
it can be easy to overlook the diverse factors of this kind which
went into its making. This is a general truth that book historians and genetic critics have been unpicking for decades now,
by exploring the fluid textual processes that lead from an author's
creative decisions to the production of a book and all the agents
that may intervene and shape those processes, from publishers to
printers and even prospective readers. As Laurel Brake has shown,
however, these considerations are heightened when it comes to
the genre to which *The Symbolist Movement* belongs:

> [...] the production process whereby writing is translated from
> the ephemeral of the periodical essay into the permanence of
> the book engineers the obscuring of the ephemeral character-
> istics and, most important, origins, even to the original readers
> of the book.[40]

The history of the *Saturday Review*, however, suggests that – in this
case, at least – some knowledge of the pre-history of the essays in
The Symbolist Movement sheds light on the conditions that made
it possible as a book. As a jobbing writer, Symons clearly needed
the income from his journalistic activities, but the *Saturday Review*
seems also to have provided a useful ideological and aesthetic
outlet for the development of his response to contemporary
French writers.

Brake is motivated, though, by the way that such transformations lie at the heart of key critical texts from the nineteenth
century: both Matthew Arnold's *Culture and Anarchy* (1869) and
Walter Pater's *The Renaissance* (1877) began life as articles or essays
published in periodicals. Brake's concern is that book publication
may 'obscure' the fractured origins of these apparent monoliths of
Victorian critical thinking. But this seems to have been precisely
Symons' intention: his previous volume of criticism, *Studies in Two*

---

39 Laurel Brake, *Subjugated Knowledges: Journalism, Gender and Literature in the
   Nineteenth Century* (New York: New York University Press, 1994), pp. 67–68.
40 Brake, *Subjugated Knowledges*, p. 66.

Literatures, included an explicit acknowledgement that its contents originated in periodical essays and reviews.[41] No such acknowledgement is found in *The Symbolist Movement*, even though its origins are diverse: the essays on Rimbaud, Laforgue, Huysmans, Verlaine and Mallarmé all derive from material that appeared in the *Saturday Review*, but Symons' essays appeared there at intervals over four years. The essay on Huysmans, for example, knits together material from the *Saturday Review* published in March 1895 and February 1898 and the essay on Mallarmé yokes material published on separate occasions, January 1897 and November 1898, in different publications – the *Saturday Review* and *Fortnightly Review* respectively.

The coherence of *The Symbolist Movement* as a volume rests on the period during 1898 and 1899 when Symons began compiling and revising his material. As the project neared completion and Symons received proofs from his publisher, William Heinemann, he wrote to Yeats in June 1899:

> I have rewritten the Laforgue essay, and am in all haste to start on the Rimbaud; and I am even contemplating a new essay on Huysmans – besides the Introduction, and some enlarging of the Villiers. And the book should appear in September![42]

His work on Laforgue mostly involved moving bibliographical information from the body of the essay to the notes at the back of the volume, and adding the extensive direct quotations from Laforgue that appealed so strongly to Eliot's imagination. But elsewhere, Symons clearly took steps to smooth out traces of the journalistic occasions for his original articles. His essay on Verlaine derived largely from an obituary article published on 11 January 1896, three days after the poet's death. For *The Symbolist Movement*, Symons altered a phrase which began 'two years ago' so that it referred in less relative fashion to 1894, eradicating these 'ephemeral characteristics'.

Other changes speak to the general themes of the book. In 1898, Symons had generalised about the 'visionary' insights granted by Nerval's experience of mental illness: 'with the approach of night,

---

41 Arthur Symons, *Studies in Two Literatures* (London: Leonard Smithers, 1897), p. x.
42 To W.B. Yeats, mid-June 1899 (*Selected Letters*, pp. 130–31).

even the most sordid and short-sighted of us becomes a little visionary'.[43] A year later, his 'visionary' terms had shifted subtly: 'with the approach of night, is not every one a little readier to believe in the mystery lurking behind the world?' (pp. 12–13). It can be seen from this that the essay where Yeats found the beginnings of Symons' interests in mysticism is, in its publication history, a palimpsest of his increasing receptivity to 'mystery'. Symons is not simply smoothing away the origins of his material here, but attempting to work out his central claim for the occult status of Symbolism as an aesthetic and a movement.

★★★

Laurel Brake's work on Pater and Arnold helps to confirm that Symons is embedded in nineteenth-century critical practice – both in his activities as a journalist and his attempt to preserve his criticism in the less 'ephemeral' form of a book. The journalistic origins of *The Symbolist Movement in Literature*, then, are inseparable from its status as a work that mediates both between French and English writings and between the nineteenth and twentieth centuries. They help to connect the contents of Symons' work with the historical and cultural conditions under which it was produced.

This is one of the reasons that Symons' book remains important to readers today. Read and absorbed by Eliot and his contemporaries, *The Symbolist Movement* remains a key source for our understanding of the influence of nineteenth-century French writers upon Modernism, but it is also valuable in its own right as an intervention in late nineteenth-century debates about the value and nature of Symbolism and Decadence, and it is an important witness to critical practice in that period too.

Of course it is not without faults: Symons may not have been wholly successful in forging coherence out of his materials; his understanding of Symbolism is highly individual; and his intimations of mystic truths can be very ambiguous. Upon its publication in 1900, an anonymous reviewer in the *Athenaeum* began by praising *The Symbolist Movement* for being 'charmingly written',

---

43 Arthur Symons, 'The Problem of Gérard de Nerval', *Fortnightly Review* 63 (January 1898), p. 84.

but then confessed to experiencing difficulties: 'We have been unable to extract from what he has written any very lucid or consistent account of what symbolism is supposed to be, or of how it is related to mysticism'.[44] Even Yeats found it 'curiously vague in its philosophy', although he praised it as 'really very fine criticism'.[45] Symons' publisher was also cautious, printing a first run of only 750 copies (his first book, *An Introduction to the Study of Browning*, had a print run of 2000 copies).[46]

And yet the book sold 250 copies in less than three weeks, bringing Symons temporary celebrity (Mary Colum describes it as the topic of a public debate at University College, Dublin). This popularity spread across the globe: the second edition published in 1908 by Archibald Constable was simultaneously printed in America by E.P. Dutton. There was sufficient demand for the book in America to merit a reprint only two years later. By this time, however, Symons was in a poor condition to benefit: he experienced a mental breakdown while on holiday in Italy during 1908 and although he made an eventual recovery, his career and reputation did not. Other factors no doubt played their role, but it is hard to exclude the stigma associated with mental illness from the general neglect of Symons' works that followed; and the publication of this volume is in part an invitation to see and reassess his criticism in the original contexts outlined here. *The Symbolist Movement in Literature* will always be remembered as the book which influenced T.S. Eliot, but its engagement with French writing of the nineteenth century, its place within late nineteenth-century critical practice and its exploration of Symbol and revolutionary poetic forms all repay closer scrutiny.

44 [Unsigned] 'Poetry and Mysticism', *Athenaeum* (24 March 1900), pp. 360–61.
45 To Lady Gregory, 29 March 1900 (*Letters*, II, p. 506).
46 Beckson, *A Life*, p. 193.

A Note on the Text and Annotations

Section I of this edition reprints the text of the second edition of *The Symbolist Movement in Literature*, published by Constable in 1908. This is substantially the same as the text of the first edition published by Leonard Smithers in 1899, except that it incorporates some minor corrections and one major change: Symons added considerable material to his essay on Huysmans and changed its title from 'Huysmans as a Symbolist' to 'The Later Huysmans' to reflect, as his endnote records, the emphasis upon that particular phase of Huysmans' career.

The 1908 text has been chosen as a text corrected by Symons and because it formed the basis of the first American edition of *The Symbolist Movement* published by E.P. Dutton in the same year; hence the historical value of that edition as the book that T.S. Eliot encountered in the library of the Harvard Union in 1908.

I have supplied translations to French phrases and texts where the sense may not be obvious from the context. Prose translations of poems are my own unless otherwise noted.

Section II supplies the essays that Symons added to *The Symbolist Movement in Literature* for the 1919 edition. Original publication information is provided in the notes at the back of the book.

Appendix 1 reproduces the text of Symons' essay 'The Decadent Movement in Literature' as it first appeared in *Harper's New Monthly Magazine* during 1893.

Appendix 2 supplies the translations from Mallarmé and Verlaine that Symons added to the 1919 edition.

The Notes section includes Symons' original endnotes, which contain reference to contemporary translations of his chosen writers, followed by my own annotations providing detail about sources quoted by Symons and unfamiliar points of reference.

The glossary provides information about writers cited by Symons and expands on some key terms relevant to the essays in this book.

The bibliography includes details of English translations of the Symbolist writers as well as works on Symons and general suggestions for further reading.

The Life of Arthur Symons

1865   Arthur Symons born.

1882   Publishes his first article (on Robert Browning), aged 17.

1884   Begins editing Shakespeare for Frederick J. Furnivall.

1886   Publishes his first book of criticism, *An Introduction to the Study of Browning*.

1888   Meets Walter Pater in Oxford.

1889   Publishes his first collection of poetry, *Days and Nights*; makes his first visit to Paris with Havelock Ellis.

1890   Rhymers' Club founded; Symons becomes an member and meets W.B. Yeats; Symons and Ellis return to Paris, where he meets Huysmans, Verlaine and Mallarmé, as well as Irish writer George Moore; Symons becomes editor of the *Academy* (briefly); he begins an inconclusive five-year relationship with Katherine Willard (she is engaged to another man).

1891   Moves into Fountain Court; travels through Provence and Spain with Ellis, and visits Germany for the first time.

1892   *The Book of the Rhymers' Club* (Symons contributes four poems); Symons writes reviews for the *Star, St James Gazette* and *Athenaeum*; publishes *Silhouettes*; *The Minister's Call* produced by the Independent Theatre Society.

1893   Verlaine visits England and lectures in London (where he stays with Symons) and Oxford; Symons becomes involved with 'Lydia'; 'The Decadent Movement in Literature'.

1894   First issue of the *The Yellow Book* (includes 'Stella Maris' by Symons); Symons translates *L'Assommoir* by Zola.

1895   Yeats and Symons share rooms in Fountain Court; Symons publishes *London Nights*; Symons issues then withdraws a writ against *Pall Mall Gazette* claiming damages for a hostile review of *London Nights*; Symons meets with Leonard Smithers and Aubrey Beardsley in Dieppe to plan the *Savoy*.

1896   First issue of the *Savoy* published (January); Symons travels to Ireland with Yeats in the Summer; Symons and Yeats visit Paris where they see a performance of Albert Jarry's *Ubu Roi*; in December the last issue of the *Savoy* includes an advert for *The Decadent Movement in Literature*; Symons visits Rome, meets writer and politician Gabriele D'Annunzio and his mistress, the actress Eleonora Duse.

1897   Symons publishes *Amoris Victima* (narrating his extended affair with 'Lydia').

1898   Symons meets Rhoda Bowser (later his wife); he works on *The Symbolist Movement* while travelling in France and Spain.

1899   Sends draft of 'Introduction' to *The Symbolist Movement* to Yeats in June, while working on the proofs.

1900   Publishes *The Symbolist Movement in Literature* and *Images of Good and Evil*.

1901   Marries Rhoda Bowser and moves out of Fountain Court; *The Loom of Dreams*.

1902   Symons and his wife make an extended tour of Europe; *Poems* (in two volumes).

1903   Attends a reading of J.M. Synge's *Riders to the Sea*.

1904   Meets John Quinn, New York lawyer and major patron of the arts; meets James Joyce in London to help with publication of his first collection of poems; publishes *Studies in Verse and Prose*.

1905   Publishes semi-autobiographical short stories, *Spiritual Adventures*.

1906   *The Fool of the World and Other Poems* and *Studies in Seven Arts*.

1907   *William Blake* and *Cities of Italy*.

1908   Second edition of *The Symbolist Movement in Literature* (simultaneously published in the USA); Symons suffers nervous breakdown in Italy. He is brought home under supervision, certified as insane and committed to Brooke House in London.

1909   Doctors tell Symons' wife, Rhoda, that there is no chance of his recovery; *Dante Gabriel Rossetti* and *The Romantic Movement in English Poetry*.

1910   Symons is allowed to leave Brooke House and moves to Island Cottage under his wife's supervision; Joseph Conrad visits Symons at Island Cottage; Symons starts to show signs of recovery.

1913   *Knave of Hearts*.

1916   *Figures of Several Centuries*.

1918   *Colour Studies in Paris*.

1919   *Studies in Elizabethan Drama*.

1920   *Charles Baudelaire: A Study* and *Lesbia and Other Poems*.

1923   *Love's Cruelty* and *Dramatis Personae*.

1924   *Collected Works*.

1925   *Studies in Modern Painters* and *Notes on Joseph Conrad*.

1927   *Parisian Nights* and *Eleonora Duse*.

1929   *Studies in Strange Souls* and *From Toulouse-Lautrec to Rodin*.

1930   *Confessions* and *A Study of Oscar Wilde*.

1931   *Jezebel Mort and Other Poems* and *Wanderings*.

1932   *A Study of Walter Pater*.

1936   Death of Rhoda Symons.

1948   Death of Arthur Symons.

The Symbolist Movement in Literature

Section I
Essays Included in the 1908 Edition

To W.B. Yeats[1]

May I dedicate to you this book on the Symbolist movement in literature, both as an expression of a deep personal friendship and because you, more than any one else, will sympathise with what I say in it, being yourself the chief representative of that movement in our country? France is the country of movements, and it is naturally in France that I have studied the development of a principle which is spreading throughout other countries, perhaps not less effectually, if with less definite outlines. Your own Irish literary movement is one of its expressions; your own poetry and A.E.'s poetry belong to it in the most intimate sense.[2] In Germany it seems to be permeating the whole of literature, its spirit is that which is deepest in Ibsen, it has absorbed the one new force in Italy, Gabriele d'Annunzio. I am told of a group of Symbolists in Russian Literature,[3] there is another in Dutch literature,[4] in Portugal it has a little school of its own under Eugenio de Castro;[5] I even saw some faint strivings that way in Spain, and the aged Spanish poet Campoamor has always fought on behalf of a 'transcendental' art in which we should recognise much of what is most essential in the doctrine of Symbolism.[6] How often have you and I discussed all these questions, rarely arguing about them, for we rarely had an essential difference of opinion, but bringing them more and more clearly into light, turning our instincts into logic, digging until we reached the bases of our convictions. And all the while we were working as well as thinking out a philosophy of art; you, at all events, creating beautiful things, as beautiful, it seems to me, as anything that is being done in our time.

And we talked of other things besides art, and there are other sympathies, besides purely artistic ones, between us. I speak often in this book of Mysticism, and that I, of all people, should venture to speak, not quite as an outsider, of such things, will probably be a surprise to many. It will be no surprise to you, for you have seen me gradually finding my way, uncertainly but inevitably, in that direction which has always been to you your natural direction. Still, as I am, so meshed about with the variable and too clinging appearances of things, so weak before the delightfulness of earthly circumstance, I hesitate sometimes in saying what I have in my mind, lest I should seem to be saying more than I have any personal right to say. But what, after all, is one's personal right? How insignificant a matter to any one but oneself, a matter how deliberately to be disregarded in that surely impersonal utterance which comes to one in one's most intimate thinking about beauty and truth and the deeper issues of things!

It is almost worth writing a book to have one perfectly sympathetic reader, who will understand everything that one has said, and more than one has said, who will think one's own thought whenever one has said exactly the right thing, who will complete what is imperfect in reading it, and be too generous to think that it is imperfect. I feel that I shall have that reader in you; so here is my book in token of that assurance.

Arthur Symons
London, June 1899

Introduction

> It is in and through Symbols that man, consciously or uncon-
> sciously, lives, works, and has his being: those ages, moreover,
> are accounted the noblest which can the best recognise symbol-
> ical worth, and prize it highest.
>
> Carlyle[1]

Without symbolism there can be no literature; indeed, not even
language. What are words themselves but symbols, almost as arbitrary as the letters which compose them, mere sounds of the voice
to which we have agreed to give certain significations, as we have
agreed to translate these sounds by those combinations of letters?
Symbolism began with the first words uttered by the first man,
as he named every living thing; or before them, in heaven, when
God named the world into being. And we see, in these beginnings, precisely what Symbolism in literature really is: a form of
expression, at the best but approximate, essentially but arbitrary,
until it has obtained the force of a convention, for an unseen reality
apprehended by the consciousness. It is sometimes permitted to us
to hope that our convention is indeed the reflection rather than
merely the sign of that unseen reality. We have done much if we
have found a recognisable sign.

'A symbol,' says Comte Goblet d'Alviella, in his book on *The
Migration of Symbols*, 'might be defined as a representation which
does not aim at being a reproduction.'[2] Originally, as he points
out, used by the Greeks to denote 'the two halves of the tablet
they divided between themselves as a pledge of hospitality,' it
came to be used of every sign, formula, or rite by which those
initiated in any mystery made themselves secretly known to one
another. Gradually the word extended its meaning, until it came
to denote every conventional representation of idea by form, of
the unseen by the visible. 'In a Symbol,' says Carlyle, 'there is
concealment and yet revelation: hence therefore, by Silence and
by Speech acting together, comes a double significance.' And, in
that fine chapter of *Sartor Resartus*, he goes further, vindicating for
the word its full value: 'In the Symbol proper, what we can call

a Symbol, there is ever, more or less distinctly and directly, some embodiment and revelation of the Infinite; the Infinite is made to blend itself with the Finite, to stand visible, and as it were, attainable there.'

It is in such a sense as this that the word Symbolism has been used to describe a movement which, during the last generation, has profoundly influenced the course of French literature. All such words, used of anything so living, variable, and irresponsible as literature, are, as symbols themselves must so often be, mere compromises, mere indications. Symbolism, as seen in the writers of our day, would have no value if it were not seen also, under one disguise or another, in every great imaginative writer. What distinguishes the Symbolism of our day from the Symbolism of the past is that it has now become conscious of itself, in a sense in which it was unconscious even in Gérard de Nerval, to whom I trace the particular origin of the literature which I call Symbolist. The forces which mould the thought of men change, or men's resistance to them slackens; with the change of men's thought comes a change of literature, alike in its inmost essence and in its outward form: after the world has starved its soul long enough in the contemplation and the rearrangement of material things, comes the turn of the soul; and with it comes the literature of which I write in this volume, a literature in which the visible world is no longer a reality, and the unseen world no longer a dream.

The great epoch in French literature which preceded this epoch was that of the offshoot of Romanticism which produced Baudelaire, Flaubert, the Goncourts, Taine, Zola, Leconte de Lisle. Taine was the philosopher both of what had gone before him and of what came immediately after; so that he seems to explain at once Flaubert and Zola. It was the age of Science, the age of material things; and words, with that facile elasticity which there is in them, did miracles in the exact representation of everything that visibly existed, exactly as it existed. Even Baudelaire, in whom the spirit is always an uneasy guest at the orgie of life, had a certain theory of Realism which tortures many of his poems into strange, metallic shapes, and fills them with imitative odours, and disturbs them with a too deliberate rhetoric of the flesh. Flaubert, the one impeccable novelist who has ever lived, was resolute to be the novelist of a world in which art, formal art, was the only escape from the burden of reality, and in which the soul was of use mainly as the agent of fine literature. The Goncourts caught at Impressionism to render the fugitive aspects of a world which existed only as a thing of flat spaces, and angles, and coloured movement, in which sun and shadow were the artists; as moods, no less flitting, were the artists of the merely receptive consciousnesses of men and women. Zola has tried to build in brick and mortar inside the covers of a book; he is quite sure that the soul is a nervous fluid, which he is quite sure some man of science is about to catch for us, as a man of science has bottled the air, a pretty, blue liquid. Leconte de Lisle turned the world to stone, but saw, beyond the world, only a pause from misery in a Nirvana never subtilised to the Eastern ecstasy. And, with all these writers, form aimed above all things at being precise, at saying rather than suggesting, at saying what they had to say so completely that nothing remained over, which it might be the business of the reader to divine. And so they have expressed, finally, a certain aspect of the world; and some of them have carried style to a point beyond which the style that says, rather than suggests, cannot go. The whole of that movement comes to a splendid funeral in Heredia's sonnets, in which the literature of form says its last word, and dies.

Meanwhile, something which is vaguely called Decadence had come into being. That name, rarely used with any precise meaning, was usually either hurled as a reproach or hurled back as a defiance. It pleased some young men in various countries to call themselves Decadents, with all the thrill of unsatisfied virtue masquerading as uncomprehended vice. As a matter of fact, the term is in its place only when applied to style; to that ingenious deformation of the language, in Mallarmé, for instance, which can be compared with what we are accustomed to call the Greek and Latin of the Decadence. No doubt perversity of form and perversity of matter are often found together, and, among the lesser men especially, experiment was carried far, not only in the direction of style. But a movement which in this sense might be called Decadent could but have been a straying aside from the main road of literature. Nothing, not even conventional virtue, is so provincial as conventional vice; and the desire to 'bewilder the middle-classes' is itself middle-class. The interlude, half a mock-interlude, of Decadence, diverted the attention of the critics while something more serious was in preparation. That something more serious has crystallised,

for the time, under the form of Symbolism, in which art returns
to the one pathway, leading through beautiful things to the eternal
beauty.

In most of the writers whom I have dealt with as summing
up in themselves all that is best in Symbolism, it will be noticed
that the form is very carefully elaborated, and seems to count
for at least as much as in those writers of whose over-possession
by form I have complained. Here, however, all this elaboration
comes from a very different motive, and leads to other ends. There
is such a thing as perfecting form that form may be annihilated.
All the art of Verlaine is in the bringing verse to a bird's song, the
art of Mallarmé in bringing verse to the song of an orchestra. In
Villiers de l'Isle-Adam drama becomes an embodiment of spiritual
forces, in Maeterlinck not even their embodiment, but the remote
sound of their voices. It is all an attempt to spiritualise literature,
to evade the old bondage of rhetoric, the old bondage of exteriority. Description is banished that beautiful things may be evoked,
magically; the regular beat of verse is broken in order that words
may fly, upon subtler wings. Mystery is no longer feared, as the
great mystery in whose midst we are islanded was feared by those
to whom that unknown sea was only a great void. We are coming
closer to nature, as we seem to shrink from it with something of
horror, disdaining to catalogue the trees of the forest. And as we
brush aside the accidents of daily life, in which men and women
imagine that they are alone touching reality, we come closer to
humanity, to everything in humanity that may have begun before
the world and may outlast it.

Here, then, in this revolt against exteriority, against rhetoric,
against a materialistic tradition; in this endeavour to disengage
the ultimate essence, the soul, of whatever exists and can be
realised by the consciousness; in this dutiful waiting upon every
symbol by which the soul of things can be made visible; literature,
bowed down by so many burdens, may at last attain liberty, and
its authentic speech. In attaining this liberty, it accepts a heavier
burden; for in speaking to us so intimately, so solemnly, as only
religion had hitherto spoken to us, it becomes itself a kind of religion, with all the duties and responsibilities of the sacred ritual.

Gérard de Nerval

I.

This is the problem of one who lost the whole world and gained his own soul.

'I like to arrange my life as if it were a novel,' wrote Gérard de Nerval,[1] and, indeed, it is somewhat difficult to disentangle the precise facts of an existence which was never quite conscious where began and where ended that 'overflowing of dreams into real life,' of which he speaks. 'I do not ask of God,' he said, 'that he should change anything in events themselves, but that he should change me in regard to things, so that I might have the power to create my own universe about me, to govern my dreams, instead of enduring them.'[2] The prayer was not granted, in its entirety; and the tragedy of his life lay in the vain endeavour to hold back the irresistible empire of the unseen, which it was the joy of his life to summon about him. Briefly, we know that Gérard Labrunie (the name de Nerval was taken from a little piece of property, worth some 1500 francs, which he liked to imagine had always been in the possession of his family) was born at Paris, May 22, 1808. His father was surgeon-major; his mother died before he was old enough to remember her, following the *Grande Armée* on the Russian campaign;[3] and Gérard was brought up, largely under the care of a studious and erratic uncle, in a little village called Montagny, near Ermenonville. He was a precocious schoolboy, and by the age of eighteen had published six little collections of verses. It was during one of his holidays that he saw, for the first and last time, the young girl whom he calls Adrienne, and whom, under many names, he loved to the end of his life. One evening she had come from the château to dance with the young peasant girls on the grass. She had danced with Gérard, he had kissed her cheek, he had crowned her hair with laurels, he had heard her sing an old song telling of the sorrows of a princess whom her father had shut in a tower because she had loved. To Gérard it seemed that already he remembered her, and certainly he was never to forget her. Afterwards, he heard that Adrienne had taken the veil;

then, that she was dead. To one who had realised that it is 'we, the living, who walk in a world of phantoms,' death could not exclude hope;[4] and when, many years later, he fell seriously and fantastically in love with a little actress called Jenny Colon, it was because he seemed to have found, in that blonde and very human person, the re-incarnation of the blonde Adrienne.

Meanwhile Gérard was living in Paris, among his friends the Romantics, writing and living in an equally desultory fashion. *Le bon Gérard* was the best loved, and, in his time, not the least famous, of the company. He led, by choice, now in Paris, now across Europe, the life of a vagabond, and more persistently than others of his friends who were driven to it by need. At that time, when it was the aim of every one to be as eccentric as possible, the eccentricities of Gérard's life and thought seemed, on the whole, less noticeable than those of many really quite normal persons. But with Gérard there was no pose; and when, one day, he was found in the Palais-Royal, leading a lobster at the end of a blue ribbon (because, he said, it does not bark, and knows the secrets of the sea), the visionary had simply lost control of his visions, and had to be sent to Dr. Blanche's asylum at Montmartre.[5] He entered March 21, 1841, and came out, apparently well again, on the 21st of November. It would seem that this first access of madness was, to some extent, the consequence of the final rupture with Jenny Colon; on June 5, 1842, she died, and it was partly in order to put as many leagues of the earth as possible between him and that memory that Gérard set out, at the end of 1842, for the East. It was also in order to prove to the world, by his consciousness of external things, that he had recovered his reason. While he was in Syria, he once more fell in love with a new incarnation of Adrienne, a young Druse, Saléma, the daughter of a Sheikh of Lebanon; and it seems to have been almost by accident that he did not marry her. He returned to Paris at the end of 1843 or the beginning of 1844, and for the next few years he lived mostly in Paris, writing charming, graceful, remarkably sane articles and books, and wandering about the streets, by day and night, in a perpetual dream, from which, now and again, he was somewhat rudely awakened. When, in the spring of 1853, he went to see Heine, for whom he was doing an admirable prose translation of his poems, and told him he had come to return the money he had received in advance, because the times were accomplished, and the end of the world, announced by the Apocalypse, was at hand, Heine sent for a cab, and Gérard found himself at Dr. Dubois' asylum, where he remained two months. It was on coming out of the asylum that he wrote *Sylvie*, a delightful idyl, chiefly autobiographical, one of his three actual achievements.[6] On August 27, 1853, he had to be taken to Dr. Blanche's asylum at Passy, where he remained till May 27, 1854. Thither, after a month or two spent in Germany, he returned on August 8, and on October 19 he came out for the last time, manifestly uncured. He was now engaged on the narrative of his own madness, and the first part of *Le Rêve et la Vie* appeared in the *Revue de Paris* of January 1, 1855. On the 20th he came into the office of the review, and showed Gautier and Maxime du Camp an apron-string which he was carrying in his pocket. 'It is the girdle,' he said, 'that Madame de Maintenon wore when she had *Esther* performed at Saint-Cyr.'[7] On the 24th he wrote to a friend: 'Come and prove my identity at the police-station of the Châtelet.' The night before he had been working at his manuscript in a pot-house of Les Halles, and had been arrested as a vagabond. He was used to such little misadventures, but he complained of the difficulty of writing. 'I set off after an idea,' he said, 'and lose myself; I am hours in finding my way back. Do you know I can scarcely write twenty lines a day, the darkness comes about me so close!' He took out the apron-string. 'It is the garter of the Queen of Sheba,' he said. The snow was freezing on the ground, and on the night of the 25th, at three in the morning, the landlord of a 'penny doss' in the Rue de la Vieille-Lanterne, a filthy alley lying between the quays and the Rue de Rivoli, heard some one knocking at the door, but did not open, on account of the cold. At dawn, the body of Gérard de Nerval was found hanging by the apron-string to a bar of the window.

It is not necessary to exaggerate the importance of the half-dozen volumes which make up the works of Gérard de Nerval. He was not a great writer; he had moments of greatness; and it is the particular quality of these moments which is of interest for us. There is the entertaining, but not more than entertaining, *Voyage en Orient*; there is the estimable translation of *Faust*, and the admirable versions from Heine; there are the volumes of short stories and sketches, of which even *Les Illuminés*, in spite of the promise of its title, is little more than an agreeable compilation.

But there remain three compositions: the sonnets, *Le Rêve et la Vie*, and *Sylvie*; of which *Sylvie* is the most objectively achieved, a wandering idyl, full of pastoral delight, and containing some folk-songs of Valois, two of which have been translated by Rossetti;[8] *Le Rêve et la Vie* being the most intensely personal, a narrative of madness, unique as madness itself; and the sonnets, a kind of miracle, which may be held to have created something at least of the method of the later Symbolists. These three compositions, in which alone Gérard is his finest self, all belong to the periods when he was, in the eyes of the world, actually mad. The sonnets belong to two of these periods, *Le Rêve et la Vie* to the last, *Sylvie* was written in the short interval between the two attacks in the early part of 1853. We have thus the case of a writer, graceful and elegant when he is sane, but only inspired, only really wise, passionate, collected, only really master of himself, when he is insane. It may be worth looking at a few of the points which so suggestive a problem presents to us.

II.

Gérard de Nerval lived the transfigured inner life of the dreamer. 'I was very tired of life!' he says. And like so many dreamers, who have all the luminous darkness of the universe in their brains, he found his most precious and uninterrupted solitude in the crowded and more sordid streets of great cities. He who had loved the Queen of Sheba, and seen the seven Elohims dividing the world, could find nothing more tolerable in mortal conditions, when he was truly aware of them, than the company of the meanest of mankind, in whom poverty and vice, and the hard pressure of civilisation, still leave some of the original vivacity of the human comedy. The real world seeming to be always so far from him, and a sort of terror of the gulfs holding him, in spite of himself, to its flying skirts, he found something at all events realisable, concrete, in these drinkers of Les Halles, these vagabonds of the Place du Carrousel, among whom he so often sought refuge.[9] It was literally, in part, a refuge. During the day he could sleep, but night wakened him, and that restlessness, which the night draws out in those who are really under lunar influences, set his feet wandering, if only in order that his mind might wander the less. The sun, as he mentions, never appears in dreams; but, with the approach of night, is not every one a little readier to believe in the mystery lurking behind the world?

Crains, dans le mur aveugle, un regard qui t'épie!*

he writes in one of his great sonnets; and that fear of the invisible watchfulness of nature was never absent from him. It is one of the terrors of human existence that we may be led at once to seek and to shun solitude; unable to bear the mortal pressure of its embrace, unable to endure the nostalgia of its absence. 'I think man's happiest when he forgets himself,' says an Elizabethan dramatist;[10] and, with Gérard, there was Adrienne to forget, and Jenny Colon the actress, and the Queen of Sheba. But to have drunk of the cup of dreams is to have drunk of the cup of eternal memory. The past, and, as it seemed to him, the future were continually with him; only the present fled continually from under his feet. It was only by the effort of this contact with people who lived so sincerely in the day, the minute, that he could find even a temporary foothold. With them, at least, he could hold back all the stars, and the darkness beyond them, and the interminable approach and disappearance of all the ages, if only for the space between tavern and tavern, where he could open his eyes on so frank an abandonment to the common drunkenness of most people in this world, here for once really living the symbolic intoxication of their ignorance.

Like so many dreamers of illimitable dreams, it was the fate of Gérard to incarnate his ideal in the person of an actress. The fatal transfiguration of the footlights, in which reality and the artificial change places with so fantastic a regularity, has drawn many moths into its flame, and will draw more, as long as men persist in demanding illusion of what is real, and reality in what is illusion. The Jenny Colons of the world are very simple, very real, if one will but refrain from assuming them to be a mystery. But it is the penalty of all imaginative lovers to create for themselves the veil which hides from them the features of the beloved. It is their privilege, for it is incomparably more entrancing to fancy oneself in love with Isis than to know that one is in love with Manon Lescaut.[11] The picture of Gérard, after many hesitations, revealing to the astonished Jenny that she is the incarnation of another, the

___

* ['Fear, in the blind wall, a gaze which spies on you!']

shadow of a dream, that she has been Adrienne and is about to be
the Queen of Sheba; her very human little cry of pure incompre-
hension, *Mais vous ne m'aimez pas!* ['But you don't love me!'] and
her prompt refuge in the arms of the *jeune premier ridé* [young male
lead], if it were not of the acutest pathos, would certainly be of the
most quintessential comedy. For Gérard, so sharp an awakening
was but like the passage from one state to another, across that little
bridge of one step which lies between heaven and hell, to which
he was so used in his dreams. It gave permanency to the trivial,
crystallising it, in another than Stendhal's sense;[12] and when death
came, changing mere human memory into the terms of eternity,
the darkness of the spiritual world was lit with a new star, which
was henceforth the wandering, desolate guide of so many visions.
The tragic figure of Aurélia, which comes and goes through all
the labyrinths of dream, is now seen always 'as if lit up by a light-
ning-flash, pale and dying, hurried away by dark horsemen.'

The dream or doctrine of the re-incarnation of souls, which has
given so much consolation to so many questioners of eternity, was
for Gérard (need we doubt?) a dream rather than a doctrine, but
one of those dreams which are nearer to a man than his breath.
'This vague and hopeless love,' he writes in *Sylvie*, 'inspired by an
actress, which night by night took hold of me at the hour of the
performance, leaving me only at the hour of sleep, had its germ
in the recollection of Adrienne, flower of the night, unfolding
under the pale rays of the moon, rosy and blonde phantom, gliding
over the green grass, half bathed in white mist. ... To love a nun
under the form of an actress! ... and if it were the very same! It is
enough to drive one mad!' Yes, *il y a de quoi devenir fou*, as Gérard
had found; but there was also, in this intimate sense of the unity,
perpetuity, and harmoniously recurring rhythm of nature, not a
little of the inner substance of wisdom. It was a dream, perhaps
refracted from some broken, illuminating angle by which madness
catches unseen light, that revealed to him the meaning of his own
superstition, fatality, malady: 'During my sleep, I had a marvellous vision. It seemed to me that the goddess appeared before me,
saying to me "I am the same as Mary, the same as thy mother,
the same also whom, under all forms, thou hast always loved. At
each of thine ordeals I have dropt yet one more of the masks with
which I veil my countenance, and soon thou shalt see me as I
am!"' And in perhaps his finest sonnet, the mysterious *Artémis*, we

have, under other symbols, and with the deliberate inconsequence of these sonnets, the comfort and despair of the same faith.

La Treizième revient … C'est encor la première;
Et c'est toujours la seule, – ou c'est le seul moment:
Car es-tu reine, ô toi! la première ou dernière?
Es-tu roi, toi le seul ou le dernier amant? …

Aimez qui vous aima du berceau dans la bière;
Celle que j'aimai seul m'aime encor tendrement;
C'est la mort – ou la morte … Ô délice! ô tourment!
La Rose qu'elle tient, c'est la Rose trémière.

Sainte napolitaine aux mains pleines de feux,
Rose au cœur violet, fleur de sainte Gudule:
As-tu trouvé ta croix dans le désert des cieux?

Roses blanches, tombez! vous insultez nos dieux:
Tombez, fantômes blancs, de votre ciel qui brûle:
– La Sainte de l'abîme est plus sainte à mes yeux!*

Who has not often meditated, above all what artist, on the slightness, after all, of the link which holds our faculties together in that sober health of the brain which we call reason? Are there not moments when that link seems to be worn down to so fine a tenuity that the wing of a passing dream might suffice to snap it? The consciousness seems, as it were, to expand and contract at once, into something too wide for the universe, and too narrow for the thought of self to find room within it. Is it that the sense of identity is about to evaporate, annihilating all, or is it that a more profound identity, the identity of the whole sentient universe, has been at last realised? Leaving the concrete world on these brief voyages, the fear is that we may not have strength to return, or that we may lose the way back. Every artist lives a double life,

---

* ['The Thirteenth returns … she is the first once more; / And she's still the only one, – or it is the only moment: / For are you, queen, you! the first or the last? Are you, king, you the only lover or the last one? … // Love in her grave whoever loved you from the cradle; / The one I loved alone loves me still tenderly; / She is death – or dead … O delight! O torment! / The rose she holds is the *Rose trémière*. // Holy neapolitan with hands full of fire / Rose with a violet heart, flower of Saint Gudula: / Did you find your cross in the deserted skies? // Fall, white roses! You insult our gods: / Fall, white ghosts, from your burning sky; / The Saint of the abyss is more holy in my eyes!']

in which he is for the most part conscious of the illusions of the imagination. He is conscious also of the illusions of the nerves, which he shares with every man of imaginative mind. Nights of insomnia, days of anxious waiting, the sudden shock of an event, any one of these common disturbances may be enough to jangle the tuneless bells of one's nerves. The artist can distinguish these causes of certain of his moods from those other causes which come to him because he is an artist, and are properly concerned with that invention which is his own function. Yet is there not some danger that he may come to confuse one with the other, that he may 'lose the thread' which conducts him through the intricacies of the inner world?

The supreme artist, certainly, is the furthest of all men from this danger; for he is the supreme intelligence. Like Dante, he can pass through hell unsinged. With him, imagination is vision; when he looks into the darkness, he sees. The vague dreamer, the insecure artist and the uncertain mystic at once, sees only shadows, not recognising their outlines. He is mastered by the images which have come at his call; he has not the power which chains them for his slaves. 'The kingdom of Heaven suffers violence,' and the dreamer who has gone tremblingly into the darkness is in peril at the hands of those very real phantoms who are the reflection of his fear.[13]

The madness of Gérard de Nerval, whatever physiological reasons may be rightly given for its outbreak, subsidence, and return, I take to have been essentially due to the weakness and not the excess of his visionary quality, to the insufficiency of his imaginative energy, and to his lack of spiritual discipline. He was an unsystematic mystic; his 'Tower of Babel in two hundred volumes,' that medley of books of religion, science, astrology, history, travel, which he thought would have rejoiced the heart of Pico della Mirandola, of Meursius, or of Nicholas of Cusa, was truly, as he says, 'enough to drive a wise man mad.'[14] 'Why not also,' he adds, 'enough to make a madman wise?' But precisely because it was this *amas bizarre*, this jumble of the perilous secrets in which wisdom is so often folly, and folly so often wisdom. He speaks vaguely of the Kabbala; the Kabbala would have been safety to him, as the Catholic Church would have been, or any other reasoned scheme of things. Wavering among intuitions, ignorances, half-truths, shadows of falsehood, now audacious, now hesitating, he was blown hither and thither by conflicting winds, a prey to the indefinite.

La Rêve et la Vie, the last fragments of which were found in his pockets after his suicide, scrawled on scraps of paper, interrupted with Kabbalistic signs and 'a demonstration of the Immaculate Conception by geometry,' is a narrative of a madman's visions by the madman himself, yet showing, as Gautier says, 'cold reason seated by the bedside of hot fever, hallucination analysing itself by a supreme philosophic effort.'[15] What is curious, yet after all natural, is that part of the narrative seems to be contemporaneous with what it describes, and part subsequent to it; so that it is not as when De Quincey says to us, such or such was the opium-dream that I had on such a night; but as if the opium-dreamer had begun to write down his dream while he was yet within its coils. 'The descent into hell,' he calls it twice; yet does he not also write: 'At times I imagined that my force and my activity were doubled; it seemed to me that I knew everything, understood everything; and imagination brought me infinite pleasures. Now that I have recovered what men call reason, must I not regret having lost them?' But he had not lost them; he was still in that state of double consciousness which he describes in one of his visions, when, seeing people dressed in white, 'I was astonished,' he says, 'to see them all dressed in white; yet it seemed to me that this was an optical illusion.' His cosmical visions are at times so magnificent that he seems to be creating myths; and it is with a worthy ingenuity that he plays the part he imagines to be assigned to him in his astral influences.

First of all I imagined that the persons collected in the garden (of the madhouse) all had some influence on the stars, and that the one who always walked round and round in a circle regulated the course of the sun. An old man, who was brought there at certain hours of the day, and who made knots as he consulted his watch, seemed to me to be charged with the notation of the course of the hours. I attributed to myself an influence over the course of the moon, and I believed that this star had been struck by the thunderbolt of the Most High, which had traced on its face the imprint of the mask which I had observed.

I attributed a mystical signification to the conversations of the warders and of my companions. It seemed to me that they

were the representatives of all the races of the earth, and that we
had undertaken between us to re-arrange the course of the stars,
and to give a wider development to the system. An error, in my
opinion, had crept into the general combination of numbers,
and thence came all the ills of humanity. I believed also that
the celestial spirits had taken human forms, and assisted at this
general congress, seeming though they did to be concerned
with but ordinary occupations. My own part seemed to me to
be the re-establishment of universal harmony by Kabbalistic
art, and I had to seek a solution by evoking the occult forces of
various religions.

So far we have, no doubt, the confusions of madness, in which
what may indeed be the symbol is taken for the thing itself. But
now observe what follows:

I seemed to myself a hero living under the very eyes of the
gods; everything in nature assumed new aspects, and secret
voices came to me from the plants, the trees, animals, the
meanest insects, to warn and to encourage me. The words of
my companions had mysterious messages, the sense of which
I alone understood; things without form and without life lent
themselves to the designs of my mind; out of combinations of
stones, the figures of angles, crevices, or openings, the shape
of leaves, out of colours, odours, and sounds, I saw unknown
harmonies come forth. 'How is it,' I said to myself, 'that I can
possibly have lived so long outside nature, without identifying
myself with her! All things live, all things are in motion, all
things correspond; the magnetic rays emanating from myself
or others traverse without obstacle the infinite chain of created
things: a transparent network covers the world, whose loose
threads communicate more and more closely with the planets
and the stars. Now a captive upon the earth, I hold converse
with the starry choir, which is feelingly a part of my joys and
sorrows.

To have thus realised that central secret of the mystics, from
Pythagoras onwards,[16] the secret which the Smaragdine Tablet of
Hermes betrays in its 'As things are below, so are they above';[17]
which Boehme has classed in his teaching of 'signatures,' and
Swedenborg has systematised in his doctrine of 'correspondences';

does it matter very much that he arrived at it by way of the obscure and fatal initiation of madness? Truth, and especially that soul of truth which is poetry, may be reached by many roads; and a road is not necessarily misleading because it is dangerous or forbidden. Here is one who has gazed at light till it has blinded him; and for us all that is important is that he has seen something, not that his eyesight has been too weak to endure the pressure of light over-flowing the world from beyond the world.

III.

And here we arrive at the fundamental principle which is at once the substance and the aesthetics of the sonnets 'composed,' as he explains, 'in that state of meditation which the Germans would call "super-naturalistic."' In one, which I will quote, he is explicit, and seems to state a doctrine.

VERS DORÉS.

Homme, libre penseur! te crois-tu seul pensant
Dans ce monde où la vie éclate en toute chose?
Des forces que tu tiens ta liberté dispose,
Mais de tous tes conseils l'univers est absent.

Respecte dans la bête un esprit agissant:
Chaque fleur est une âme à la Nature éclose;
Un mystère d'amour dans le métal repose;
'Tout est sensible!' Et tout sur ton être est puissant.

Crains, dans le mur aveugle, un regard qui t'épie!
A la matière même un verbe est attaché …
Ne la fais pas servir à quelque usage impie!

Souvent dans l'être obscur habite un Dieu caché;
Et comme un oeil naissant couvert par ses paupières,
Un pur esprit s'accroît sous l'écorce des pierres!*

---

* ['Man, free thinker! Do you believe you are the only thinking being / in this world where life breaks out of all things? / You are free to dispose of the forces you have at your command / But the universe doesn't take your advice. // Respect the spirit which moves each beast; / Each flower is a soul where Nature buds; / A mysterious love sleeps in each metal; / 'Everything is conscious' and everything exercises power over your being. // Fear a gaze

But in the other sonnets, in *Artémis*, which I have quoted, in *El Desdichado*, *Myrtho*, and the rest, he would seem to be deliberately obscure; or at least, his obscurity results, to some extent, from the state of mind which he describes in *Le Rêve et la Vie*: 'I then saw, vaguely drifting into form, plastic images of antiquity, which outlined themselves, became definite, and seemed to represent symbols, of which I only seized the idea with difficulty.' Nothing could more precisely represent the impression made by these sonnets, in which, for the first time in French, words are used as the ingredients of an evocation, as themselves not merely colour and sound, but symbol. Here are words which create an atmosphere by the actual suggestive quality of their syllables, as, according to the theory of Mallarmé, they should do; as, in the recent attempts of the Symbolists, writer after writer has endeavoured to lure them into doing. Persuaded, as Gérard was, of the sensitive unity of all nature, he was able to trace resemblances where others saw only divergences; and the setting together of unfamiliar and apparently alien things, which comes so strangely upon us in his verse, was perhaps an actual sight of what it is our misfortune not to see. His genius, to which madness had come as the liberating, the precip- itating, spirit, disengaging its finer essence, consisted in a power of materialising vision, whatever is most volatile and unseizable in vision, and without losing the sense of mystery, or that quality which gives its charm to the intangible. Madness, then, in him, had lit up, as if by lightning-flashes, the hidden links of distant and divergent things; perhaps in somewhat the same manner as that in which a similarly new, startling, perhaps over-true sight of things is gained by the artificial stimulation of·haschisch, opium, and those other drugs by which vision is produced deliberately, and the soul, sitting safe within the perilous circle of its own magic, looks out on the panorama which either rises out of the darkness before it, or drifts from itself into the darkness. The very imagery of these sonnets is the imagery which is known to all dreamers of bought dreams. *Rose au coeur violet, fleur de sainte Gudule; le Temple au péristyle immense; la grotte où nage la syrène*: the dreamer

---

within the blind wall which spies on you! / The word is inseparable from matter itself ... / Don't use it for impious purposes! // Obscure beings often house a hidden God; / and like a nascent eye, covered by eyelids, / A pure spirit grows beneath the stony crust.']

of bought dreams has seen them all. But no one before Gérard realised that such things as these might be the basis of almost a new aesthetics. Did he himself realise all that he had done, or was it left for Mallarmé to theorise upon what Gérard had but divined?[18]

That he made the discovery, there is no doubt; and we owe to the fortunate accident of madness one of the foundations of what may be called the practical aesthetics of Symbolism. Look again at that sonnet *Artémis*, and you will see in it not only the method of Mallarmé, but much of the most intimate manner of Verlaine. The first four lines, with their fluid rhythm, their repetitions and echoes, their delicate evasions, might have been written by Verlaine; in the later part the firmness of the rhythms and the jewelled significance of the words are like Mallarmé at his finest, so that in a single sonnet we may fairly claim to see a foreshadowing of the styles of Mallarmé and Verlaine at once. With Verlaine the resemblance goes, perhaps, no further; with Mallarmé it goes to the very roots, the whole man being, certainly, his style.

Gérard de Nerval, then, had divined, before all the world, that poetry should be a miracle; not a hymn to beauty, nor the description of beauty, nor beauty's mirror; but beauty itself, the colour, fragrance, and form of the imagined flower, as it blossoms again out of the page. Vision, the over-powering vision, had come to him beyond, if not against, his will; and he knew that vision is the root out of which the flower must grow. Vision had taught him symbol, and he knew that it is by symbol alone that the flower can take visible form. He knew that the whole mystery of beauty can never be comprehended by the crowd, and that while clearness is a virtue of style, perfect explicitness is not a necessary virtue. So it was with disdain, as well as with confidence, that he allowed these sonnets to be overheard. It was enough for him to say:

J'ai rêvé dans la grotte où nage le syrène;*

and to speak, it might be, the siren's language, remembering her. 'It will be my last madness,' he wrote, 'to believe myself a poet: let criticism cure me of it.' Criticism, in his own day, even Gautier's criticism, could but be disconcerted by a novelty so unexampled. It is only now that the best critics in France are beginning to realise how great in themselves, and how great in their influence,

---

* ['I have dreamed in the grotto where the siren swims']

are these sonnets, which, forgotten by the world for nearly fifty years, have all the while been secretly bringing new aesthetics into French poetry.

Villiers de l'Isle-Adam
À chacun son infini

I.

Count Philippe Auguste Mathias de Villiers de l'Isle-Adam was born at St. Brieuc, in Normandy, November 28, 1838; he died at Paris, under the care of the Frères Saint-Jean-de-Dieu, August 19, 1889. Even before his death, his life had become a legend, and the legend is even now not to be disentangled from the actual occurrences of an existence so heroically visionary. The Don Quixote of idealism, it was not only in philosophical terms that life, to him, was the dream, and the spiritual world the reality; he lived his faith, enduring what others called reality with contempt, whenever, for a moment, he became conscious of it.[1] The basis of the character of Villiers was pride, and it was a pride which covered more than the universe. And this pride, first of all, was the pride of race.

Descendent of the original Rodolphe le Bel, Seigneur de Villiers (1067), through Jean de Villiers and Marie de l'Isle and their son Pierre the first Villiers de l'Isle-Adam, a Villiers de l'Isle-Adam, born in 1384, had been Marshal of France under Jean-sans-Peur, Duke of Burgundy; he took Paris during the civil war, and after being imprisoned in the Bastille, reconquered Pontoise from the English, and helped to reconquer Paris. Another Villiers de l'Isle-Adam, born in 1464, Grand Master of the Order of St. John of Jerusalem, defended Rhodes against 200,000 Turks for a whole year, in one of the most famous sieges in history; it was he who obtained from Charles V. the concession of the isle of Malta for his Order, henceforth the Order of the Knights of Malta.

For Villiers, to whom time, after all, was but a metaphysical abstraction, the age of the Crusaders had not passed. From a descendant of the Grand Master of the Knights of St. John of Jerusalem, the nineteenth century demanded precisely the virtues which the sixteenth century had demanded of that ancestor. And these virtues were all summed up in one word, which, in its double significance, single to him, covered the whole attitude of life: the word 'nobility.' No word returns oftener to the lips in speaking of what is most characteristic in his work, and to Villiers moral and spiritual nobility seemed but the inevitable consequence of that other kind of nobility by which he seemed to himself still a Knight of the Order of St. John of Jerusalem. It was his birthright.

To the aristocratic conception of things, nobility of soul is indeed a birthright, and the pride with which this gift of nature is accepted is a pride of exactly the opposite kind to that democratic pride to which nobility of soul is a conquest, valuable in proportion to its difficulty. This duality, always essentially aristocratic and democratic, typically Eastern and Western also, finds its place in every theory of religion, philosophy and the ideal life. The pride of *being*, the pride of *becoming*: these are the two ultimate contradictions set before every idealist. Villiers' choice, inevitable indeed, was significant. In its measure, it must always be the choice of the artist, to whom, in his contemplation of life, the means is often so much more important than the end. That nobility of soul which comes without effort, which comes only with an unrelaxed diligence over oneself, that I should be I: there can at least be no comparison of its beauty with the stained and dusty onslaught on a never quite conquered fort of the enemy, in a divided self. And, if it be permitted to choose among degrees of sanctity, that, surely, is the highest in which a natural genius for such things accepts its own attainment with the simplicity of a birthright.

And the Catholicism of Villiers was also a part of his inheritance. His ancestors had fought for the Church, and Catholicism was still a pompous flag, under which it was possible to fight on behalf of the spirit, against that materialism which is always, in one way or another, atheist. Thus he dedicates one of his stories to the Pope, chooses ecclesiastical splendours by preference among the many splendours of the world which go to make up his stage-pictures, and is learned in the subtleties of the Fathers. The Church is his favourite symbol of austere intellectual beauty; one way, certainly, by which the temptations of external matter may be vanquished, and a way, also, by which the desire of worship may be satisfied.

But there was also, in his attitude towards the mysteries of the spiritual world, that 'forbidden' curiosity which had troubled the obedience of the Templars, and which came to him, too, as a kind of knightly quality. Whether or not he was actually a Kabbalist, questions of magic began, at an early age, to preoccupy him, and, from the first wild experiment of *Isis* to the deliberate summing up of *Axël*, the 'occult' world finds its way into most of his pages.

Fundamentally, the belief of Villiers is the belief common to all Eastern mystics.* 'Know, once for all, that there is for thee no other universe than that conception thereof which is reflected at the bottom of thy thoughts.' 'What is knowledge but a recognition?' Therefore, 'forgetting for ever that which was the illusion of thyself,' hasten to become 'an intelligence freed from the bonds and the desires of the present moment.' 'Become the flower of thyself! Thou art but what thou thinkest: therefore think thyself eternal.' 'Man, if thou cease to limit in thyself a thing, that is, to desire it, if, so doing, thou withdraw thyself from it, it will follow thee, woman-like, as the water fills the place that is offered to it in the hollow of the hand. For thou possessest the real being of all things, in thy pure will, and thou art the God that thou art able to become.'[3]

To have accepted the doctrine which thus finds expression in *Axël*, is to have accepted this among others of its consequences: 'Science states, but does not explain: she is the oldest offspring of the chimeras; all the chimeras, then, on the same terms as the world (the oldest of them!), are *something more* than nothing!' And in *Elën* there is a fragment of conversation between two young students, which has its significance also:

> *Goetze.* There's my philosopher in full flight to the regions of the sublime! Happily we have Science, which is a torch, dear mystic; we will analyse your sun, if the planet does not burst into pieces sooner than it has any right to!
>
> *Samuel.* Science will not suffice. Sooner or later you will end by coming to your knees.
>
> *Goetze.* Before what?
>
> *Samuel.* Before the darkness![4]

Such avowals of ignorance are possible only from the height of a great intellectual pride. Villiers' revolt against Science, so far as Science is materialistic, and his passionate curiosity in that chimera's flight towards the invisible, are one and the same impulse of a mind to which only mind is interesting. *Toute cette vieille Extériorité,*

---

* [Symons' footnote:] 'I am far from sure,' wrote Verlaine, 'that the philosophy of Villiers will not one day become the formula of our century.'[2]

maligne, compliquée, inflexible,* that illusion which Science accepts for the one reality: it must be the whole effort of one's consciousness to escape from its entanglements, to dominate it, or to ignore it, and one's art must be the building of an ideal world beyond its access, from which one may indeed sally out, now and again, in a desperate enough attack upon the illusions in the midst of which men live.

And just that, we find, makes up the work of Villiers, work which divides itself roughly into two divisions: one, the ideal world, or the ideal in the world (*Axël, Elën, Morgane, Isis,* some of the *contes,* and, intermediary, *La Révolte*); the other, satire, the mockery of reality (*L'Eve Future,* the *Contes Cruels, Tribulat Bonhomet*). It is part of the originality of Villiers that the two divisions constantly flow into one another; the idealist being never more the idealist than in his buffooneries.

II.

Axël is the Symbolist drama, in all its uncompromising conflict with the 'modesty' of Nature and the limitations of the stage. It is the drama of the soul, and at the same time it is the most pictorial of dramas; I should define its manner as a kind of spiritual romanticism. The earlier dramas, *Elën, Morgane,* are fixed at somewhat the same point in space; *La Révolte,* which seems to anticipate *The Doll's House,* shows us an aristocratic Ibsen, touching reality with a certain disdain, certainly with far less skill, certainly with far more beauty.[5] But *Axël,* meditated over during a lifetime, shows us Villiers' ideal of his own idealism.

The action takes place, it is true, in this century, but it takes place in corners of the world into which the modern spirit has not yet passed; this *Monastère de Religieuses-trinitaires, le cloître de Sainte Apollodora, situé sur les confins du littoral de l'ancienne Flandre française,* and the *très vieux château fort, le burg des margraves d'Auërsperg, isolé au milieu du Schwartzswald.*[6] The characters, Axël d'Auërsperg, Eve Sara Emmanuèle de Maupers, Maître Janus, the Archidiacre, the Commandeur Kaspar d'Auërsperg, are at once more and less than human beings: they are the types of different ideals, and they are clothed with just enough humanity to give form to what would

* ['All this old, malign, complicated, inflexible Exteriority']

otherwise remain disembodied spirit. The religious ideal, the occult ideal, the worldly ideal, the passionate ideal, are all presented, one after the other, in these dazzling and profound pages; Axël is the disdainful choice from among them, the disdainful rejection of life itself, of the whole illusion of life, 'since infinity alone is not a deception.' And Sara? Sara is a superb part of that life which is rejected, which she herself comes, not without reluctance, to reject. In that motionless figure, during the whole of the first act silent but for a single 'No,' and leaping into a moment's violent action as the act closes, she is the haughtiest woman in literature.[7] But she is a woman, and she desires life, finding it in Axël. Pride, and the woman's devotion to the man, aid her to take the last cold step with Axël, in that transcendental giving up of life at the moment when life becomes ideal.

And the play is written, throughout, with a curious solemnity, a particular kind of eloquence, which makes no attempt to imitate the level of the speech of every day, but which is a sort of ideal language in which beauty is aimed at as exclusively as if it were written in verse. The modern drama, under the democratic influence of Ibsen, the positive influence of Dumas *fils*,[8] has limited itself to the expression of temperaments in the one case, of theoretic intelligences in the other, in as nearly as possible the words which the average man would use for the statement of his emotions and ideas. The form, that is, is degraded below the level of the characters whom it attempts to express; for it is evident that the average man can articulate only a small enough part of what he obscurely feels or thinks; and the theory of Realism is that his emotions and ideas are to be given only in so far as the words at his own command can give them. Villiers, choosing to concern himself only with exceptional characters, and with them only in the absolute, invents for them a more elaborate and a more magnificent speech than they would naturally employ, the speech of their thoughts, of their dreams.

And it is a world thought or dreamt in some more fortunate atmosphere than that in which we live, that Villiers has created for the final achievement of his abstract ideas. I do not doubt that he himself always lived in it, through all the poverty of the precipitous Rue des Martyrs.[9] But it is in *Axël*, and in *Axël* only, that he has made us also inhabitants of that world. Even in *Elën* we are spectators, watching a tragical fairy play (as if *Fantasio* became

suddenly in deadly earnest), watching some one else's dreams.[10]
Axël envelops us in its own atmosphere; it is as if we found
ourselves on a mountain-top, on the other side of the clouds, and
without surprise at finding ourselves there.

The ideal, to Villiers, being the real, spiritual beauty being the
essential beauty, and material beauty its reflection, or its revelation,
it is with a sort of fury that he attacks the materialising forces of
the world: science, progress, the worldly emphasis on 'facts,' on
what is 'positive,' 'serious,' 'respectable.' Satire, with him, is the
revenge of beauty upon ugliness, the persecution of the ugly; it is
not merely social satire, it is a satire on the material universe by one
who believes in a spiritual universe. Thus it is the only laughter of
our time which is fundamental, as fundamental as that of Swift or
Rabelais. And this lacerating laughter of the idealist is never surer
in its aim than when it turns the arms of science against itself, as
in the vast buffoonery of *L'Eve Future*. A Parisian wit, sharpened
to a fineness of irony such as only wit which is also philosophy
can attain, brings in another method of attack; humour, which
is almost English, another; while again satire becomes tragic,
fantastic, macabre. In those enigmatic 'tales of the grotesque and
arabesque,' in which Villiers rivals Poe on his own ground, there
is, for the most part, a multiplicity of meaning which is, as it is
meant to be, disconcerting. I should not like to say how far Villiers
does not, sometimes, believe in his own magic.

It is characteristic of him, at all events, that he employs what
we call the supernatural alike in his works of pure idealism and
in his works of sheer satire. The moment the world ceased to be
the stable object, solidly encrusted with houses in brick and stone,
which it is to most of its so temporary inhabitants, Villiers was at
home. When he sought the absolute beauty, it was beyond the
world that he found it; when he sought horror, it was a breath
blowing from an invisible darkness which brought it to his nerves;
when he desired to mock the pretensions of knowledge or of
ignorance, it was always with the unseen that his tragic buffoonery
made familiar.

There is, in everything which Villiers wrote, a strangeness,
certainly both instinctive and deliberate, which seems to me to be
the natural consequence of that intellectual pride which, as I have
pointed out, was at the basis of his character. He hated every kind
of mediocrity: therefore he chose to analyse exceptional souls,

to construct exceptional stories, to invent splendid names, and to evoke singular landscapes. It was part of his curiosity in souls to prefer the complex to the simple, the perverse to the straight-forward, the ambiguous to either. His heroes are incarnations of spiritual pride, and their tragedies are the shock of spirit against matter, the invasion of spirit by matter, the temptation of spirit by spiritual evil. They seek the absolute, and find death; they seek wisdom, find love, and fall into spiritual decay; they seek reality, and find crime; they seek phantoms, and find themselves. They are on the borders of a wisdom too great for their capacity; they are haunted by dark powers, instincts of ambiguous passions; they are too lucid to be sane in their extravagances; they have not quite systematically transposed their dreams into action. And his hero-ines, when they are not, like *L'Eve Future*, the vitalised mechanism of an Edison, have the solemnity of dead people, and a hieratic speech. *Songe, des coeurs condamnés à ce supplice, de ne pas m'aimer!* says Sara, in *Axël. Je ne l'aime pas, ce jeune homme. Qu'ai-je donc fait à Dieu?* says Elën.* And their voice is always like the voice of Elën: 'I listened attentively to the sound of her voice; it was taciturn, subdued, like the murmur of the river Lethe, flowing through the region of shadows.' They have the immortal weariness of beauty, they are enigmas to themselves, they desire and know not why they refrain, they do good and evil with the lifting of an eyelid, and are innocent and guilty of all the sins of the earth.

And these strange inhabitants move in as strange a world. They are the princes and châtelaines of ancient castles lost in the depths of the Black Forest; they are the last descendants of a great race about to come to an end; students of magic, who have the sharp and swift swords of the soldier; enigmatic courtesans, at the table of strange feasts; they find incalculable treasures, *tonnantes et sonnantes cataractes d'or liquide*, only to disdain them.† All the pomp of the world approaches them, that they may the better abnegate it, or that it may ruin them to a deeper degree of their material hell. And we see them always at the moment of a crisis, before the two ways of a decision, hesitating in the entanglements of a great temptation.

---

* ['Just think of those hearts condemned to the agony of never loving me!' – *Axël* Part IV, Scene IV; 'I don't love this young man. What have I done to God then?' – *Elën* Act II, Scene 6 (omitting a stage direction).]

† ['Thundering and resounding cataracts of liquid gold' – a stage direction from *Axël* Part IV, Scene IV.]

And this casuist of souls will drag forth some horribly stunted or horribly overgrown soul from under its obscure covering, setting it to dance naked before our eyes. He has no mercy on those who have no mercy on themselves.

In the sense in which that word is ordinarily used, Villiers has no pathos. This is enough to explain why he can never, in the phrase he would have disliked so greatly, 'touch the popular heart.' His mind is too abstract to contain pity, and it is in his lack of pity that he seems to put himself outside humanity. *À chacun son infini*, he has said, and in the avidity of his search for the infinite he has no mercy for the blind weakness which goes stumbling over the earth, without so much as knowing that the sun and stars are overhead. He sees only the gross multitude, the multitude which has the contentment of the slave. He cannot pardon stupidity, for it is incomprehensible to him. He sees, rightly, that stupidity is more criminal than vice; if only because vice is curable, stupidity incurable. But he does not realise, as the great novelists have realised, that stupidity can be pathetic, and that there is not a peasant, nor even a self-satisfied bourgeois, in whom the soul has not its part, in whose existence it is not possible to be interested.

Contempt, noble as it may be, anger, righteous though it may be, cannot be indulged in without a certain lack of sympathy; and lack of sympathy comes from a lack of patient understanding. It is certain that the destiny of the greater part of the human race is either infinitely pathetic or infinitely ridiculous. Under which aspect, then, shall that destiny, and those obscure fractions of humanity, be considered? Villiers was too sincere an idealist, too absolute in his idealism, to hesitate. 'As for living,' he cries, in that splendid phrase of *Axël*, 'our servants will do that for us!'[11] And, in the *Contes Cruels*, there is this not less characteristic expression of what was always his mental attitude: 'As at the play, in a central stall, one sits out, so as not to disturb one's neighbours – out of courtesy, in a word – some play written in a wearisome style and of which one does not like the subject, so I lived, out of politeness': *je vivais par politesse*. In this haughtiness towards life, in this disdain of ordinary human motives and ordinary human beings, there is at once the distinction and the weakness of Villiers. And he has himself pointed the moral against himself in these words of the story which forms the epilogue to the *Contes Cruels*: 'When the forehead alone contains the existence of a man, that man is enlightened only from above his head; then his jealous shadow, prostrate under him, draws him by the feet, that it may drag him down into the invisible.'

III.

All his life Villiers was a poor man; though, all his life, he was awaiting that fortune which he refused to anticipate by any mean employment. During most of his life, he was practically an unknown man. Greatly loved, ardently admired, by that inner circle of the men who have made modern French literature, from Verlaine to Maeterlinck, he was looked upon by most people as an amusing kind of madman, a little dangerous, whose ideas, as they floated freely over the café-table, it was at times highly profitable to steal. For Villiers talked his works before writing them, and sometimes he talked them instead of writing them, in his too royally spend-thrift way. To those who knew him he seemed genius itself, and would have seemed so if he had never written a line; for he had the dangerous gift of a personality which seems to have already achieved all that it so energetically contemplates. But personality tells only within hands' reach; and Villiers failed even to startle, failed even to exasperate, the general reader. That his *Premières Poésies*, published at the age of nineteen, should have brought him fame was hardly to be expected, remarkable, especially in its ideas, as that book is. Nor was it to be expected of the enigmatic fragment of a romance, *Isis* (1862), anticipating, as it does, by so long a period, the esoteric and spiritualistic romances which were to have their vogue. But *Elën* (1864) and *Morgane* (1865), those two poetic dramas in prose, so full of distinction, of spiritual rarity; but two years later, *Claire Lenoir* (afterwards incorporated in one of his really great books, *Tribulat Bonhomet*), with its macabre horror; but *La Révolte* (1870), for Villiers so 'actual,' and which had its moment's success when it was revived in 1896 at the Odéon; but *Le Nouveau Monde* (1880), a drama which, by some extraordinary caprice, won a prize; but *Les Contes Cruels* (1880), that collection of masterpieces, in which the essentially French *conte* is outdone on its own ground! It was not till 1886 that Villiers ceased to be an unknown writer, with the publication of that phosphorescent buffoonery of science, that vast parody of humanity, *L'Eve Future*. *Tribulat Bonhomet* (which he himself defined as *bouffonnerie énorme* *et sombre, couleur du siècle)** was to come, in its final form, and the superb poem in prose *Akëdysséril*; and then, more and more indifferent collections of stories, in which Villiers, already dying, is but the shadow of himself: *L'Amour Suprême* (1886), *Histoires Insolites* (1888), *Nouveaux Contes Cruels* (1888). He was correcting the proofs of *Axël* when he died; the volume was published in 1890, followed by *Propos d'au-delà*, and a series of articles, *Chez les Passants*. Once dead, the fame which had avoided him all his life began to follow him; he had *une belle presse* at his funeral.

Meanwhile, he had been preparing the spiritual atmosphere of the new generation. Living among believers in the material world, he had been declaring, not in vain, his belief in the world of the spirit; living among Realists and Parnassians, he had been creating a new form of art, the art of the Symbolist drama, and of Symbolism in fiction. He had been lonely all his life, for he had been living, in his own lifetime, the life of the next generation. There was but one man among his contemporaries to whom he could give, and from whom he could receive, perfect sympathy. That man was Wagner. Gradually the younger men came about him; at the end he was not lacking in disciples.

And after all, the last word of Villiers is faith; faith against the evidence of the senses, against the negations of materialistic science, against the monstrous paradox of progress, against his own pessimism in the face of these formidable enemies. He affirms; he 'believes in soul, is very sure of God;' requires no witness to the spiritual world of which he is always the inhabitant; and is content to lose his way in the material world, brushing off its mud from time to time with a disdainful gesture, as he goes on his way (to apply a significant word of Pater) 'like one on a secret errand.'[12]

---

*   ['an enormous, gloomy tomfoolery, that captured an era' – from 'Le Tzar et les Grand Ducs', a short story in *L'Amour suprême* (1888).]

Arthur Rimbaud

That story of the Arabian Nights, which is at the same time a true story, the life of Rimbaud, has been told, for the first time, in the extravagant but valuable book of an anarchist of letters, who writes under the name of Paterne Berrichon, and who has since married Rimbaud's sister.[1] *La Vie de Jean-Arthur Rimbaud* is full of curiosity for those who have been mystified by I know not what legends, invented to give wonder to a career, itself more wonderful than any of the inventions. The man who died at Marseilles, at the Hospital of the Conception, on March 10, 1891, at the age of thirty-seven, *négociant* [salesman], as the register of his death describes him, was a writer of genius, an innovator in verse and prose, who had written all his poetry by the age of nineteen, and all his prose by a year or two later. He had given up literature to travel hither and thither, first in Europe, then in Africa; he had been an engineer, a leader of caravans, a merchant of precious merchandise. And this man, who had never written down a line after those astonishing early experiments, was heard, in his last delirium, talking of precisely such visions as those which had haunted his youth, and using, says his sister, 'expressions of a singular and penetrating charm' to render these sensations of visionary countries. Here certainly is one of the most curious problems of literature: is it a problem of which we can discover the secret?

Jean-Nicolas-Arthur Rimbaud was born at Charleville, in the Ardennes, October 28, 1854. His father, of whom he saw little, was a captain in the army; his mother, of peasant origin, was severe, rigid, and unsympathetic. At school he was an unwilling but brilliant scholar, and by his fifteenth year was well acquainted with Latin literature and intimately with French literature. It was in that year that he began to write poems, from the first curiously original: eleven poems dating from that year are to be found in his collected works. When he was sixteen he decided that he had had enough of school, and enough of home. Only Paris existed: he must go to Paris. The first time he went without a ticket; he spent, indeed, fifteen days in Paris, but he spent them in Mazas, from which he was released and restored to his home by his schoolmaster.[2] The second time, a few days later, he sold his watch, which paid for his railway ticket. This time he threw himself on the hospitality of André Gill, a painter and verse-writer, of some little noto-riety then, whose address he had happened to come across.[3] The uninvited guest was not welcomed, and after some penniless days in Paris he tramped back to Charleville. The third time (he had waited five months, writing poems, and discontented to be only writing poems) he made his way to Paris on foot, in a heat of revolutionary sympathy, to offer himself to the insurgents of the Commune. Again he had to return on foot. Finally, having learnt with difficulty that a man is not taken at his own valuation until he has proved his right to be so accepted, he sent up the manuscript of his poems to Verlaine. The manuscript contained *Le Bateau Ivre*, *Les Premières Communions*, *Ma Bohème*, *Roman*, *Les Effarés*, and, indeed, all but a few of the poems he ever wrote. Verlaine was overwhelmed with delight, and invited him to Paris. A local admirer lent him the money to get there, and from October 1871 to July 1872 he was Verlaine's guest.

The boy of seventeen, already a perfectly original poet, and beginning to be an equally original prose-writer, astonished the whole Parnasse, Banville, Hugo himself. On Verlaine his influ-ence was more profound. The meeting brought about one of those lamentable and admirable disasters which make and unmake careers. Verlaine has told us in his *Confessions* that, 'in the begin-ning, there was no question of any sort of affection or sympathy between two natures so different as that of the poet of the *Assis* and mine, but simply of an extreme admiration and astonishment before this boy of sixteen, who had already written things, as Fénélon has excellently said, "perhaps outside literature."' This admiration and astonishment passed gradually into a more personal feeling, and it was under the influence of Rimbaud that the long vagabondage of Verlaine's life began. The two poets wandered together through Belgium, England, and again Belgium, from July 1872 to August 1873, when there occurred that tragic parting at Brussels which left Verlaine a prisoner for eighteen months, and sent Rimbaud back to his family.[4] He had already written all the poetry and prose that he was ever to write, and in 1873 he printed at Brussels *Une Saison en Enfer*. It was the only book he himself ever gave to the press, and no sooner was it printed than he destroyed the whole edition, with the exception of a few copies, of which only Verlaine's copy, I believe, still exists. Soon began new wanderings, with their invariable return to the starting-point of Charleville: a few days in Paris, a year in England, four months in Stuttgart (where he was visited by Verlaine), Italy, France again, Vienna, Java, Holland, Sweden, Egypt, Cyprus, Abyssinia, and then nothing but Africa, until the final return to France. He had been a teacher of French in England, a seller of key-rings in the streets of Paris, had unloaded vessels in the ports, and helped to gather in the harvest in the country; he had been a volunteer in the Dutch army, a military engineer, a trader; and now physical sciences had begun to attract his insatiable curiosity, and dreams of the fabulous East began to resolve themselves into dreams of a romantic commerce with the real East. He became a merchant of coffee, perfumes, ivory, and gold, in the interior of Africa; then an explorer, a predecessor, and in his own regions, of Marchand.[5] After twelve years' wandering and exposure in Africa he was attacked by a malady of the knee, which rapidly became worse. He was transported first to Aden, then to Marseilles, where, in May 1891, his leg was amputated. Further complications set in. He insisted, first, on being removed to his home, then on being taken back to Marseilles. His sufferings were an intolerable torment, and more cruel to him was the torment of his desire to live. He died inch by inch, fighting every inch; and his sister's quiet narrative of those last months is agonising. He died at Marseilles in November, 'prophesying,' says his sister, and repeating 'Allah Kerim! Allah Kerim!'[6]

The secret of Rimbaud, I think, and the reason why he was able to do the unique thing in literature which he did, and then to disappear quietly and become a legend in the East, is that his mind was not the mind of the artist but of the man of action. He was a dreamer, but all his dreams were discoveries. To him it was an identical act of his temperament to write the sonnet of the *Vowels* and to trade in ivory and frankincense with the Arabs. He lived with all his faculties at every instant of his life, abandoning himself to himself with a confidence which was at once his strength and (looking at things less absolutely) his weakness. To the student of success, and what is relative in achievement, he illustrates the danger of one's over-possession by one's own genius, just as aptly as the saint in the cloister does, or the mystic too full of God to speak intelligibly to the world, or the spilt wisdom of the drunkard.

The artist who is above all things an artist cultivates a little choice corner of himself with elaborate care; he brings miraculous flowers to growth there, but the rest of the garden is but mown grass or tangled bushes. That is why many excellent writers, very many painters, and most musicians are so tedious on any subject but their own. Is it not tempting, does it not seem a devotion rather than a superstition, to worship the golden chalice in which the wine has been made God, as if the chalice were the reality, and the Real Presence the symbol? The artist, who is only an artist, circumscribes his intelligence into almost such a fiction, as he reverences the work of his own hands. But there are certain natures (great or small, Shakespeare or Rimbaud, it makes no difference) to whom the work is nothing; the act of working, everything. Rimbaud was a small, narrow, hard, precipitate nature, which had the will to live, and nothing but the will to live; and his verses, and his follies, and his wanderings, and his traffickings were but the breathing of different hours in his day.

That is why he is so swift, definite, and quickly exhausted in vision; why he had his few things to say, each an action with consequences. He invents new ways of saying things, not because he is a learned artist, but because he is burning to say them, and he has none of the hesitations of knowledge. He leaps right over or through the conventions that had been standing in everybody's way; he has no time to go round, and no respect for trespass-boards, and so he becomes the *enfant terrible* of literature, playing pranks (as in that sonnet of the *Vowels*), knocking down barriers for the mere amusement of the thing, getting all the possible advantage of his barbarisms in mind and conduct. And so, in life, he is first of all conspicuous as a disorderly liver, a revolter against morals as against prosody, though we may imagine that, in his heart, morals meant as little to him, one way or the other, as prosody. Later on, his revolt seems to be against civilisation itself, as he disappears into the deserts of Africa. And it is, if you like, a revolt against civilisation, but the revolt is instinctive, a need of the organism; it is not doctrinal, cynical, a conviction, a sentiment.

Always, as he says, *rêvant univers fantastiques*, he is conscious of the danger as well the ecstasy of that divine imitation; for he says: 'My life will always be too vast to be given up wholly to force and beauty.' *J'attends Dieu avec gourmandise*, he cries in a fine rapture; and then, sadly enough: 'I have created all the feasts, all the triumphs, all the dramas of the world. I have set myself to invent new flowers, a new flesh, a new language. I have fancied that I have attained supernatural power. Well, I have now only to put my imagination and my memories in the grave. What a fine artist's and storyteller's fame thrown away!' See how completely he is conscious, and how completely he is at the mercy, of that hallucinatory rage of vision, vision to him being always force, power, creation, which on some of his pages seems to become sheer madness, and on others a kind of wild but absolute insight. He will be silent, he tells us, as to all that he contains within his mind, 'greedy as the sea,' for otherwise poets and visionaries would envy him his fantastic wealth. And, in that *Nuit d'Enfer*, which does not bear that title in vain, he exalts himself as a kind of saviour; he is in the circle of pride in Dante's hell, and he has lost all sense of limit, really believes himself to be 'no one and some one.' Then, in the *Alchimie du Verbe*, he becomes the analyst of his own hallucinations 'I believe in all the enchantments,' he tells us; 'I invented the colour of the vowels: A, black; E, white; I, red; O, blue; U, green.* I regulated the form and the movement of every

---

* [Symons' footnote:] Here is the famous sonnet, which must be taken, as it was meant, without undue seriousness, and yet as something more than a mere joke.

VOYELLES

A noir, E blanc, I rouge, U vert, O bleu, voyelles,
 Je dirai quelque jour vos naissances latentes.
 A, noir corset velu des mouches éclatantes
 Qui bombillent autour des puanteurs cruelles,

Golfe d'ombre; E, candeur des vapeurs et des tentes,
 Lance des glaciers fiers, rois blancs, frissons d'ombelles;
 I, pourpres, sang craché, rire des lèvres belles
 Dans la colère ou les ivresses pénitentes;

U, cycles, vibrements divins des mers virides,
 Paix des pâtis semés d'animaux, paix des rides
 Que l'alchimie imprime aux grands fronts studieux;

O, suprême Clarion plein de strideurs étranges,
 Silences traversés des mondes et des Anges;
 – O l'Oméga, rayon violet de Ses Yeux!

[A black, E white, I red, U green, O blue, vowels, / Some day I'll recite your latent births. / A, black velvet corset of dazzling flies / Who buzz around cruel

consonant, and, with instinctive rhythms, I flattered myself that I had invented a poetic language accessible, one day or another, to every shade of meaning. I reserved to myself the right of translation ... I accustomed myself to simple hallucination: I saw, quite frankly, a mosque in place of a factory, a school of drums kept by the angels, post-chaises on the roads of heaven, a drawing-room at the bottom of a lake; monsters, mysteries; the title of a vaudeville raised up horrors before me. Then I explained my magical sophisms by the hallucination of words! I ended by finding something sacred in the disorder of my mind.' Then he makes the great discovery. Action, one sees, this fraudulent and insistent will to live, has been at the root of all these mental and verbal orgies, in which he has been wasting the very substance of his thought. Well, 'action,' he discovers, 'is not life, but a way of spoiling something.' Even this is a form of enervation, and must be rejected from the absolute. *Mon devoir m'est remis. Il ne faut plus songer à cela. Je suis réellement d'outre-tombe, et pas de commissions.**

It is for the absolute that he seeks, always; the absolute which the great artist, with his careful wisdom, has renounced seeking. And he is content with nothing less; hence his own contempt for what he has done, after all, so easily; for what has come to him, perhaps through his impatience, but imperfectly. He is a dreamer in whom dream is swift, hard in outline, coming suddenly and going suddenly, a real thing, but seen only in passing. Visions rush past him, he cannot arrest them; they rush forth from him, he cannot restrain their haste to be gone, as he creates them in the

---

stenches, // Gulf of shadows; E, candour of fumes and tents / Lance of proud glaciers, white kings, shudder of cowslips; / I, purple, blood spat out, laughter of beautiful lips / In anger or drunken sadness; // U, cycles, divine vibrations of viridian seas, / The peace of pastures sown with animals, the peace of those wrinkles / That alchemy prints upon studious foreheads; // O, the last Trump filled with bizarre stridulations, / Silences crossed by worlds and angels; / O, Omega, the violet beam from His Eyes!]

Coincidence or origin, it has lately been pointed out that Rimbaud may formerly have seen an old A B C book in which the vowels are coloured for the most part as his are (A, black; E, yellow; I, red; O, blue; U, green). In the little illustrative pictures around them some are oddly in keeping with the images of Rimbaud.

* ['My job is over. I shouldn't even dream of that any more. I am really beyond the grave, and no more errands.' – from Section III of 'Vies' [Lives] in *Illuminations*.]

mere indiscriminate idleness of energy. And so this seeker after the absolute leaves but a broken medley of fragments, into each of which he has put a little of his personality, which he is for ever dramatising, by multiplying one facet, so to speak, after another. Very genuinely, he is now a beaten and wandering ship, flying in a sort of intoxication before the wind, over undiscovered seas; now a starving child outside a baker's window, in the very ecstasy of hunger; now *la victime et la petite épouse* of the first communion; now:

> Je ne parlerai pas, je ne penserai rien;
> Mais l'amour infini me montera dans l'âme,
> Et j'irai loin, bien loin, comme un bohémien,
> Par la Nature, heureux comme avec une femme!*

He catches at verse, at prose, invents a sort of *vers libre* before any one else, not quite knowing what to do with it, invents a quite new way of writing prose, which Laforgue will turn to account later on; and having suggested, with some impatience, half the things that his own and the next generation are to busy themselves with developing, he gives up writing, as an inadequate form, to which he is also inadequate.

What, then, is the actual value of Rimbaud's work, in verse and prose, apart from its relative values of so many kinds? I think, considerable; though it will probably come to rest on two or three pieces of verse, and a still vaguer accomplishment in prose. He brought into French verse something of that 'gipsy way of going with nature, as with a woman'; a very young, very crude, very defiant and sometimes very masterly sense of just those real things which are too close to us to be seen by most people with any clearness. He could render physical sensation, of the subtlest kind, without making any compromise with language, forcing language to speak straight, taming it as one would tame a dangerous animal. And he kneaded prose as he kneaded verse, making it a disartic-ulated, abstract, mathematically lyrical thing. In verse, he pointed the way to certain new splendours, as to certain new *naïvetés*; there is the *Bateau Ivre*, without which we might never have had

---

* ['I will speak no more, I will think of nothing; / But infinite love will rise in my soul, / And I will go far, very far, just like a gypsy / In a natural way, happy as if I were with a woman.' – 'Sensation'.]

Verlaine's *Crimen Amoris*.[7] And, inter-tangled with what is ingenuous, and with what is splendid, there is a certain irony, which comes into that youthful work as if youth were already reminiscent of itself, so conscious is it that youth is youth, and that youth is passing.

In all these ways, Rimbaud had his influence upon Verlaine, and his influence upon Verlaine was above all the influence of the man of action upon the man of sensation; the influence of what is simple, narrow, emphatic, upon what is subtle, complex, growing. Verlaine's rich, sensitive nature was just then trying to realise itself. Just because it had such delicate possibilities, because there were so many directions in which it could grow, it was not at first quite sure of its way. Rimbaud came into the life and art of Verlaine, troubling both, with that trouble which reveals a man to himself. Having helped to make Verlaine a great poet, he could go. Note that he himself could never have developed: writing had been one of his discoveries; he could but make other discoveries, personal ones. Even in literature he had his future; but his future was Verlaine.

Paul Verlaine

I.

'Bien affectueusement … yours, P. Verlaine.' So, in its gay and friendly mingling of French and English, ended the last letter I had from Verlaine. A few days afterwards came the telegram from Paris telling me of his death, in the Rue Descartes, on that 8th January 1896.

'Condemned to death,' as he was, in Victor Hugo's phrase of men in general, 'with a sort of indefinite reprieve,' and gravely ill as I had for some time known him to be, it was still with a shock, not only of sorrow, but of surprise, that I heard the news of his death.[1] He had suffered and survived so much, and I found it so hard to associate the idea of death with one who had always been so passionately in love with life, more passionately in love with life than any man I ever knew. Rest was one of the delicate privileges of life which he never loved: he did but endure it with grumbling gaiety when a hospital-bed claimed him. And whenever he spoke to me of the long rest which has now sealed his eyelids, it was with a shuddering revolt from the thought of ever going away into the cold, out of the sunshine which had been so warm to him. With all his pains, misfortunes, and the calamities which followed him step by step all his life, I think few men ever got so much out of their lives, or lived so fully, so intensely, with such a genius for living. That, indeed, is why he was a great poet. Verlaine was a man who gave its full value to every moment, who got out of every moment all that that moment had to give him. It was not always, not often, perhaps, pleasure. But it was energy, the vital force of a nature which was always receiving and giving out, never at rest, never passive, or indifferent, or hesitating. It is impossible for me to convey to those who did not know him any notion of how sincere he was. The word 'sincerity' seems hardly to have emphasis enough to say, in regard to this one man, what it says, adequately enough, of others. He sinned, and it was with all his humanity; he repented, and it was with all his soul. And to every occurrence of the day, to every mood of the mind, to every impulse of the creative instinct, he brought the same unparalleled sharpness of sensation. When, in 1894, he was my guest in London, I was amazed by the exactitude of his memory of the mere turnings of the streets, the shapes and colours of the buildings, which he had not seen for twenty years.[2] He saw, he felt, he remembered, everything, with an unconscious mental selection of the fine shades, the essential part of things, or precisely those aspects which most other people would pass by.

Few poets of our time have been more often drawn, few have been easier to draw, few have better repaid drawing, than Paul Verlaine. A face without a beautiful line, a face all character, full of somnolence and sudden fire, in which every irregularity was a kind of aid to the hand, could not but tempt the artist desiring at once to render a significant likeness and to have his own part in the creation of a picture. Verlaine, like all men of genius, had something of the air of the somnambulist: that profound slumber of the face, as it was in him, with its startling awakenings. It was a face devoured by dreams, feverish and somnolent; it had earthly passion, intellectual pride, spiritual humility; the air of one who remembers, not without an effort, who is listening, half distractedly to something which other people do not hear; coming back so suddenly, and from so far, with the relief of one who steps out of that obscure shadow into the noisier forgetfulness of life. The eyes, often half closed, were like the eyes of a cat between sleeping and waking; eyes in which contemplation was 'itself an act.' A remarkable lithograph by Mr. Rothenstein (the face lit by oblique eyes, the folded hand thrust into the cheek) gives with singular truth the sensation of that restless watch on things which this prisoner of so many chains kept without slackening.[3] To Verlaine every corner of the world was alive with tempting and consoling and terrifying beauty. I have never known any one to whom the sight of the eyes was so intense and imaginative a thing. To him, physical sight and spiritual vision, by some strange alchemical operation of the brain, were one. And in the disquietude of his face, which seemed to take such close heed of things, precisely because it was sufficiently apart from them to be always a spectator, there was a realisable process of vision continually going on, in which all the loose ends of the visible world were being caught up into a new mental fabric.

And along with this fierce subjectivity, into which the egoism of the artist entered so unconsciously, and in which it counted for so much, there was more than the usual amount of childishness, always in some measure present in men of genius. There was a real, almost blithe, childishness in the way in which he would put on his 'Satanic' expression, of which it was part of the joke that every one should not be quite in the secret. It was a whim of this kind which made him put at the beginning of *Romances sans Paroles* that very criminal image of a head which had so little resemblance with even the shape, indeed curious enough, of his actual head. 'Born under the sign of Saturn,' as he no doubt was, with that 'old prisoner's head' of which he tells us, it was by his amazing faculty for a simple kind of happiness that he always impressed me. I have never seen so cheerful an invalid as he used to be at that hospital, the Hôpital Saint-Louis, where at one time I used to go and see him every week. His whole face seemed to chuckle as he would tell me, in his emphatic, confiding way, everything that entered into his head; the droll stories cut short by a groan, a lamentation, a sudden fury of reminiscence, at which his face would cloud or convulse, the wild eyebrows slanting up and down; and then, suddenly, the good laugh would be back, clearing the air. No one was ever so responsive to his own moods as Verlaine, and with him every mood had the vehemence of a passion. Is not his whole art a delicate waiting upon moods, with that perfect confidence in them as they are, which it is a large part of ordinary education to discourage in us, and a large part of experience to repress? But to Verlaine, happily, experience taught nothing; or rather, it taught him only to cling the more closely to those moods in whose succession lies the more intimate part of our spiritual life.

It is no doubt well for society that man should learn by experience; for the artist the benefit is doubtful. The artist, it cannot be too clearly understood, has no more part in society than a monk in domestic life: he cannot be judged by its rules, he can be neither praised nor blamed for his acceptance or rejection of its conventions. Social rules are made by normal people for normal people, and the man of genius is fundamentally abnormal. It is the poet against society, society against the poet, a direct antagonism; the shock of which, however, it is often possible to avoid by a compromise. So much licence is allowed on the one side, so much liberty foregone on the other. The consequences are not always of the best, art being generally the loser. But there are certain natures to which compromise is impossible; and the nature of Verlaine was one of these natures.

'The soul of an immortal child,' says one who has understood him better than others, Charles Morice, 'that is the soul of Verlaine, with all the privileges and all the perils of so being: with the sudden despair so easily distracted, the vivid gaieties without a cause, the excessive suspicions and the excessive confidences, the whims so easily outwearied, the deaf and blind infatuations, with, especially, the unceasing renewal of impressions in the incorruptible integrity of personal vision and sensation. Years, influences, teachings, may pass over a temperament such as this, may irritate it, may fatigue it; transform it, never – never so much as to alter that particular unity which consists in a dualism, in the division of forces between the longing after what is evil and the adoration of what is good; or rather, in the antagonism of spirit and flesh. Other men "arrange" their lives, take sides, follow one direction; Verlaine hesitates before a choice, which seems to him monstrous, for, with the integral *naïveté* of irrefutable human truth, he cannot resign himself, however strong may be the doctrine, however enticing may be the passion, to the necessity of sacrificing one to the other, and from one to the other he oscillates without a moment's repose.'[4]

It is in such a sense as this that Verlaine may be said to have learnt nothing from experience, in the sense that he learnt everything direct from life, and without comparing day with day. That the exquisite artist of the *Fêtes Galantes* should become the great poet of *Sagesse*, it was needful that things should have happened as disastrously as they did: the marriage with the girl-wife, that brief idyl, the passion for drink, those other forbidden passions, vaga-bondage, an attempted crime, the eighteen months of prison, conversion; followed, as it had to be, by relapse, bodily sickness, poverty, beggary almost, a lower and lower descent into mean distresses. It was needful that all this should happen, in order that the spiritual vision should eclipse the material vision; but it was needful that all this should happen in vain, so far as the conduct of life was concerned. Reflection, in Verlaine, is pure waste; it is the speech of the soul and the speech of the eyes, that we must listen to in his verse, never the speech of the reason. And I call him fortunate because, going through life with a great unconsciousness of what most men spend their lives in considering, he was able to abandon himself entirely to himself, to his unimpeded vision, to his unchecked emotion, to the passionate sincerity which in him was genius.

II.

French poetry, before Verlaine, was an admirable vehicle for a really fine, a really poetical, kind of rhetoric. With Victor Hugo, for the first time since Ronsard (the two or three masterpieces of Ronsard and his companions) it had learnt to sing;[5] with Baudelaire it had invented a new vocabulary for the expression of subtle, often perverse, essentially modern emotion and sensation. But with Victor Hugo, with Baudelaire, we are still under the dominion of rhetoric. 'Take eloquence, and wring its neck!' said Verlaine in his *Art Poétique*; and he showed, by writing it, that French verse could be written without rhetoric. It was partly from his study of English models that he learnt the secret of liberty in verse, but it was much more a secret found by the way, in the mere endeavour to be absolutely sincere, to express exactly what he saw, to give voice to his own temperament, in which intensity of feeling seemed to find its own expression, as if by accident. *L'art, mes enfants, c'est d'être absolument soi-même*, he tells us in one of his later poems;* and, with such a personality as Verlaine's to express, what more has art to do, if it would truly, and in any interesting manner, hold the mirror up to nature?[6]

For, consider the natural qualities which this man had for the task of creating a new poetry. 'Sincerity, and the impression of the moment followed to the letter': that is how he defined his theory of style, in an article written about himself.

> Car nous voulons la nuance encor,
> Pas la couleur, rien que la nuance!†

as he cries, in his famous *Art Poétique*. Take, then, his suscepti-bility of the senses, an emotional susceptibility not less delicate; a life sufficiently troubled to draw out every emotion of which he was capable, and, with it, that absorption in the moment, that inability to look before or after; the need to love and the need

---

* ['The art, my children, is to be absolutely oneself' – Poem XVIII ('J'ai dit à l'esprit vain, à l'ostentation') in *Bonheur* (1891).]

† ['For we still want nuance, / Not colour – nothing but nuance!']

to confess, each a passion; an art of painting the fine shades of landscape, of evoking atmosphere, which can be compared only with the art of Whistler; a simplicity of language which is the direct outcome of a simplicity of temperament, with just enough consciousness of itself for a final elegance; and, at the very depth of his being, an almost fierce humility, by which the passion of love, after searching furiously through all his creatures, finds God by the way, and kneels in the dust before him. Verlaine was never a theorist: he left theories to Mallarmé. He had only his divination; and he divined that poetry, always desiring that miracles should happen, had never waited patiently enough upon the miracle. It was by that proud and humble mysticism of his temperament that he came to realise how much could be done by, in a sense, trying to do nothing.

And then: *De la musique avant toute chose; De la musique encore et toujours!*[*] There are poems of Verlaine which go as far as verse can go to become pure music, the voice of a bird with a human soul. It is part of his simplicity, his divine childishness, that he abandons himself, at times, to the song which words begin to sing in the air, with the same wise confidence with which he abandons himself to the other miracles about him. He knows that words are living things, which we have not created, and which go their way without demanding of us the right to live. He knows that words are suspicious, not without their malice, and that they resist mere force with the impalpable resistance of fire or water. They are to be caught only with guile or with trust. Verlaine has both, and words become Ariel to him. They bring him not only that submission of the slave which they bring to others, but all the soul, and in a happy bondage. They transform themselves for him into music, colour, and shadow; a disembodied music, diaphanous colours, luminous shadow. They serve him with so absolute a self-negation that he can write *romances sans paroles*, songs almost without words, in which scarcely a sense of the interference of human speech remains. The ideal of lyric poetry, certainly, is to be this passive, flawless medium for the deeper consciousness of things, the mysterious voice of that mystery which lies about us, out of which we have come, and into which we shall return. It is not without reason that we cannot analyse a perfect lyric.

[*]   ['Music before anything else; more music for evermore' – 'Art poétique'.]

With Verlaine the sense of hearing and the sense of sight are almost interchangeable: he paints with sound, and his line and atmosphere become music. It was with the most precise accuracy that Whistler applied the terms of music to his painting, for painting, when it aims at being the vision of reality, *pas la couleur, rien que la nuance*, passes almost into the condition of music.[7] Verlaine's landscape painting is always an evocation, in which outline is lost in atmosphere.

> C'est des beaux yeux derrière des voiles,
> > C'est le grand jour tremblant de midi,
> > C'est, par un ciel d'automne attiédi,
> Le bleu fouillis des claires étoiles!*

He was a man, certainly, 'for whom the visible world existed,' but for whom it existed always as a vision.[8] He absorbed it through all his senses, as the true mystic absorbs the divine beauty. And so he created in verse a new voice for nature, full of the humble ecstasy with which he saw, listened, accepted.

> Cette âme qui se lamente
> En cette plaine dormante
> > C'est la nôtre, n'est-ce pas?
> La mienne, dis, et la tienne,
> Dont s'exhale l'humble antienne
> > Par ce tiède soir, tout bas?†

And with the same attentive simplicity with which he found words for the sensations of hearing and the sensations of sight, he found words for the sensations of the soul, for the fine shades of feeling. From the moment when his inner life may be said to have begun, he was occupied with the task of an unceasing confession, in which one seems to overhear him talking to himself, in that vague, preoccupied way which he often had. Here again are words which startle one by their delicate resemblance to thoughts, by

---

* ['"Tis veils of beauty for beautiful eyes, / 'Tis the trembling light of the naked noon, / 'Tis a medley of blue and gold, the moon / And stars in the cool of autumn skies.' – Symons' translation of 'Art poétique'.]

† ['What soul is this that complains / Over the sleeping plains, / And what is it that it saith? / Is it mine, is it thine, / This lowly hymn I divine / In the warm night, low as a breath?' – Symons' translation from 'Ariettes oubliées I', *Romances sans paroles*.]

their winged flight from so far, by their alighting so close. The verse murmurs, with such an ingenuous confidence, such intimate secrets. That 'setting free' of verse, which is one of the achievements of Verlaine, was itself mainly an attempt to be more and more sincere, a way of turning poetic artifice to new account, by getting back to nature itself, hidden away under the eloquent rhetoric of Hugo, Baudelaire, and the Parnassians. In the devotion of rhetoric to either beauty or truth, there is a certain consciousness of an audience, of an external judgment: rhetoric would convince, be admired. It is the very essence of poetry to be unconscious of anything between its own moment of flight and the supreme beauty which it will never attain. Verlaine taught French poetry that wise and subtle unconsciousness. It was in so doing that he 'fused his personality,' in the words of Verhaeren, 'so profoundly with beauty, that he left upon it the imprint of a new and henceforth eternal attitude.'[9]

III.

J'ai la fureur d'aimer, says Verlaine, in a passage of very personal significance.

> J'ai la fureur d'aimer. Mon cœur si faible est fou.
> N'importe quand, n'importe quel et n'importe où,
> Qu'un éclair de beauté, de vertu, de vaillance,
> Luise, il s'y précipite, il y vole, il y lance,
> Et, le temps d'une étreinte, il embrasse cent fois
> L'être ou l'objet qu'il a poursuivi de son choix;
> Puis, quand l'illusion a replié son aile,
> Il revient triste et seul bien souvent, mais fidèle,
> Et laissant aux ingrats quelque chose de lui,
> Sang ou chair ….
> J'ai la fureur d'aimer. Qu'y faire? Ah, laissez faire!*

---

* ['I have a rage for love. My feeble heart is mad / No matter when, no matter what and no matter where, / If a beam of beauty, of virtue, of courage / Shines forth, it rushes to it, it flies to it, it leaps to it, / And for the length of a clinch, it embraces one hundred times / The being or the object it sought as its choice; / Then, when the illusion has folded its wing, / It comes back sad and often alone, but faithful, / And leaving something of itself to the ingrates, / Blood or flesh … / I have a rage for love. What to do? Ah, let it happen!'[10]]

And certainly this admirable, and supremely dangerous, quality was at the root of Verlaine's nature. Instinctive, unreasoning as he was, entirely at the mercy of the emotion or impression which, for the moment, had seized upon him, it was inevitable that he should be completely at the mercy of the most imperious of instincts, of passions, and of intoxications. And he had the simple and ardent nature, in this again consistently childlike, to which love, some kind of affection, given or returned, is not the luxury, the exception, which it is to many natures, but a daily necessity. To such a temperament there may or may not be the one great passion; there will certainly be many passions. And in Verlaine I find that single, childlike necessity of loving and being loved, all through his life and on every page of his works; I find it, unchanged in essence, but constantly changing form, in his chaste and unchaste devotions to women, in his passionate friendships with men, in his supreme mystical adoration of God.

To turn from *La Bonne Chanson*, written for a wedding present to a young wife, to *Chansons pour Elle*, written more than twenty years later, in dubious honour of a middle-aged mistress, is to travel a long road, the hard, long road which Verlaine had travelled during those years. His life was ruinous, a disaster, more sordid perhaps than the life of any other poet; and he could write of it, from a hospital-bed, with this quite sufficient sense of its deprivations. 'But all the same, it is hard,' he laments, in *Mes Hôpitaux*, 'after a life of work, set off, I admit, with accidents in which I have had a large share, catastrophes perhaps vaguely premeditated – it is hard, I say, at forty-seven years of age, in full possession of all the reputation (of the *success*, to use the frightful current phrase) to which my highest ambitions could aspire – hard, hard, hard indeed, worse than hard, to find myself – good God! – to find myself *on the streets*, and to have nowhere to lay my head and support an ageing body save the pillows and the *menus* of a public charity, even now uncertain, and which might at any moment be withdrawn – God forbid! – without, apparently, the fault of any one, oh! not even, and above all, not mine.' Yet, after all, these sordid miseries, this poor man's vagabondage, all the misfortunes of one certainly 'irreclaimable,' on which so much stress has been laid, alike by friends and by foes, are externalities; they are not the man; the man, the eternal lover, passionate and humble, remains unchanged, while only his shadow wanders, from morning to night of the long day.

The poems to Rimbaud, to Lucien Létinois, to others, the whole volume of *Dédicaces*, cover perhaps as wide a range of sentiment as *La Bonne Chanson* and *Chansons pour Elle*. The poetry of friendship has never been sung with such plaintive sincerity, such simple human feeling, as in some of these poems, which can only be compared, in modern poetry, with a poem for which Verlaine had a great admiration, Tennyson's *In Memoriam*.[11] Only, with Verlaine, the thing itself, the affection or the regret, is everything; there is no room for meditation over destiny, or search for a problematical consolation. Other poems speak a more difficult language, in which, doubtless, *l'ennui de vivre avec les gens et dans les choses* [the boredom of living with people and things] counts for much, and *la fureur d'aimer* for more.

In spite of the general impression to the contrary, an impression which by no means displeased him himself, I must contend that the sensuality of Verlaine, brutal as it could sometimes be, was after all simple rather than complicated, instinctive rather than perverse. In the poetry of Baudelaire, with which the poetry of Verlaine is so often compared, there is a deliberate science of sensual perversity which has something almost monachal in its accentuation of vice with horror, in its passionate devotion to passions. Baudelaire brings every complication of taste, the exasperation of perfumes, the irritant of cruelty, the very odours and colours of corruption, to the creation and adornment of a sort of religion, in which an eternal mass is served before a veiled altar. There is no confession, no absolution, not a prayer is permitted which is not set down in the ritual. With Verlaine, however often love may pass into sensuality, to whatever length sensuality may be hurried, sensuality is never more than the malady of love. It is love desiring the absolute, seeking in vain, seeking always, and, finally, out of the depths, finding God.

Verlaine's conversion took place while he was in prison, during those solitary eighteen months in company with his thoughts, that enforced physical inactivity, which could but concentrate his whole energy on the only kind of sensation then within his capacity, the sensations of the soul and of the conscience. With that promptitude of abandonment which was his genius, he grasped feverishly at the succour of God and the Church, he abased himself before the immaculate purity of the Virgin. He had not, like others who have risen from the same depths to the same height of humiliation, to despoil his nature of its pride, to conquer his intellect, before he could become *l'enfant vêtu de laine et d'innocence* [the child clothed in wool and innocence].[12] All that was simple, humble, childlike in him accepted that humiliation with the loving child's joy in penitence; all that was ardent, impulsive, indomitable in him burst at once into a flame of adoration.

He realised the great secret of the Christian mystics: that it is possible to love God with an extravagance of the whole being, to which the love of the creature cannot attain. All love is an attempt to break through the loneliness of individuality, to fuse oneself with something not oneself, to give and to receive, in all the warmth of natural desire, that inmost element which remains, so cold and so invincible, in the midst of the soul. It is a desire of the infinite in humanity, and, as humanity has its limits, it can but return sadly upon itself when that limit is reached. Thus human love is not only an ecstasy but a despair, and the more profound a despair the more ardently it is returned.

But the love of God, considered only from its human aspect, contains at least the illusion of infinity. To love God is to love the absolute, so far as the mind of man can conceive the absolute, and thus, in a sense, to love God is to possess the absolute, for love has already possessed that which it apprehends. What the earthly lover realises to himself as the image of his beloved is, after all, his own vision of love, not her. God must remain *deus absconditus*, even to love; but the lover, incapable of possessing infinity, will have possessed all of infinity of which he is capable. And his ecstasy will be flawless. The human mind, meditating on infinity, can but discover perfection beyond perfection; for it is impossible to conceive of limitation in any aspect of that which has once been conceived as infinite. In place of that deception which comes from the shock of a boundary-line beyond which humanity cannot conceive of humanity, there is only a divine rage against the limits of human perception, which by their own failure seem at last to limit for us the infinite itself. For once, love finds itself bounded only by its own capacity; so far does the love of God exceed the love of the creature, and so far would it exceed that love if God did not exist.

But if he does exist! if, outside humanity, a conscient, eternal perfection, who has made the world in his image, loves the humanity he has made, and demands love in return! If the spirit of his love is as a breath over the world, suggesting, strengthening, the love which it desires, seeking man that man may seek God, itself the impulse which it humbles itself to accept at man's hands; if, indeed,

Mon Dieu m'a dit: mon fils, il faut m'aimer;*

how much more is this love of God, in its inconceivable acceptance and exchange, the most divine, the only unending, intoxication in the world! Well, it is this realised sense of communion, point by point realised, and put into words, more simple, more human, more instinctive than any poet since the mediaeval mystics has found for the delights of this intercourse, that we find in *Sagesse*, and in the other religious poems of Verlaine.

But, with Verlaine, the love of God is not merely a rapture, it is a thanksgiving for forgiveness. Lying in wait behind all the fair appearances of the world, he remembers the old enemy, the flesh; and the sense of sin (that strange paradox of the reason) is childishly strong in him. He laments his offence, he sees not only the love but the justice of God, and it seems to him, as in a picture, that the little hands of the Virgin are clasped in petition for him. Verlaine's religion is the religion of the Middle Ages. *Je suis catholique*, he said to me, *mais ... catholique du moyen-âge!*† He might have written the ballad which Villon made for his mother, and with the same visual sense of heaven and hell. Like a child, he tells his sins over, promises that he has put them behind him, and finds such *naïve*, human words to express his gratitude. The Virgin is really, to him, mother and friend; he delights in the simple, peasant humanity, still visible in her who is also the Mystical Rose, the Tower of Ivory, the Gate of Heaven, and who now extends her hands, in the gesture of pardon, from a throne only just lower than the throne of God.[13]

IV.

Experience, I have said, taught Verlaine nothing; religion had no more stable influence upon his conduct than experience. In that apology for himself which he wrote under the anagram of 'Pauvre

---

* ['My God said to me: my son, you must love me' – from *Sagesse*.]
† ['I am a Catholic, but ... a Catholic from the Middle Ages!']

Lelian,' he has stated the case with his usual sincerity.[14] 'I believe,' he says, 'and I sin in thought, as in action; I believe, and I repent in thought, if no more. Or again, I believe, and I am a good Christian at this moment; I believe, and I am a bad Christian the instant after. The remembrance, the hope, the invocation of a sin delights me, with or without remorse, sometimes under the very form of sin, and hedged with all its natural consequences; more often – so strong, so natural and *animal*, are flesh and blood – just in the same manner as the remembrances, hopes, invocations of any carnal freethinker. This delight, I, you, someone else, writers, it pleases us to put to paper and publish more or less well expressed: we consign it, in short, into literary form, forgetting all religious ideas, or not letting one of them escape us. Can any one in good faith condemn us as poet? A hundred times no.' And, indeed, I would echo, a hundred times no! It is just this apparent complication of what is really a great simplicity which gives its singular value to the poetry of Verlaine, permitting it to sum up in itself the whole paradox of humanity, and especially the weak, passionate, uncertain, troubled century to which we belong, in which so many doubts, negations, and distresses seem, now more than ever, to be struggling towards at least an ideal of spiritual consolation. Verlaine is the poet of these weaknesses and of that ideal.

Jules Laforgue

Jules Laforgue was born at Montevideo, of Breton parents, August 20, 1860. He died in Paris in 1887, two days before his twenty-seventh birthday. From 1880 to 1886 he had been reader to the Empress Augusta at Berlin. He married only a few months before his death. *D'allures?* says M. Gustave Kahn, *fort correctes, de hauts gibus, des cravates sobres, des vestons anglais, des pardessus clergymans, et de par les nécessités, un parapluie immuablement placé sous le bras.** His portraits show us a clean-shaved, reticent face, betraying little. With such a personality anecdotes have but small chance of appropriating those details by which expansive natures express themselves to the world. We know nothing about Laforgue which his work is not better able to tell us, even now that we have all his notes, unfinished fragments, and the letters of an almost virginal *naïveté* which he wrote to the woman whom he was going to marry. His entire work, apart from these additions, is contained in two small volumes, one of prose, the *Moralités Légendaires*, the other of verse, *Les Complaintes, L'Imitation de Notre-Dame la Lune*, and a few other pieces, all published during the last three years of his life.

The prose and verse of Laforgue, scrupulously correct, but with a new manner of correctness, owe more than any one has realised to the half-unconscious prose and verse of Rimbaud. Verse and prose are alike a kind of travesty, making subtle use of colloquialism, slang, neologism, technical terms, for their allusive, their factitious, their reflected meanings, with which one can play, very seriously. The verse is alert, troubled, swaying, deliberately uncertain, hating rhetoric so piously that it prefers, and finds its piquancy in, the ridiculously obvious. It is really *vers libre*, but at the same time correct verse, before *vers libre* had been invented. And it carries, as far as that theory has ever been carried, the theory which demands an instantaneous notation (Whistler, let us say) of

---

* ['His looks? ... very correct, high-sided hats, plain ties, English jackets, clergyman's overcoats, and – according to necessity, an umbrella immutably held beneath the arm.' – *Les Hommes d'aujourd'hui* (1886).]

the figure or landscape which one has been accustomed to define with such rigorous exactitude. Verse, always elegant, is broken into a kind of mockery of prose.

> Encore un de mes pierrots mort;
>   Mort d'un chronique orphelinisme;
>   C'était un coeur plein de dandysme
> Lunaire, en un drôle de corps;*

he will say to us, with a familiarity of manner, as of one talking languidly, in a low voice, the lips always teased into a slightly bitter smile; and he will pass suddenly into the ironical lilt of

> Hotel garni
> De l'infini,

> Sphinx et Joconde
> Des défunts mondes;†

and from that into this solemn and smiling end of one of his last poems, his own epitaph, if you will:

> Il prit froid l'autre automne,
> S'étant attardi vers les peines des cors,
> Sur la fin d'un beau jour.
> Oh! ce fut pour vos cors, et ce fut pour l'automne,
> Qu'il nous montra qu' 'on meurt d'amour!'
> On ne le verra plus aux fêtes nationales,
> S'enfermer dans l'Histoire et tirer les verrous,
> Il vint trop tard, il est reparti sans scandale;
> O vous qui m'écoutez, rentrez chacun chez vous.‡

---

* ['Another of my pierrots dead; / Dead from chronic orphanism; / He had the heart of a lunar dandy / And a funny little body' – from 'Locutions des Pierrots', *L'Imitation de Notre-Dame La Lune*.]

† ['The well-stocked hotel / Of infinity, // Sphinx and Mona Lisa / From outdated worlds' – from 'Litanies des derniers quartiers de la lune', *L'Imitation de Notre-Dame la Lune*.]

‡ ['He took cold last autumn, / Staying out late for the horns' sufferings, / At the end of a fine day. / Oh! Because of your horns, and because of autumn, / He showed us that "one dies of love". / You won't see him any more on national holidays / Stuffing himself into History and turning the keys. / He came too late, he left again without a scandal; / O you who listen to me, go back to your own homes.' – a slight misquotation from 'Simple Agonie' in *Derniers vers* (1890): 'Il vint trop tard' (he came too late) should read 'Il vint trop tôt' (he came too early).]

The old cadences, the old eloquence, the ingenuous seriousness of poetry, are all banished, on a theory as self-denying as that which permitted Degas to dispense with recognisable beauty in his figures.[1] Here, if ever, is modern verse, verse which dispenses with so many of the privileges of poetry, for an ideal quite of its own. It is, after all, a very self-conscious ideal, becoming artificial through its extreme naturalness; for in poetry it is not 'natural' to say things quite so much in the manner of the moment, with however ironical an intention.

The prose of the *Moralités Légendaires* is perhaps even more of a discovery. Finding its origin, as I have pointed out, in the experimental prose of Rimbaud, it carries that manner to a singular perfection. Disarticulated, abstract, mathematically lyrical, it gives expression, in its icy ecstasy, to a very subtle criticism of the universe, with a surprising irony of cosmical vision. We learn from books of mediaeval magic that the embraces of the devil are of a coldness so intense that it may be called, by an allowable figure of speech, fiery. Everything may be as strongly its opposite as itself, and that is why this balanced, chill, colloquial style of Laforgue has, in the paradox of its intensity, the essential heat of the most obviously emotional prose. The prose is more patient than the verse, with its more compassionate laughter at universal experience. It can laugh as seriously, as profoundly, as in that graveyard monologue of Hamlet, Laforgue's Hamlet, who, Maeterlinck ventures to say, 'is at moments more Hamlet than the Hamlet of Shakespeare.'[2] Let me translate a few sentences from it.

> Perhaps I have still twenty or thirty years to live, and I shall pass that way like the others. Like the others? O Totality, the misery of being there no longer! Ah! I would like to set out tomorrow, and search all through the world for the most adamantine processes of embalming. They, too, were the little people of History, learning to read, trimming their nails, lighting the dirty lamp every evening, in love, gluttonous, vain, fond of compliments, handshakes, and kisses, living on bell-tower gossip, saying, 'What sort of weather shall we have tomorrow? Winter has really come .... We have had no plums this year.' Ah! everything is good, if it would not come to an end. And thou, Silence, pardon the Earth; the little madcap hardly knows what she is doing; on the day of the great summing-up of

consciousness before the Ideal, she will be labelled with a pitiful *idem* in the column of the miniature evolutions of the Unique Evolution, in the column of negligible quantities ... To die! Evidently, one dies without knowing it, as, every night, one enters upon sleep. One has no consciousness of the passing of the last lucid thought into sleep, into swooning, into death. Evidently. But to be no more, to be here no more, to be ours no more! Not even to be able, any more, to press against one's human heart, some idle afternoon, the ancient sadness contained in one little chord on the piano!

In these always 'lunar' parodies, *Salomé, Lohengrin, Fils de Parsifal, Persée et Andromède*, each a kind of metaphysical myth, he realises that *la créature va hardiment à être cérébrale, anti-naturelle,** and he has invented these fantastic puppets with an almost Japanese art of spiritual dislocation. They are, in part, a way of taking one's revenge upon science, by an ironical borrowing of its very terms, which dance in his prose and verse, derisively, at the end of a string.

In his acceptance of the fragility of things as actually a principle of art, Laforgue is a sort of transformed Watteau, showing his disdain for the world which fascinates him, in quite a different way. He has constructed his own world, lunar and actual, speaking slang and astronomy, with a constant disengaging of the visionary aspect, under which frivolity becomes an escape from the arrogance of a still more temporary mode of being, the world as it appears to the sober majority. He is terribly conscious of daily life, cannot omit, mentally, a single hour of the day; and his flight to the moon is in sheer desperation. He sees what he calls *l'Inconscient* in every gesture, but he cannot see it without these gestures. And he sees, not only as an imposition, but as a conquest, the possibilities for art which come from the sickly modern being, with his clothes, his nerves: the mere fact that he flowers from the soil of his epoch.

It is an art of the nerves, this art of Laforgue, and it is what all art would tend towards if we followed our nerves on all their journeys. There is in it all the restlessness of modern life, the haste

---

* ['the creature is boldly going to become cerebral, anti-natural' – a slight misquotation from Laforgue's 'Notes d'esthetique' [Notes on Aesthetics] in *Mélanges posthumes* (1902). Symons omits the word 'purement' before 'cérébrale' ('The creature is boldly going to become purely cerebral').]

to escape from whatever weighs too heavily on the liberty of the moment, that capricious liberty which demands only room enough to hurry itself weary. It is distressingly conscious of the unhappiness of mortality, but it plays, somewhat uneasily, at a disdainful indifference. And it is out of these elements of caprice, fear, contempt, linked together by an embracing laughter, that it makes its existence.

Il n'y a pas de type, il y a la vie, Laforgue replies to those who come to him with classical ideals. *Votre idéal est bien vite magnifiquement submergé,** in life itself, which should form its own art, an art deliberately ephemeral, with the attaching pathos of passing things. There is a great pity at the root of this art of Laforgue: self-pity, which extends, with the artistic sympathy, through mere clearness of vision, across the world. His laughter, which Maeterlinck has defined so admirably as 'the laughter of the soul,' is the laughter of Pierrot, more than half a sob, and shaken out of him with a deplorable gesture of the thin arms, thrown wide. He is a metaphysical Pierrot, *Pierrot lunaire,* and it is of abstract notions, the whole science of the unconscious, that he makes his showman's patter. As it is part of his manner not to distinguish between irony and pity, or even belief, we need not attempt to do so. Heine should teach us to understand at least so much of a poet who could not otherwise resemble him less. In Laforgue, sentiment is squeezed out of the world before one begins to play at ball with it.

And so, of the two, he is the more hopeless. He has invented a new manner of being René or Werther: an inflexible politeness towards man, woman, and destiny.[3] He composes love-poems hat in hand, and smiles with an exasperating tolerance before all the transformations of the eternal feminine. He is very conscious of death, but his *blague* of death is, above all things, gentlemanly. He will not permit himself, at any moment, the luxury of dropping the mask: not at any moment.

Read this *Autre Complainte de Lord Pierrot*, with the singular pity of its cruelty, before such an imagined dropping of the mask.

Celle qui doit me mettre au courant de la Femme!
    Nous lui dirons d'abord, de mon air le moins froid:

___

* ['There is no type, there is life … And your ideal is very quickly drowned magnificently' – from *Mélanges posthumes*.]

'La somme des angles d'un triangle, chère âme,
    Est égale à deux droits.'

Et si ce cri lui part: 'Dieu de Dieu que je t'aime!'
    – 'Dieu reconnaîtra les siens.' Ou piquée au vif:
– 'Mes claviers ont du cœur, tu sera mon seul thème.'
    Moi: 'Tout est relatif.'

De tous ses yeux, alors! se sentant trop banale:
    'Ah! tu ne m'aime[s] pas; tant d'autres sont jaloux!'
Et moi, d'un œil qui vers l'Inconscient s'emballe:
    'Merci, pas mal; et vous?'

'Jouons au plus fidèle!' – A quoi bon, ô Nature!
    'Autant à qui perd gagne.' Alors, autre couplet:
– 'Ah! tu te lasseras le premier, j'en suis sûr.'
    – 'Après vous, s'il vous plaît.'

Enfin, si, par un soir, elle meurt dans mes livres,
    Douce; feignant de n'en pas croire encor mes yeux,
J'aurai un: 'Ah çà, mais, nous avions De Quoi vivre!
    C'était donc sérieux?'*

And yet one realises, if one but reads him attentively enough, how much suffering and despair, and resignation to what is, after all, the inevitable, are hidden away under this disguise, and also why this disguise is possible. Laforgue died at twenty-seven: he had been a dying man all his life, and his work has the fatal evasiveness of those who shrink from remembering the one thing which they are unable to forget. Coming as he does after Rimbaud, turning

* ['This one should bring me up to speed with Woman! / We say to her first, with my least cold air: / "The sum of the angles of a triangle, dear soul, / is equal to two right angles." // And if this cry escapes her: "God of Gods how I love you!" / "God will recognise his own." Or pricked to the quick: / "There's feeling in my playing; you will be my only theme." / Me: "Everything is relative." // With all her eyes, then! feeling too banal: / "Ah! You don't love me: so many others are jealous!" / And I, with an eye towards the Unconscious, lose it: / "Not bad, thank you; and you?" // "Let's see who is most faithful" – "To what good, o Nature! / The loser wins." And then, another couplet: / – "Ah, you'll get tired first, I'm sure of it." / "After you, if you please." // Finally, if she dies in my books one evening, / Quiet; pretending not to trust my eyes yet, / I'd try: "Ah that, but we would have Something to Live For! / You were serious then?"']

the divination of the other into theories, into achieved results, he is the eternally grown up, mature to the point of self-negation, as the other is the eternal *enfant terrible*. He thinks intensely about life, seeing what is automatic, pathetically ludicrous in it, almost as one might who has no part in the comedy. He has the double advantage, for his art, of being condemned to death, and of being, in the admirable phrase of Villiers, 'one of those who come into the world with a ray of moonlight in their brains.'[4]

Stéphane Mallarmé

I.

Stéphane Mallarmé was one of those who love literature too much to write it except by fragments; in whom the desire of perfection brings its own defeat. With either more or less ambition he would have done more to achieve himself; he was always divided between an absolute aim at the absolute, that is, the unattainable, and a too logical disdain for the compromise by which, after all, literature is literature. Carry the theories of Mallarmé to a practical conclusion, multiply his powers in a direct ratio, and you have Wagner. It is his failure not to be Wagner. And, Wagner having existed, it was for him to be something more, to complete Wagner. Well, not being able to be that, it was a matter of sincere indifference to him whether he left one or two little, limited masterpieces of formal verse and prose, the more or the less. It was 'the work' that he dreamed of, the new art, more than a new religion, whose precise form in the world he was never quite able to settle.

Un auteur difficile, in the phrase of Catulle Mendès,[1] it has always been to what he himself calls 'a labyrinth illuminated by flowers' that Mallarmé has felt it due to their own dignity to invite his readers.[2] To their own dignity, and also to his. Mallarmé was obscure, not so much because he wrote differently, as because he thought differently, from other people. His mind was elliptical, and, relying with undue confidence on the intelligence of his readers, he emphasised the effect of what was unlike other people in his mind by resolutely ignoring even the links of connection that existed between them. Never having aimed at popularity, he never needed, as most writers need, to make the first advances. He made neither intrusion upon nor concession to those who, after all, were not obliged to read him. And when he spoke, he considered it neither needful nor seemly to listen in order to hear whether he was heard. To the charge of obscurity he replied, with sufficient disdain, that there are many who do not know how to read – except the newspaper, he adds, in one of those disconcerting, oddly-printed parentheses, which make his work, to those who rightly apprehend it, so full of wise limitations, so safe from hasty or seemingly final conclusions. No one in our time has more significantly vindicated the supreme right of the artist in the aristocracy of letters; wilfully, perhaps, not always wisely, but nobly, logically. Has not every artist shrunk from that making of himself 'a motley to the view,'[3] that handing over of his naked soul to the laughter of the multitude? But who, in our time, has wrought so subtle a veil, shining on this side, where the few are, a thick cloud on the other, where are the many? The oracles have always had the wisdom to hide their secrets in the obscurity of many meanings, or of what has seemed meaningless; and might it not, after all, be the finest epitaph for a self-respecting man of letters to be able to say, even after the writing of many books: I have kept my secret, I have not betrayed myself to the multitude?

But to Mallarmé, certainly, there might be applied the significant warning of Rossetti:

> Yet woe to thee if once thou yield
> Unto the act of doing nought![4]

After a life of persistent devotion to literature, he has left enough poems to make a single small volume (less, certainly, than a hundred poems in all), a single volume of prose, a few pamphlets, and a prose translation of the poems of Poe. It is because among these there are masterpieces, poems which are among the most beautiful poems written in our time, prose which has all the subtlest qualities of prose, that, quitting the abstract point of view, we are forced to regret the fatal enchantments, fatal for him, of theories which are so greatly needed by others, so valuable for our instruction, if we are only a little careful in putting them into practice.

In estimating the significance of Stéphane Mallarmé, it is necessary to take into account not only his verse and prose, but, almost more than these, the Tuesdays of the Rue de Rome, in which he gave himself freely to more than one generation.[5] No one who has ever climbed those four flights of stairs will have forgotten the narrow, homely interior, elegant with a sort of scrupulous Dutch comfort; the heavy, carved furniture, the tall clock, the portraits, Manet's,[6] Whistler's, on the walls; the table on which the china bowl, odorous with tobacco, was pushed from hand to hand; above all, the rocking-chair, Mallarmé's, from which he would rise quietly, to stand leaning his elbow on the mantelpiece, while one hand, the hand which did not hold the cigarette, would sketch out one of those familiar gestures: *un peu de prêtre, un peu de danseuse* (in M. Rodenbach's admirable phrase), *avec lesquels il avait l'air chaque fois d'*entrer *dans la conversation, comme on entre en scène.*★ One of the best talkers of our time, he was, unlike most other fine talkers, harmonious with his own theories in giving no monologues, in allowing every liberty to his guests, to the conversation; in his perfect readiness to follow the slightest indication, to embroider upon any frame, with any material presented him. There would have been something almost of the challenge of the improvisatore in this easily moved alertness of mental attitude, had it not been for the singular gentleness with which Mallarmé's intelligence moved, in these considerable feats, with the half-apologetic negligence of the perfect acrobat. He seemed to be no more than brushing the dust off your own ideas, settling, arranging them a little, before he gave them back to you, surprisingly luminous. It was only afterwards that you realised how small had been your own part in the matter, as well as what it meant to have enlightened without dazzling you. But there was always a feeling of comradeship, the comradeship of a master, whom, while you were there at least, you did not question; and that very feeling lifted you, in your own estimation, nearer to art.

Invaluable, it seems to me, those Tuesdays must have been to the young men of two generations who have been making French literature; they were unique, certainly, in the experience of the young Englishman who was always so cordially received there, with so flattering a cordiality. Here was a house in which art, literature, was the very atmosphere, a religious atmosphere; and the master of the house, in his just a little solemn simplicity, a priest. I never heard the price of a book mentioned, or the number of thousand francs which a popular author had been paid for his last volume; here, in this one literary house, literature was unknown as a trade. And, above all, the questions that were discussed were never, at least, in Mallarmé's treatment, in his guidance of them, other than essential questions, considerations of art in the abstract,

★ ['one of those gestures (with a bit of the priest, a bit of the dancer about it), with which [Mallarmé] had the air of *entering* into a conversation each time, like an actor coming on stage' – from an obituary for Mallarmé in *Le Figaro*, 13 September 1898.]

of literature before it coagulates into a book, of life as its amusing and various web spins the stuff of art. When, indeed, the conversation, by some untimely hazard, drifted too near to one, became for a moment, perhaps inconveniently, practical, it was Mallarmé's solicitous politeness to wait, a little constrained, almost uneasy, rolling his cigarette in silence, until the disturbing moment had passed.

There were other disturbing moments, sometimes. I remember one night, rather late, the sudden irruption of M. de Heredia, coming on after a dinner-party, and seating himself, in his well-filled evening dress, precisely in Mallarmé's favourite chair. He was intensely amusing, voluble, floridly vehement; Mallarmé, I am sure, was delighted to see him; but the loud voice was a little trying to his nerves, and then he did not know what to do without his chair. He was like a cat that has been turned out of its favourite corner, as he roamed uneasily about the room, resting an unaccustomed elbow on the sideboard, visibly at a disadvantage.

For the attitude of those young men, some of them no longer exactly young, who frequented the Tuesdays, was certainly the attitude of the disciple. Mallarmé never exacted it, he seemed never to notice it; yet it meant to him, all the same, a good deal; as it meant, and in the best sense, a good deal to them. He loved art with a supreme disinterestedness, and it was for the sake of art that he wished to be really a master. For he knew that he had something to teach, that he had found out some secrets worth knowing, that he had discovered a point of view which he could to some degree perpetuate in those young men who listened to him. And to them this free kind of apprenticeship was, beyond all that it gave in direct counsels, in the pattern of work, a noble influence. Mallarmé's quiet, laborious life was for some of them the only counterpoise to the Bohemian example of the *d'Harcourt* or the *Taverne*, where art is loved, but with something of haste, in a very changing devotion.[7] It was impossible to come away from Mallarmé's without some tranquillising influence from that quiet place, some impersonal ambition towards excellence, the resolve, at least, to write a sonnet, a page of prose, that should be in its own way as perfect as one could make it, worthy of Mallarmé.

II.

'Poetry,' said Mallarmé, 'is the language of a state of crisis';[8] and all his poems are the evocation of a passing ecstasy, arrested in mid–flight. This ecstasy is never the mere instinctive cry of the heart, the simple human joy or sorrow, which, like the Parnassians, but for not quite the same reason, he did not admit in poetry. It is a mental transposition of emotion or sensation, veiled with atmosphere, and becoming, as it becomes a poem, pure beauty. Here, for instance, in a poem which I have translated line for line, and almost word for word, a delicate emotion, a figure vaguely divined, a landscape magically evoked, blend in a single effect.

SIGH

My soul, calm sister, towards thy brow, whereon scarce grieves
An autumn strewn already with its russet leaves,
And towards the wandering sky of thine angelic eyes,
Mounts, as in melancholy gardens may arise
Some faithful fountain sighing whitely towards the blue!
– Towards the blue pale and pure that sad October knew,
When, in those depths, it mirrored languors infinite,
And agonising leaves upon the waters white,
Windily drifting, traced a furrow cold and dun,
Where, in one long last ray, lingered the yellow sun.

Another poem comes a little closer to nature, but with what exquisite precautions, and with what surprising novelty in its unhesitating touch on actual things!

SEA-WIND

The flesh is sad, alas! and all the books are read,
Flight, only flight! I feel that birds are wild to tread
The floor of unknown foam, and to attain the skies!
Nought, neither ancient gardens mirrored in the eyes,
Shall hold this heart that bathes in waters its delight,
O nights! nor yet my waking lamp, whose lonely light
Shadows the vacant paper, whiteness profits best,
Nor the young wife who rocks her baby on her breast.
I will depart. O steamer, swaying rope and spar,
Lift anchor for exotic lands that lie afar!
A weariness, outworn by cruel hopes, still clings

To the last farewell handkerchief's last beckonings!
And are not these, the masts inviting storms, not these
That an awakening wind bends over wrecking seas,
Lost, not a sail, a sail, a flowering isle, ere long?
But, O my heart, hear thou, hear thou the sailors' song!

These (need I say?) belong to the earlier period, in which Mallarmé had not yet withdrawn his light into the cloud; and to the same period belong the prose-poems, one of which, perhaps the most exquisite, I will translate here.

AUTUMN LAMENT

Ever since Maria left me, for another star – which? Orion, Altair, or thou, green Venus? – I have always cherished solitude. How many long days I have passed, alone with my cat! By *alone*, I mean without a material being, and my cat is a mystical companion, a spirit. I may say, then, that I have passed long days alone with my cat, and alone, with one of the last writers of the Roman decadence; for since the white creature is no more, strangely and singularly, I have loved all that may be summed up in the word: fall. Thus, in the year, my favourite season is during those last languid summer days which come just before the autumn; and, in the day, the hour when I take my walk is the hour when the sun lingers before fading, with rays of copper-yellow on the grey walls, and of copper-red on the window-panes. And, just so, the literature from which my soul demands delight must be the poetry dying out of the last moments of Rome, provided, nevertheless, that it breathes nothing of the rejuvenating approach of the Barbarians, and does not stammer the infantile Latin of the first Christian prose.

I read, then, one of those beloved poems (whose streaks of rouge have more charm for me than the fresh cheek of youth), and buried my hand in the fur of the pure animal, when a barrel-organ began to sing, languishingly and melancholy, under my window. It played in the long alley of poplars, whose leaves seem mournful to me even in spring, since Maria passed that way with the tapers, for the last time. Yes, sad people's instrument, truly: the piano glitters, the violin brings one's torn fibres to the light, but the barrel-organ, in the twilight of memory, has set me despairingly dreaming. While it murmured a gaily vulgar air, such as puts mirth into the heart of the suburbs, an old-fashioned, an empty air, how came it that its refrain went to my very soul, and made me weep like a romantic ballad? I drank it in, and I did not throw a penny out of the window, for fear of disturbing my own impression, and of perceiving that the instrument was not singing by itself.

Between these characteristic, clear, and beautiful poems, in verse and in prose, and the opaque darkness of the later writings, come one or two poems, perhaps the finest of all, in which already clearness is 'a secondary grace,'[9] but in which a subtle rapture finds incomparable expression. *L'Après-midi d'un Faune* and *Hérodiade* have already been introduced, in different ways, to English readers: the former by Mr. Gosse, in a detailed analysis; the latter by a translation into verse.[10] And Debussy in his new music, has taken *L'Après-midi d'un Faune* almost for his new point of departure, interpreting it, at all events, faultlessly. In these two poems I find Mallarmé at the moment when his own desire achieves itself; when he attains Wagner's ideal, that 'the most complete work of the poet should be that which, in its final achievement, becomes a perfect music':[11] every word is a jewel, scattering and recapturing sudden fire, every image is a symbol, and the whole poem is visible music. After this point began that fatal 'last period' which comes to most artists who have thought too curiously, or dreamed too remote dreams, or followed a too wandering beauty. Mallarmé had long been too conscious that all publication is 'almost a speculation, on one's modesty, for one's silence'; that 'to unclench the fists, breaking one's sedentary dream, for a ruffling face to face with the idea,' was after all unnecessary to his own conception of himself, a mere way of convincing the public that one exists; and having achieved, as he thought, 'the right to abstain from doing anything exceptional,' he devoted himself, doubly, to silence.[12] Seldom condescending to write, he wrote now only for himself, and in a manner which certainly saved him from intrusion. Some of Meredith's poems, and occasional passages of his prose, can alone give in English some faint idea of the later prose and verse of Mallarmé.[13] The verse could not, I think, be translated; of the prose, in which an extreme lucidity of thought comes to us but glimmeringly through the entanglements of a construction, part Latin, part English, I shall endeavour to translate some fragments, in speaking of the theoretic writings, contained in the two volumes of *Vers et Prose* and *Divagations*.

III.

It is the distinction of Mallarmé to have aspired after an impossible liberation of the soul of literature from what is fretting and constraining in 'the body of that death,' which is the mere literature of words. Words, he has realised, are of value only as a notation of the free breath of the spirit; words, therefore, must be employed with an extreme care, in their choice and adjustment, in setting them to reflect and chime upon one another; yet least of all for their own sake, for what they can never, except by suggestion, express. 'Every soul is a melody,' he has said, 'which needs to be readjusted; and for that are the flute or viol of each.' The word, treated indeed with a kind of 'adoration,' as he says, is so regarded in a magnificent sense, in which it is apprehended as a living thing, itself the vision rather than the reality; at least the philtre of the evocation. The word, chosen as he chooses it, is for him a liberating principle, by which the spirit is extracted from matter; takes form, perhaps assumes immortality. Thus an artificiality, even, in the use of words, that seeming artificiality which comes from using words as if they had never been used before, that chimerical search after the virginity of language, is but the paradoxical outward sign of an extreme discontent with even the best of their service. Writers who use words fluently, seeming to disregard their importance, do so from an unconscious confidence in their expressiveness, which the scrupulous thinker, the precise dreamer, can never place in the most carefully chosen among them. To evoke, by some elaborate, instantaneous magic of language, without the formality of an after all impossible description; to be, rather than to express: that is what Mallarmé has consistently, and from the first, sought in verse and prose. And he has sought this wandering, illusive, beckoning butterfly, the soul of dreams, over more and more entangled ground; and it has led him into the depths of many forests, far from the sunlight. To say that he has found what he sought is impossible; but (is it possible to avoid saying?) how heroic a search, and what marvellous discoveries by the way!

I think I understand, though I cannot claim his own authority for my supposition, the way in which Mallarmé wrote verse, and the reason why it became more and more abstruse, more and more unintelligible. Remember his principle: that to name is to destroy, to suggest is to create.[14] Note, further, that he condemns the inclusion in verse of anything but, 'for example, the horror of the forest, of the silent thunder afloat in the leaves; not the intrinsic, dense wood of the trees.' He has received, then, a mental sensation: let it be the horror of the forest. This sensation begins to form in his brain, at first probably no more than a rhythm, absolutely without words. Gradually thought begins to concentrate itself (but with an extreme care, lest it should break the tension on which all depends) upon the sensation, already struggling to find its own consciousness. Delicately, stealthily, with infinitely timid precaution, words present themselves, at first in silence. Every word seems like a desecration, seems, the clearer it is, to throw back the original sensation farther and farther into the darkness. But, guided always by the rhythm, which is the executive soul (as, in Aristotle's definition, the soul is the form of the body),[15] words come slowly, one by one, shaping the message. Imagine the poem already written down, at least composed. In its very imperfection, it is clear, it shows the links by which it has been riveted together; the whole process of its construction can be studied. Now most writers would be content; but with Mallarmé the work has only begun. In the final result there must be no sign of the making, there must be only the thing made. He works over it, word by word, changing a word here, for its colour, which is not precisely the colour required, a word there, for the break it makes in the music. A new image occurs to him, rarer, subtler, than the one he has used; the image is transferred. By the time the poem has reached, as it seems to him, a flawless unity, the steps of the progress have been only too effectually effaced; and while the poet, who has seen the thing from the beginning, still sees the relation of point to point, the reader, who comes to it only in its final stage, finds himself in a not unnatural bewilderment. Pursue this manner of writing to its ultimate development; start with an enigma, and then withdraw the key of the enigma; and you arrive, easily, at the frozen impenetrability of those latest sonnets, in which the absence of all punctuation is scarcely a recognisable hindrance.

That, I fancy to myself, was his actual way of writing; here, in what I prefer to give as a corollary, is the theory. 'Symbolist, Decadent, or Mystic, the schools thus called by themselves, or thus hastily labelled by our information-press, adopt, for meet-ing-place, the point of an Idealism which (similarly as in fugues, in sonatas) rejects the "natural" materials, and, as brutal, a direct thought ordering them; to retain no more than suggestion. To be instituted, a relation between images, exact; and that therefrom should detach itself a third aspect, fusible and clear, offered to the divination. Abolished, the pretension, aesthetically an error, despite its dominion over almost all the masterpieces, to enclose within the subtle paper other than, for example, the horror of the forest, or the silent thunder afloat in the leaves; not the intrinsic, dense wood of the trees. Some few bursts of personal pride, verid-ically trumpeted, awaken the architecture of the palace, alone habitable; not of stone, on which the pages would close but ill.' For example (it is his own): 'I say: a flower! and out of the oblivion to which my voice consigns every contour, so far as anything save the known calyx, musically arises, idea, and exquisite, the one flower absent from all bouquets.' 'The pure work,' then, 'implies the elocutionary disappearance of the poet, who yields place to the words, immobilised by the shock of their inequality; they take light from mutual reflection, like an actual trail of fire over precious stones, replacing the old lyric afflatus or the enthusiastic personal direction of the phrase.' 'The verse which out of many vocables remakes an entire word, new, unknown to the language, and as if magical, attains this isolation of speech.' Whence, it being 'music which rejoins verse, to form, since Wagner, Poetry,' the final conclusion: 'That we are now precisely at the moment of seeking, before that breaking up of the large rhythms of literature, and their scattering in articulate, almost instrumental, nervous waves, an art which shall complete the transposition, into the Book, of the symphony, or simply recapture our own: for, it is not in elementary sonorities of brass, strings, wood, unquestionably, but in the intellectual word at its utmost, that, fully and evidently, we should find, drawing to itself all the correspondences of the universe, the supreme Music.'[16]

Here, literally translated, in exactly the arrangement of the original, are some passages out of the theoretic writings, which I have brought together, to indicate what seem to me the main lines of Mallarmé's doctrine. It is the doctrine which, as I have already said, had been divined by Gérard de Nerval; but what, in Gérard, was pure vision, becomes in Mallarmé a logical sequence of meditation. Mallarmé was not a mystic, to whom anything came unconsciously; he was a thinker, in whom an extraordinary subtlety of mind was exercised on always explicit, though by no means the common, problems. 'A seeker after something in the world, that is there in no satisfying measure, or not at all,'[17] he pursued his search with unwearying persistence, with a sharp mental division of dream and idea, certainly very lucid to himself, however he may have failed to render his expression clear to others. And I, for one, cannot doubt that he was, for the most part, entirely right in his statement and analysis of the new conditions under which we are now privileged or condemned to write. His obscurity was partly his failure to carry out the spirit of his own directions; but, apart from obscurity, which we may all be fortunate enough to escape, is it possible for a writer, at the present day, to be quite simple, with the old, objective simplicity, in either thought or expression? To be *naïf*, to be archaic, is not to be either natural or simple; I affirm that it is not natural to be what is called 'natural' any longer. We have no longer the mental attitude of those to whom a story was but a story, and all stories good; we have realised, since it was proved to us by Poe, not merely that the age of epics is past, but that no long poem was ever written;[18] the finest long poem in the world being but a series of short poems linked together by prose. And, naturally, we can no longer write what we can no longer accept. Symbolism, implicit in all literature from the beginning, as it is implicit in the very words we use, comes to us now, at last quite conscious of itself, offering us the only escape from our many imprisonments. We find a new, an older, sense in the so worn out forms of things; the world, which we can no longer believe in as the satisfying material object it was to our grandparents, becomes transfigured with a new light; words, which long usage had darkened almost out of recognition, take fresh lustre. And it is on the lines of that spiritualising of the word, that perfecting of form in its capacity for allusion and suggestion, that confidence in the eternal correspondences between the visible and the invisible universe, which Mallarmé taught, and too intermittently practised, that literature must now move, if it is in any sense to move forward.

The Later Huysmans

In the preface to his first novel, *Marthe: histoire d'une fille*, thirty years ago, Huysmans defined his theory of art in this defiant phrase: 'I write what I see, what I feel, and what I have experienced, and I write it as well as I can: that is all.' Ten or twelve years ago, he could still say, in answer to an interviewer who asked him his opinion of Naturalism: 'At bottom, there are writers who have talent and others who have not; let them be Naturalists, Romantics, Decadents, what you will, it is all the same to me: I only want to know if they have talent.'[1] Such theoretical liberality, in a writer of original talent, is a little disconcerting: it means that he is without a theory of his own, that he is not yet conscious of having chosen his own way. And, indeed, it is only with *En Route* that Huysmans can be said to have discovered the direction in which he had really been travelling from the beginning.

In a preface written not long since for a limited edition of *À Rebours*, Huysmans confessed that he had never been conscious of the direction in which he was travelling. 'My life and my literature,' he affirmed, 'have undoubtedly a certain amount of passivity, of the incalculable, of a direction not mine. I have simply obeyed; I have been led by what are called "mysterious ways."' He is speaking of the conversion which took him to La Trappe in 1892, but the words apply to the whole course of his career as a man of letters. In *Là-Bas*, which is a sort of false start, he had, indeed, realised, though for himself, at that time ineffectually, that 'it is essential to preserve the veracity of the document, the precision of detail, the fibrous and nervous language of Realism, but it is equally essential to become the well-digger of the soul, and not to attempt to explain what is mysterious by mental maladies. ... It is essential, in a word, to follow the great road so deeply dug out by Zola, but it is necessary also to trace a parallel pathway in the air, and to grapple with the within and the after, to create, in a word, a spiritual Naturalism.' This is almost a definition of the art of *En Route*, where this spiritual realism is applied to the history of a soul, a conscience; in *La Cathédrale* the method has still further developed, and Huysmans becomes, in his own way, a Symbolist.

To the student of psychology few more interesting cases could be presented than the development of Huysmans. From the first he has been a man 'for whom the visible world existed,'[2] indeed, but as the scene of a slow martyrdom. The world has always appeared to him to be a profoundly uncomfortable, unpleasant, and ridiculous place; and it has been a necessity of his temperament to examine it minutely, with all the patience of disgust, and a necessity of his method to record it with an almost ecstatic hatred. In his first book, *Le Drageoir à Epices*, published at the age of twenty-six, we find him seeking his colour by preference in a drunkard's cheek or a carcase outside a butcher's shop. *Marthe*, published at Brussels in 1876, anticipates *La Fille Elisa* and *Nana*, but it has a crude brutality of observation in which there is hardly a touch of pity. *Les Soeurs Vatard* is a frame without a picture, but in *En Ménage* the dreary tedium of existence is chronicled in all its insignificance with a kind of weary and aching hate. 'We, too,' is its conclusion, 'by leave of the everlasting stupidity of things, may, like our fellow-citizens, live stupid and respected.' The fantastic unreality, the exquisite artificiality of *A Rebours*, the breviary of the decadence, is the first sign of that possible escape which Huysmans has always foreseen in the direction of art, but which he is still unable to make into more than an artificial paradise, in which beauty turns to a cruel hallucination and imprisons the soul still more fatally. The end is a cry of hopeless hope, in which Huysmans did not understand the meaning till later: 'Lord, have pity of the Christian who doubts, of the sceptic who would fain believe, of the convict of life who sets sail alone by night, under a firmament lighted only by the consoling watch-lights of the old hope.'

In *Là-Bas* we are in yet another stage of this strange pilgrim's progress. The disgust which once manifested itself in the merely external revolt against the ugliness of streets, the imbecility of faces, has become more and more internalised, and the attraction of what is perverse in the unusual beauty of art has led, by some obscure route, to the perilous halfway house of a corrupt mysticism. The book, with its monstrous pictures of the Black Mass and of the spiritual abominations of Satanism, is one step further in the direction of the supernatural; and this, too, has its desperate, unlooked-for conclusion: 'Christian glory is a laughing-stock to our age; it contaminates the supernatural and casts out the world

to come.' In *Là-Bas* we go down into the deepest gulf; *En Route*
sets us one stage along a new way, and at this turning-point begins
the later Huysmans.

The old conception of the novel as an amusing tale of adventures, though it has still its apologists in England, has long since
ceased in France to mean anything more actual than powdered
wigs and lace ruffles. Like children who cry to their elders for 'a
story, a story,' the English public still wants its plot, its heroine, its
villain. That the novel should be psychological was a discovery as
early as Benjamin Constant, whose *Adolphe* anticipates *Le Rouge
et le Noir*, that rare, revealing, yet somewhat arid masterpiece of
Stendhal.[3] But that psychology could be carried so far into the
darkness of the soul, that the flaming walls of the world themselves
faded to a glimmer, was a discovery which had been made by no
novelist before Huysmans wrote *En Route*. At once the novel
showed itself capable of competing, on their own ground, with
poetry, with the great 'confessions,' with philosophy. *En Route*
is perhaps the first novel which does not set out with the aim
of amusing its readers. It offers you no more entertainment than
Paradise Lost or the *Confessions* of St. Augustine, and it is possible
to consider it on the same level.[4] The novel, which, after having
chronicled the adventures of the Vanity Fairs of this world, has set
itself with admirable success to analyse the amorous and ambitious
and money-making intelligence of the conscious and practical self,
sets itself at last to the final achievement: the revelation of the
sub-conscious self, no longer the intelligence, but the soul. Here,
then, purged of the distraction of the incident, liberated from the
bondage of a too realistic conversation, in which the aim had
been to convey the very gesture of breathing life, internalised to a
complete liberty, in which, just because it is so absolutely free, art
is able to accept, without limiting itself, the expressive medium of
a convention, we have in the novel a new form, which may be at
once a confession and a decoration, the soul and a pattern.

The story of a conversion is a new thing in modern French;
it is a confession, a self-ascultation of the soul; a kind of thinking
aloud. It fixes, in precise words, all the uncertainties, the contradictions, the absurd unreasonableness and not less absurd logic,
which distract man's brain in the passing over him of sensation and
circumstance. And all this thinking is concentrated on one end, is
concerned with the working out, in his own singular way, of one

man's salvation. There is a certain dry hard casuistry, a subtlety and closeness almost ecclesiastical, in the investigation of an obscure and yet definite region, whose intellectual passions are as varied and as tumultuous as those of the heart. Every step is taken deliberately, is weighed, approved, condemned, viewed from this side and from that, and at the same time one feels behind all this reasoning an impulsion urging a soul onward against its will. In this astonishing passage, through Satanism to faith, in which the cry, 'I am so weary of myself, so sick of my miserable existence,' echoes through page after page, until despair dies into conviction, the conviction of the 'uselessness of concerning oneself about anything but mysticism and the liturgy, of thinking about anything but about God,' it is impossible not to see the sincerity of an actual, unique experience. The force of mere curiosity can go far, can penetrate to a certain depth; yet there is a point at which mere curiosity, even that of genius, comes to an end; and we are left to the individual soul's apprehension of what seems to it the reality of spiritual things. Such a personal apprehension comes to us out of this book, and at the same time, just as in the days when he forced language to express, in a more coloured and pictorial way than it had ever expressed before, the last escaping details of material things, so, in this analysis of the aberrations and warfares, the confessions and trials of the soul in penitence, Huysmans has found words for even the most subtle and illusive aspects of that inner life which he has come, at the last, to apprehend.

In *La Cathédrale* we are still occupied with this sensitive, lethargic, persevering soul, but with that soul in one of its longest halts by the way, as it undergoes the slow, permeating influence of '*la Cathédrale mystique par excellence*,' the cathedral of Chartres. And the greater part of the book is taken up with a study of this cathedral, of that elaborate and profound symbolism by which 'the soul of sanctuaries' slowly reveals itself (*quel laconisme hermétique!*)* with a sort of parallel interpretation of the symbolism which the Church of the Middle Ages concealed or revealed in colours, precious stones, plants, animals, numbers, odours, and in the Bible itself, in the setting together of the Old and New Testaments.

No doubt, to some extent, this book is less interesting than *En Route*, in the exact proportion in which everything in the world is

---

* ['what hermetic concision' – from Chapter V of *La Cathédrale*.]

less interesting than the human soul. There are times when Durtal is almost forgotten, and, unjustly enough, it may seem as if we are given this archaeology, these bestiaries, for their own sake. To fall into this error is to mistake the whole purpose of the book, the whole extent of the discovery in art which Huysmans has been one of the first to make.

For in *La Cathédrale*, Huysmans does but carry further the principle which he had perceived in *En Route*, showing, as he does, how inert matter, the art of stones, the growth of plants, the unconscious life of beasts, may be brought under the same law of the soul, may obtain, through symbol, a spiritual existence. He is thus but extending the domain of the soul while he may seem to be limiting or ignoring it; and Durtal may well stand aside for a moment, in at least the energy of contemplation, while he sees, with a new understanding, the very sight of his eyes, the very stuff of his thoughts, taking life before him, a life of the same substance of his own. What is Symbolism if not an establishing of the links which hold the world together, the affirmation of an eternal, minute, intricate, almost invisible life, which runs through the whole universe? Every age has its own symbols; but, a symbol once perfectly expressed, that symbol remains, as Gothic architecture remains, the very soul of the Middle Ages. To get at that truth which is all but the deepest meaning of beauty, to find that symbol which is its most adequate expression, is in itself a kind of creation; and that is what Huysmans does for us in *La Cathédrale*. More and more he has put aside all the profane and accessible and outward pomp of writing for an inner and more severe beauty of perfect truth. He has come to realise that truth can be reached and revealed only by symbol. Hence, all that description, that heaping up of detail, that passionately patient elaboration: all means to an end, not, as you may hastily incline to think, ends in themselves.

It is curious to observe how often an artist perfects a particular means of expression long before he has any notion of what to do with it. Huysmans began by acquiring so astonishing a mastery of description that he could describe the inside of a cow hanging in a butcher's shop as beautifully as if it were a casket of jewels. The little work-girls of his early novels were taken for long walks, in which they would have seen nothing but the arm on which they leant and the milliners' shops which they passed; and what they did not see was described, marvellously, in twenty pages.

Huysmans is a brain all eye, a brain which sees even ideas as if they had a superficies. His style is always the same, whether he writes of a butcher's shop or a stained-glass window; it is the immediate expression of a way of seeing, so minute and so intense that it becomes too emphatic for elegance and too coloured for atmosphere or composition, always ready to sacrifice euphony to either fact or colour. He cares only to give you the thing seen, exactly as he sees it, with all his love or hate, and with all the exaggeration which that feeling brings into it. And he loves beauty as a bulldog loves its mistress: by growling at all her enemies. He honours wisdom by annihilating stupidity. His art of painting in words resembles Monet's art of painting with his brush:[5] there is the same power of rendering a vivid effect, almost deceptively, with a crude and yet sensitive realism. '*C'est pour la gourmandise de l'oeil un gala de teintes*,'[*] he says of the provision cellars at Hamburg; and this greed of the eye has eaten up in him almost every other sense. Even of music he writes as a deaf man with an eye for colour might write, to whom a musician had explained certain technical means of expression in music. No one has ever invented such barbarous and exact metaphors for the rendering of visual sensations. Properly, there is no metaphor; the words say exactly what they mean; they become figurative, as we call it, in their insistence on being themselves fact.

Huysmans knows that the motive force of the sentence lies in the verbs, and his verbs are the most singular, precise, and expressive in any language. But in subordinating, as he does, every quality to that of sharp, telling truth, the truth of extremes, his style loses charm; yet it can be dazzling; it has the solidity of those walls encrusted with gems which are to be seen in a certain chapel in Prague; it blazes with colour, and arabesques into a thousand fantastic patterns.

And now all that laboriously acquired mastery finds at last its use, lending itself to the new spirit with a wonderful docility. At last the idea which is beyond reality has been found, not where des Esseintes sought it, and a new meaning comes into what had once been scarcely more than patient and wrathful observation. The idea is there, visible, in his cathedral, like the sun which flashes into unity, into meaning, into intelligible beauty, the bewildering

---

[*] ['For a greedy eye it is a carnival of colours' – from *De Tout* (1902).]

lozenges of colour, the inextricable trails of lead, which go to make up the picture in one of its painted windows. What, for instance, could be more precise in its translation of the different aspects under which the cathedral of Chartres can be seen, merely as colour, than this one sentence: 'Seen as a whole, under a clear sky, its grey silvers, and, if the sun shines upon it, turns pale yellow and then golden; seen close, its skin is like that of a nibbled biscuit, with its siliceous limestone eaten into holes; sometimes, when the sun is setting, it turns crimson, and rises up like a monstrous and delicate shrine, rose and green; and, at twilight, turns blue, then seems to evaporate as it fades into violet.' Or, again, in a passage which comes nearer to the conventional idea of eloquence, how absolute an avoidance of a conventional phrase, a word used for its merely oratorical value: 'High up, in space, like salamanders, human beings, with burning faces and flaming robes, lived in a firmament of fire; but these conflagrations were circumscribed, limited by an incombustible frame of darker glass, which beat back the clear young joy of the flames; by that kind of melancholy, that more serious and more aged aspect, which is taken by the duller colours. The hue and cry of reds, the limpid security of whites, the reiterated halleluias of yellows, the virginal glory of blues, all the quivering hearth-glow of painted glass, dies away as it came near this border coloured with the rust of iron, with the russet of sauce, with the harsh violet of sandstone, with bottle-green, with the brown of touchwood, with sooty black, with ashen grey.'

This, in its excess of exactitude (how mediaeval a quality!) becomes, on one page, a comparison of the tower without a spire to an unsharpened pencil which cannot write the prayers of earth upon the sky. But, for the most part, it is a consistent humanising of too objectively visible things, a disengaging of the sentiment which exists in them, which is one of the secrets of their appeal to us, but which for the most part we overlook as we set ourselves to add up the shapes and colours which have enchanted us. To Huysmans this artistic discovery has come, perhaps in the most effectual way, but certainly in the way least probable in these days, through faith, a definite religious faith; so that, beginning tentatively, he has come, at last, to believe in the Catholic Church as a monk of the Middle Ages believed in it. And there is no doubt that to Huysmans this abandonment to religion has brought, among other gifts, a certain human charity in which he was notably lacking, removing at once one of his artistic limitations. It has softened his contempt of humanity; it has broadened his outlook on the world. And the sense, diffused through the whole of this book, of the living and beneficent reality of the Virgin, of her real presence in the cathedral built in her honour and after her own image, brings a strange and touching kind of poetry into these closely and soberly woven pages.

From this time forward, until his death, Huysmans is seen purging himself of his realism, coming closer and closer to that spiritual Naturalism which he had invented, an art made out of an apprehension of the inner meaning of those things which he still saw with the old tenacity of vision. Nothing is changed in him and yet all is changed. The disgust of the world deepens through *L'Oblat*, which is the last stage but one in the pilgrimage which begins with *En Route*. It seeks an escape in poring, with a dreadful diligence, over a saint's recorded miracles, in the life of *Sainte Lydwine de Schiedam*, which is mediaeval in its precise acceptance of every horrible detail of the story. *Les Foules de Lourdes* has the same minute attentiveness to horror, but with a new pity in it, and a way of giving thanks to the Virgin, which is in Huysmans yet another escape from his disgust of the world. But it is in the great chapter on Satan as the creator of ugliness that his work seems to end where it had begun, in the service of art, now come from a great way off to join itself with the service of God. And the whole soul of Huysmans characterises itself in the turn of a single phrase there: that 'art is the only clean thing on earth, except holiness.'

Maeterlinck as a Mystic

The secret of things which is just beyond the most subtle words, the secret of the expressive silences, has always been clearer to Maeterlinck than to most people; and, in his plays, he has elaborated an art of sensitive, taciturn, and at the same time highly ornamental simplicity, which has come nearer than any other art to being the voice of silence. To Maeterlinck the theatre has been, for the most part, no more than one of the disguises by which he can express himself, and with his book of meditations on the inner life, *Le Trésor des Humbles*, he may seem to have dropped his disguise.

All art hates the vague; not the mysterious, but the vague; two opposites very commonly confused, as the secret with the obscure, the infinite with the indefinite. And the artist who is also a mystic hates the vague with a more profound hatred than any other artist. Thus Maeterlinck, endeavouring to clothe mystical conceptions in concrete form, has invented a drama so precise, so curt, so arbitrary in its limits, that it can safely be confided to the masks and feigned voices of marionettes. His theatre of artificial beings, who are at once more ghostly and more mechanical than the living actors whom we are accustomed to see, in so curious a parody of life, moving with a certain freedom of action across the stage, may be taken as itself a symbol of the aspect under which what we fantastically term 'real life' presents itself to the mystic. Are we not all puppets, in a theatre of marionettes, in which the parts we play, the dresses we wear, the very emotion whose dominance gives its express form to our faces, have all been chosen for us; in which I, it may be, with curled hair and a Spanish cloak, play the romantic lover, sorely against my will, while you, a 'fair penitent' for no repented sin, pass whitely under a nun's habit? And as our parts have been chosen for us, our motions controlled from behind the curtain, so the words we seem to speak are but spoken through us, and we do but utter fragments of some elaborate invention, planned for larger ends than our personal display or convenience, but to which, all the same, we are in a humble degree necessary. This symbolical theatre, its very existence being a symbol, has perplexed many minds, to some of whom it has seemed puerile, a child's mystification of small words and repetitions, a thing of attitudes and omissions; while others, yet more unwisely, have compared it with the violent, rhetorical, most human drama of the Elizabethans, with Shakespeare himself, to whom all the world was a stage, and the stage all this world, certainly.[1] A sentence, already famous, of the *Trésor des Humbles*, will tell you what it signifies to Maeterlinck himself.

'I have come to believe,' he writes, in *Le Tragique Quotidien*, 'that an old man seated in his armchair, waiting quietly under the lamplight, listening without knowing it to all the eternal laws which reign about his house, interpreting without understanding it all that there is in the silence of doors and windows, and in the little voice of light, enduring the presence of his soul and of his destiny, bowing his head a little, without suspecting that all the powers of the earth intervene and stand on guard in the room like attentive servants, not knowing that the sun itself suspends above the abyss the little table on which he rests his elbow, and that there is not a star in the sky nor a force in the soul which is indifferent to the motion of a falling eyelid or a rising thought – I have come to believe that this motionless old man lived really a more profound, human, and universal life than the lover who strangles his mistress, the captain who gains a victory, or the husband who "avenges his honour."'

That, it seems to me, says all there is to be said of the intention of this drama which Maeterlinck has evoked; and, of its style, this other sentence, which I take from the same essay: 'It is only the words that at first sight seem useless which really count in a work.'

This drama, then, is a drama founded on philosophical ideas, apprehended emotionally; on the sense of the mystery of the universe, of the weakness of humanity, that sense which Pascal expressed when he said: *Ce qui m'étonne le plus est de voir que tout le monde n'est pas étonné de sa faiblesse;** with an acute feeling of the pathetic ignorance in which the souls nearest to one another look out upon their neighbours. It is a drama in which the interest is concentrated on vague people, who are little parts of the universal consciousness, their strange names being but the pseudonyms of

---

* ['What amazes me most is to see that everyone is not amazed at his own weakness.' – Blaise Pascal, *Pensées* (fragment 374).]

obscure passions, intimate emotions. They have the fascination which we find in the eyes of certain pictures, so much more real and disquieting, so much more permanent with us, than living people. And they have the touching simplicity of children; they are always children in their ignorance of themselves, of one another, and of fate. And, because they are so disembodied of the more trivial accidents of life, they give themselves without limitation to whatever passionate instinct possesses them. I do not know a more passionate love-scene than that scene in the wood beside the fountain, where Pelléas and Mélisande confess the strange burden which has come upon them.[2] When the soul gives itself absolutely to love, all the barriers of the world are burnt away, and all its wisdom and subtlety are as incense poured on a flame. Morality, too, is burnt away, no longer exists, any more than it does for children or for God.

Maeterlinck has realised, better than any one else, the significance, in life and art, of mystery. He has realised how unsearchable is the darkness out of which we have but just stepped, and the darkness into which we are about to pass. And he has realised how the thought and sense of that twofold darkness invade the little space of light in which, for a moment, we move; the depth to which they shadow our steps, even in that moment's partial escape. But in some of his plays he would seem to have apprehended this mystery as a thing merely or mainly terrifying; the actual physical darkness surrounding blind men, the actual physical approach of death as the intruder; he has shown to us people huddled at a window, out of which they are almost afraid to look, or beating at a door, the opening of which they dread. Fear shivers through these plays, creeping across our nerves like a damp mist coiling up out of a valley. And there is beauty, certainly, in this 'vague spiritual fear';[3] but a less obvious kind of beauty than that which gives its profound pathos to *Aglavaine et Sélysette*, the one play written since the writing of the essays. Here is mystery, which is also pure beauty, in these delicate approaches of intellectual pathos, in which suffering and death and error become transformed into something almost happy, so full is it of strange light.

And the aim of Maeterlinck, in his plays, is not only to render the soul and the soul's atmosphere, but to reveal this strangeness, pity, and beauty through beautiful pictures. No dramatist has ever been so careful that his scenes should be in themselves beautiful, or has made the actual space of forest, tower, or seashore so emotionally significant. He has realised, after Wagner, that the art of the stage is the art of pictorial beauty, of the correspondence in rhythm between the speakers, their words, and their surroundings. He has seen how, in this way, and in this way alone, the emotion, which it is but a part of the poetic drama to express, can be at once intensified and purified.

It is only after hinting at many of the things which he had to say in these plays, which have, after all, been a kind of subterfuge, that Maeterlinck has cared, or been able, to speak with the direct utterance of the essays. And what may seem curious is that this prose of the essays, which is the prose of a doctrine, is incomparably more beautiful than the prose of the plays, which was the prose of an art. Holding on this point a different opinion from one who was, in many senses, his master, Villiers de l'Isle-Adam, he did not admit that beauty of words, or even any expressed beauty of thoughts, had its place in spoken dialogue, even though it was not two living actors speaking to one another on the stage, but a soul speaking to a soul, and imagined speaking through the mouths of marionettes. But that beauty of phrase which makes the profound and sometimes obscure pages of *Axël* shine as with the crossing fire of jewels, rejoices us, though with a softer, a more equable, radiance, in the pages of these essays, in which every sentence has the indwelling beauty of an intellectual emotion, preserved at the same height of tranquil ecstasy from first page to last. There is a sort of religious calm in these deliberate sentences, into which the writer has known how to introduce that divine monotony which is one of the accomplishments of great style. Never has simplicity been more ornate or a fine beauty more visible through its self-concealment.

But, after all, the claim upon us of this book is not the claim of a work of art, but of a doctrine, and more than that, of a system. Belonging, as he does, to the eternal hierarchy, the unbroken succession, of the mystics, Maeterlinck has apprehended what is essential in the mystical doctrine with a more profound comprehension, and thus more systematically, than any mystic of recent times. He has many points of resemblance with Emerson, on whom he has written an essay which is properly an exposition of his own personal ideas; but Emerson, who proclaimed the supreme guidance of the inner light, the supreme necessity of trusting instinct, of honouring emotion, did but proclaim all this, not without a certain anti-mystical vagueness: Maeterlinck has systematised it. A more profound mystic than Emerson, he has greater command of that which comes to him unawares, is less at the mercy of visiting angels.

Also, it may be said that he surrenders himself to them more absolutely, with less reserve and discretion; and, as he has infinite leisure, his contemplation being subject to no limits of time, he is ready to follow them on unknown rounds, to any distance, in any direction, ready also to rest in any wayside inn, without fearing that he will have lost the road on the morrow.

This old gospel, of which Maeterlinck is the new voice, has been quietly waiting until certain bankruptcies, the bankruptcy of Science, of the Positive Philosophies, should allow it full credit. Considering the length even of time, it has not had an unreasonable space of waiting; and remember that it takes time but little into account. We have seen many little gospels demanding of every emotion, of every instinct, 'its certificate at the hand of some respectable authority.' Without confidence in themselves or in things, and led by Science, which is as if one were led by one's notebook, they demand a reasonable explanation of every mystery. Not finding that explanation, they reject the mystery; which is as if the fly on the wheel rejected the wheel because it was hidden from his eyes by the dust of its own raising.

The mystic is at once the proudest and the humblest of men. He is as a child who resigns himself to the guidance of an unseen hand, the hand of one walking by his side; he resigns himself with the child's humility. And he has the pride of the humble, a pride manifesting itself in the calm rejection of every accepted map of the roads, of every offer of assistance, of every painted signpost pointing out the smoothest ways on which to travel. He demands no authority for the unseen hand whose fingers he feels upon his wrist. He conceives of life, not, indeed, so much as a road on which one walks, very much at one's own discretion, but as a blown and wandering ship, surrounded by a sea from which there is no glimpse of land; and he conceives that to the currents of that sea he may safely trust himself. Let his hand, indeed, be on the rudder, there will be no miracle worked for him; it is enough miracle that the sea should be there, and the ship, and he himself.

He will never know why his hand should turn the rudder this way rather than that.

Jacob Boehme has said, very subtly, 'that man does not perceive the truth but God perceives the truth in man'; that is, that whatever we perceive or do is not perceived or done consciously by us, but unconsciously through us.[4] Our business, then, is to tend that 'inner light' by which most mystics have symbolised that which at once guides us in time and attaches us to eternity. This inner light is no miraculous descent of the Holy Spirit, but the perfectly natural, though it may finally be overcoming, ascent of the spirit within us. The spirit, in all men, being but a ray of the universal light, it can, by careful tending, by the removal of all obstruction, the cleansing of the vessel, the trimming of the wick, as it were, be increased, made to burn with a steadier, a brighter flame. In the last rapture it may become dazzling, may blind the watcher with excess of light, shutting him in within the circle of transfiguration, whose extreme radiance will leave all the rest of the world henceforth one darkness.

All mystics being concerned with what is divine in life, with the laws which apply equally to time and eternity, it may happen to one to concern himself chiefly with time seen under the aspect of eternity, to another to concern himself rather with eternity seen under the aspect of time. Thus many mystics have occupied themselves, very profitably, with showing how natural, how explicable on their own terms, are the mysteries of life; the whole aim of Maeterlinck is to show how mysterious all life is, 'what an astounding thing it is, merely to live.'[5] What he had pointed out to us, with certain solemn gestures, in his plays, he sets himself now to affirm, slowly, fully, with that 'confidence in mystery' of which he speaks. Because 'there is not an hour without its familiar miracles and its ineffable suggestions,' he sets himself to show us these miracles and these meanings where others have not always sought or found them, in women, in children, in the theatre. He seems to touch, at one moment or another, whether he is discussing *La Beauté Intérieure* or *Le Tragique Quotidien*, on all of these hours, and there is no hour so dark that his touch does not illuminate it. And it is characteristic of him, of his 'confidence in mystery,' that he speaks always without raising his voice, without surprise or triumph, or the air of having said anything more than the simplest observation. He speaks, not as if he knew more than

others, or had sought out more elaborate secrets, but as if he had
listened more attentively.

Loving most those writers 'whose works are nearest to silence,'
he begins his book, significantly, with an essay on Silence, an essay
which, like all these essays, has the reserve, the expressive reticence, of those 'active silences' of which he succeeds in revealing
a few of the secrets.

'Souls,' he tells us, 'are weighed in silence, as gold and silver are
weighed in pure water, and the words which we pronounce have
no meaning except through the silence in which they are bathed.
We seek to know that we may learn not to know'; knowledge,
that which can be known by the pure reason, metaphysics, 'indis-
pensable' on this side of the 'frontiers,' being after all precisely
what is least essential to us, since least essentially ourselves. 'We
possess a self more profound and more boundless than the self of
the passions or of pure reason. ... There comes a moment when
the phenomena of our customary consciousness, what we may call
the consciousness of the passions or of our normal relationships, no
longer mean anything to us, no longer touch our real life. I admit
that this consciousness is often interesting in its way, and that it is
often necessary to know it thoroughly. But it is a surface plant, and
its roots fear the great central fire of our being. I may commit a
crime without the least breath stirring the tiniest flame of this fire;
and, on the other hand, the crossing of a single glance, a thought
which never comes into being, a minute which passes without the
utterance of a word, may rouse it into terrible agitations in the
depths of its retreat, and cause it to overflow upon my life. Our
soul does not judge as we judge; it is a capricious and hidden thing.
It can be reached by a breath and unconscious of a tempest. Let
us find out what reaches it; everything is there, for it is there that
we ourselves are.'

And it is towards this point that all the words of this book tend.
Maeterlinck, unlike most men ('What is man but a God who is
afraid?'), is not 'miserly of immortal things.' He utters the most
divine secrets without fear, betraying certain hiding-places of the
soul in those most nearly inaccessible retreats which lie nearest
to us. All that he says we know already; we may deny it, but
we know it. It is what we are not often at leisure enough with
ourselves, sincere enough with ourselves, to realise; what we often
dare not realise; but, when he says it, we know that it is true, and

our knowledge of it is his warrant for saying it. He is what he is precisely because he tells us nothing which we do not already know, or, it may be, what we have known and forgotten.

The mystic, let it be remembered, has nothing in common with the moralist. He speaks only to those who are already prepared to listen to him, and he is indifferent to the 'practical' effect which these or others may draw from his words. A young and profound mystic of our day has figured the influence of wise words upon the foolish and headstrong as 'torches thrown into a burning city.'[6] The mystic knows well that it is not always the soul of the drunkard or the blasphemer which is farthest from the eternal beauty. He is concerned only with that soul of the soul, that life of life, with which the day's doings have so little to do; itself a mystery, and at home only among those supreme mysteries which surround it like an atmosphere. It is not always that he cares that his message, or his vision, may be as clear to others as it is to himself. But, because he is an artist, and not only a philosopher, Maeterlinck has taken especial pains that not a word of his may go astray, and there is not a word of this book which needs to be read twice, in order that it may be understood, by the least trained of attentive readers. It is, indeed, as he calls it, 'The Treasure of the Lowly.'

Conclusion

Our only chance, in this world, of a complete happiness, lies in the measure of our success in shutting the eyes of the mind, and deadening its sense of hearing, and dulling the keenness of its apprehension of the unknown. Knowing so much less than nothing, for we are entrapped in smiling and many-coloured appearances, our life may seem to be but a little space of leisure, in which it will be the necessary business of each of us to speculate on what is so rapidly becoming the past and so rapidly becoming the future, that scarcely existing present which is after all our only possession. Yet, as the present passes from us, hardly to be enjoyed except as memory or as hope, and only with an at best partial recognition of the uncertainty or inutility of both, it is with a kind of terror that we wake up, every now and then, to the whole knowledge of our ignorance, and to some perception of where it is leading us. To live through a single day with that overpowering consciousness of our real position, which, in the moments in which alone it mercifully comes, is like blinding light or the thrust of a flaming sword, would drive any man out of his senses. It is our hesitations, the excuses of our hearts, the compromises of our intelligence, which save us. We can forget so much, we can bear suspense with so fortunate an evasion of its real issues; we are so admirably finite.

And so there is a great, silent conspiracy between us to forget death; all our lives are spent in busily forgetting death. That is why we are active about so many things which we know to be unimportant; why we are so afraid of solitude, and so thankful for the company of our fellow-creatures. Allowing ourselves, for the most part, to be but vaguely conscious of that great suspense in which we live, we find our escape from its sterile, annihilating reality in many dreams, in religion, passion, art; each a forgetfulness, each a symbol of creation; religion being the creation of a new heaven, passion the creation of a new earth, and art, in its mingling of heaven and earth, the creation of heaven out of earth. Each is a kind of sublime selfishness, the saint, the lover, and the artist having each an incommunicable ecstasy which he esteems as his ultimate attainment, however, in his lower moments, he may serve God in action, or do the will of his mistress, or minister to men by showing them a little beauty. But it is, before all things, an escape; and the prophets who have redeemed the world, and the artists who have made the world beautiful, and the lovers who have quickened the pulses of the world, have really, whether they knew it or not, been fleeing from the certainty of one thought: that we have, all of us, only our one day; and from the dread of that other thought: that the day, however used, must after all be wasted.

The fear of death is not cowardice; it is, rather, an intellectual dissatisfaction with an enigma which has been presented to us, and which can be solved only when its solution is of no further use. All we have to ask of death is the meaning of life and we are waiting all through life to ask that question. That life should be happy or unhappy, as those words are used, means so very little; and the heightening or lessening of the general felicity of the world means so little to any individual. There is something almost vulgar in happiness which does not become joy, and joy is an ecstasy which can rarely be maintained in the soul for more than the moment during which we recognise that it is not sorrow. Only very young people want to be happy. What we all want is to be quite sure that there is something which makes it worth while to go on living, in what seems to us our best way, at our finest intensity; something beyond the mere fact that we are satisfying a sort of inner logic (which may be quite faulty) and that we get our best makeshift for happiness on that so hazardous assumption.

Well, the doctrine of Mysticism, with which all this symbolical literature has so much to do, of which it is all so much the expression, presents us, not with a guide for conduct, not with a plan for our happiness, not with an explanation of any mystery, but with a theory of life which makes us familiar with mystery, and which seems to harmonise those instincts which make for religion, passion, and art, freeing us at once of a great bondage. The final uncertainty remains, but we seem to knock less helplessly at closed doors, coming so much closer to the once terrifying eternity of things about us, as we come to look upon these things as shadows, through which we have our shadowy passage. 'For in the particular acts of human life,' Plotinus tells us, 'it is not the interior soul and the true man, but the exterior shadow of the man alone, which laments and weeps, performing his part on the earth as in a more ample and extended scene, in which many shadows of souls and phantom scenes appear.'[1] And as we realise the identity of a poem, a prayer, or a kiss, in that spiritual universe which we are weaving for ourselves, each out of a thread of the great fabric; as we realise the infinite insignificance of action, its immense distance from the current of life; as we realise the delight of feeling ourselves carried onward by forces which it is our wisdom to obey; it is at least with a certain relief that we turn to an ancient doctrine, so much the more likely to be true because it has so much the air of a dream. On this theory alone does all life become worth living, all art worth making, all worship worth offering. And because it might slay as well as save, because the freedom of its sweet captivity might so easily become deadly to the fool, because that is the hardest path to walk in where you are told only, walk well; it is perhaps the only counsel of perfection which can ever really mean much to the artist.

Section II
Essays Added to the 1919 Edition

In September 1908, whilst travelling through Italy with his wife, Arthur Symons experienced a profound mental breakdown which resulted in his being certified insane and committed to Brooke House, an asylum in East London. Doctors initially considered Symons' condition to be permanent, but he started to make a slow recovery during 1909 and gradually returned to his former literary career, even writing an account of his experiences with mental illness in *A Confession* (1930).

Symons continued to be active as a poet, translator and literary critic until a few years before his death in 1945. It is, however, noticeable how much of the work Symons published during the twentieth century recycled or reprinted previously published material. The second American edition of *The Symbolist Movement in Literature*, published by E.P. Dutton in 1919, is no exception. Symons added seven essays to the original volume and re-ordered the collection:

Introduction
Balzac
Prosper Mérimée
Gérard de Nerval
Théophile Gautier
Gustave Flaubert
Charles Baudelaire
Edmond and Jules de Goncourt
Villiers de L'Isle-Adam
Léon Cladel
A Note on Zola's Method
Stéphane Mallarmé
Paul Verlaine
Joris-Karl Huysmans
The Later Huysmans
Arthur Rimbaud

Jules Laforgue
Maeterlinck as a Mystic
Conclusion

Although the edition was described as 'revised and enlarged', Symons made only minor alterations to most of the essays in the previous volume, and while he added some notes for the additional essays at the end of the volume, these consisted solely of lists of publications with no explanatory material (for this reason, they are omitted from this edition).

All of the essays Symons added to this edition of *The Symbolist Movement* had been published separately in previous collections of his essays. The essays on Balzac, Merimée and Gautier had already been collected in *Studies in Prose and Verse* (1904), and the essays on Huysmans, the Goncourt brothers, Flaubert, Cladel and Baudelaire had been collected in *Figures of Several Centuries* (1916). In fact, the essay on Zola had been collected twice, in the previous collections *Studies in Two Literatures* (1897) and *Studies in Prose and Verse*.

When adding these essays to *The Symbolist Movement*, Symons took very few steps to revise or adjust them to the collection as a whole, and several bear clear signs of their previous origins in his journalistic output. The essay on Flaubert, for example, is clearly an introduction to one specific text, *Salammbô*, and accordingly limited in scope. This leaves some doubt about the integrity as of this 'revised and enlarged' account of Symbolism. The inclusion of an essay on Baudelaire as a whole constitutes an implicit recognition of the poet's genealogical importance to the movement in France, and the inclusion of the Goncourt brothers restores them, in part, to the prominence attributed to them in 'The Decadent Movement in Literature'. But Symons did not review the rationale for their inclusion explicitly or otherwise attempt to accommodate them within the general account of Symbolism he provides within the collection.

For this reason, the essays added to the 1919 edition are published here in a separate section and reproduced in the order of their first publication in periodical form or elsewhere. From this it will be seen that the essay on Baudelaire was the last to be published, appearing in the *Saturday Review* during 1907. As such, it reflects also Symons' own burgeoning interests and activities as a translator during the first decades of the twentieth century: his translation of Baudelaire's prose poems appeared in 1905, he published a study of Baudelaire in 1920 and, indeed, Symons reused material taken from the essay that appeared in the 1919 edition of *The Symbolist Movement* as a preface to his own collected translations of Baudelaire's prose and poems in 1927.

In contrast, the earliest material added in 1919 relates to J.K. Huysmans and first appeared in the *Fortnightly Review* during 1892. What's more, the majority of essays added are roughly contemporary with the pieces chosen for inclusion in the first editions of *The Symbolist Movement* (the majority being written between 1892 and 1902). As such they shed important light on Symons' general thinking about French literature in the nineteenth century, as well as reflecting shifts in his views afterwards.

Joris-Karl Huysmans

The novels of Huysmans, however we may regard them as novels are, at all events, the sincere and complete expression of a very remarkable personality. From *Marthe* to *Là-Bas* every story, every volume, disengages the same atmosphere – the atmosphere of a London November, when mere existence is a sufficient burden, and the little miseries of life loom up through the fog into a vague and formidable grotesqueness. Here, for once, is a pessimist whose philosophy is mere sensation – and sensation, after all, is the one certainty in a world which may be well or ill arranged, for ultimate purposes, but which is certainly, for each of us, what each of us feels it to be. To Huysmans the world appears to be a profoundly uncomfortable, unpleasant, ridiculous place, with a certain solace in various forms of art, and certain possibilities of at least temporary escape. Part of his work presents to us a picture of ordinary life as he conceives it, in its uniform trivial wretchedness; in another part he has made experiment in directions which have seemed to promise escape, relief; in yet other portions he has allowed himself the delight of his sole enthusiasm, the enthusiasm of art. He himself would be the first to acknowledge – indeed, practically, he has acknowledged that the particular way in which he sees life is a matter of personal temperament and constitution, a matter of nerves. The Goncourts have never tired of insisting on the fact of their *névrose*, of pointing out its importance in connection with the form and structure of their work, their touch on style, even. To them the *maladie fin de siècle* has come delicately, as to the chlorotic fine ladies of the Faubourg Saint-Germain:[1] it has sharpened their senses to a point of morbid acuteness, it has given their work a certain feverish beauty. To Huysmans it has given the exaggerated horror of whatever is ugly and unpleasant, with the fatal instinct of discovering, the fatal necessity of contemplating, every flaw and every discomfort that a somewhat imperfect world can offer for inspection. It is the transposition of the ideal. Relative values are lost, for it is the sense of the disagreeable only that is heightened; and the world, in this strange disorder of vision, assumes an aspect which can only be compared with that of a drop of impure water under the microscope. 'Nature seen through a temperament' is Zola's definition of all art.[2] Nothing, certainly, could be more exact and expressive as a definition of the art of Huysmans.

To realise how faithfully and how completely Huysmans has revealed himself in all he has written, it is necessary to know the man. 'He gave me the impression of a cat,' some interviewer once wrote of him; 'courteous, perfectly polite, almost amiable, but all nerves, ready to shoot out his claws at the least word.' And indeed, there is something of his favourite animal about him. The face is grey, wearily alert, with a look of benevolent malice. At first sight it is commonplace, the features are ordinary, one seems to have seen it at the Bourse or the Stock Exchange. But gradually that strange, unvarying expression, that look of benevolent malice, grows upon you as the influence of the man makes itself felt. I have seen Huysmans in his office – he is an employé in the Ministry of Foreign Affairs, and a model employé; I have seen him in a café, in various houses; but I always see him in memory as I used to see him at the house of the bizarre Madame X.[3] He leans back on the sofa, rolling a cigarette between his thin, expressive fingers, looking at no one and at nothing, while Madame X moves about with solid vivacity in the midst of her extraordinary menagerie of *bric-à-brac*. The spoils of all the world are there, in that incredibly tiny *salon*; they lie underfoot, they climb up walls, they cling to screens, brackets, and tables; one of your elbows menaces a Japanese toy, the other a Dresden china shepherdess; all the colours of the rainbow clash in a barbaric discord of notes. And in a corner of this fantastic room, Huysmans lies back indifferently on the sofa, with the air of one perfectly resigned to the boredom of life. Something is said by my learned friend who is to write for the new periodical, or perhaps it is the young editor of the new periodical who speaks or (if that were not impossible) the taciturn Englishman who accompanies me; and Huysmans, without looking up, and without taking the trouble to speak very distinctly, picks up the phrase, transforms it, more likely transpierces it, in a perfectly turned sentence, a phrase of impromptu elaboration. Perhaps it is only a stupid book that some one has mentioned, or a stupid woman; as he speaks, the book looms up before one, becomes monstrous in its dullness, a master-piece and miracle of imbecility; the unimportant little woman grows into a slow horror before your eyes. It is always the unpleasant aspect of things that he seizes, but the intensity of his revolt from that unpleasantness brings a touch of the sublime into the very expression of his disgust. Every sentence is an epigram, and every epigram slaughters a reputation or an idea. He speaks with an accent as of pained surprise, an amused look of contempt, so profound that it becomes almost pity, for human imbecility.

Yes, that is the true Huysmans, the Huysmans of *À Rebours*, and it is just such surroundings that seem to bring out his peculiar quality. With this contempt for humanity, this hatred of mediocrity, this passion for a somewhat exotic kind of modernity, an artist who is so exclusively an artist was sure, one day or another, to produce a work which, being produced to please himself, and being entirely typical of himself, would be, in a way, the quintessence of contemporary Decadence. And it is precisely such a book that Huysmans has written, in the extravagant, astonishing *À Rebours*. All his other books are a sort of unconscious preparation for this one book, a sort of inevitable and scarcely necessary sequel to it. They range themselves along the line of a somewhat erratic development, from Baudelaire, through Goncourt, by way of Zola, to the surprising originality of so disconcerting an exception to any and every order of things.

The descendant of a long line of Dutch painters – one of whom, Cornelius Huysmans, has a certain fame among the lesser landscape men of the great period – Joris-Karl Huysmans was born at Paris, February 5, 1848. His first book, *Le Drageoir à Épices*, published at the age of twenty-six, is a *pasticcio* of prose poems, done after Baudelaire, of little sketches, done after Dutch artists, together with a few studies of Parisian landscape, done after nature. It shows us the careful, laboured work of a really artistic temperament; it betrays here and there, the spirit of acrimonious observation which is to count for so much with Huysmans – in the crude malice of *L'Extase*, for example, in the notation of the 'richness of tone,' the 'superb colouring,' of an old drunkard. And one sees already something of the novelty and the precision of his description, the novelty and the unpleasantness of the subjects which he chooses to describe, in this vividly exact picture of the carcass of a cow hung up outside a butcher's shop:

> As in a hothouse, a marvellous vegetation flourished in the carcass. Veins shot out on every side like trails of bind-weed;

dishevelled branch-work extended itself along the body, an efflorescence of entrails unfurled their violet-tinted corollas, and big clusters of fat stood out, a sharp white, against the red medley of quivering flesh.

In *Marthe: histoire d'une fille*, which followed in 1876, two years later, Huysmans is almost as far from actual achievement as in *Le Drageoir à Épices*, but the book, in its crude attempt to deal realistically, and somewhat after the manner of Goncourt, with the life of a prostitute of the lowest depths, marks a considerable advance upon the somewhat casual experiments of his earlier manner. It is important to remember that *Marthe* preceded *La Fille Elisa* and *Nana*. 'I write what I see, what I feel, and what I have experienced,' says the brief and defiant preface, 'and I write it as well as I can: that is all. This explanation is not an excuse, it is simply the statement of the aim that I pursue in art.' Explanation or excuse notwithstanding, the book was forbidden to be sold in France. It is Naturalism in its earliest and most pitiless stage – Naturalism which commits the error of evoking no sort of interest in this unhappy creature who rises a little from her native gutter, only to fall back more woefully into the gutter again. Goncourt's Elisa at least interests us; Zola's Nana at all events appeals to our senses. But Marthe is a mere document, like her story. Notes have been taken – no doubt *sur le vif* – they have been strung together, and here they are with only an interesting brutality, a curious sordidness to note, in these descriptions that do duty for psychology and incident alike, in the general flatness of character, the general dislocation of episode.

Les Soeurs Vatard, published in 1879, and the short story *Sac au Dos*, which appeared in 1880 in the famous Zolaist manifesto, *Les Soirées de Médan*, show the influence of *Les Rougon-Macquart* rather than of *Germinie Lacerteux*. For the time the 'formula' of Zola has been accepted: the result is, a remarkable piece of work, but a story without a story, a frame without a picture. With Zola, there is at all events a beginning and an end, a chain of events, a play of character upon incident. But in *Les Soeurs Vatard* there is no reason for the narrative ever beginning or ending; there are miracles of description – the workroom, the rue de Sèvres,[4] the locomotives, the *Foire du pain d'épice*[5] – which lead to nothing; there are interiors, there are interviews, there are the two workgirls, Céline and Désirée, and their lovers; there is what Zola himself described as *tout ce milieu ouvrier, ce coin de misère et d'ignorance, de tranquille ordure et d'air naturellement empesté.** And with it all there is a heavy sense of stagnancy, a dreary lifelessness. All that is good in the book reappears, in vastly better company, in *En Ménage* (1881), a novel which is, perhaps, more in the direct line of heritage from *L'Éducation Sentimentale* – the starting-point of the Naturalistic novel – than any other novel of the Naturalists.

En Ménage is the story of '*Monsieur Tout-le-monde*, an insignificant personality, one of those poor creatures who have not even the supreme consolation of being able to complain of any injustice in their fate, for an injustice supposes at all events a misunderstood merit, a force.' André is the reduction to the bourgeois formula of the invariable hero of Huysmans. He is just enough removed from the commonplace to suffer from it with acuteness. He cannot get on either with or without a woman in his establishment. Betrayed by his wife, he consoles himself with a mistress, and finally goes back to the wife. And the moral of it all is: 'Let us be stupidly comfortable, if we can, in any way we can: but it is almost certain that we cannot.' In *À Vau-l'Eau*, a less interesting story which followed *En Ménage*, the daily misery of the respectable M. Folantin, the government employé, consists in the impossible search for a decent restaurant, a satisfactory dinner: for M. Folantin, too, there is only the same counsel of a desperate, an inevitable resignation. Never has the intolerable monotony of small inconveniences been so scrupulously, so unsparingly chronicled, as in these two studies in the heroic degree of the commonplace. It happens to André, at a certain epoch in his life, to take back an old servant who had left him many years before. He finds that she has exactly the same defects as before, and 'to find them there again,' comments the author, 'did not displease him. He had been expecting them all the time, he saluted them as old acquaintances, yet with a certain surprise, notwithstanding, to see them neither grown nor diminished. He noted for himself with satisfaction that the stupidity of his servant had remained stationary.' On another page, referring to the inventor of cards, Huysmans defines him as

---

*   ['this whole milieu of the working-man, this corner of poverty and ignorance, of tranquil shite and naturally foul air' – from the section on Huysmans' literary debut in Zola's *Le Roman experimental* (1880).]

one who 'did something towards suppressing the free exchange of human imbecility.' Having to say in passing that a girl has returned from a ball, 'she was at home again,' he observes, 'after the half-dried sweat of the waltzes.' In this invariably sarcastic turn of the phrase, this absoluteness of contempt, this insistence on the disagreeable, we find the note of Huysmans, particularly at this point in his career, when, like Flaubert, he forced himself to contemplate and to analyse the more mediocre manifestations of *la bêtise humaine* [human stupidity].

There is a certain perversity in this furious contemplation of stupidity, this fanatical insistence on the exasperating attraction of the sordid and the disagreeable; and it is by such stages that we come to *À Rebours*. But on the way we have to note a volume of *Croquis Parisiens* (1880), in which the virtuoso who is a part of the artist in Huysmans has executed some of his most astonishing feats; and a volume on *L'Art Moderne* (1883), in which the most modern of artists in literature has applied himself to the criticism – the revelation, rather – of modernity in art. In the latter, Huysmans was the first to declare the supremacy of Degas – 'the greatest artist that we possess today in France' – while announcing with no less fervour the remote, reactionary, and intricate genius of Gustave Moreau. He was the first to discover Raffaëlli,[6] 'the painter of poor people and the open sky – a sort of Parisian Millet,' as he called him; the first to discover Forain, '*le véritable peintre de la fille*' [the true painter of young girls]; the first to discover Odilon Redon, to do justice to Pissaro [*sic*] and Paul Gauguin. No literary artist since Baudelaire has made so valuable a contribution to art criticism and the *Curiosités Esthétiques* are, after all, less exact in their actual study, less revolutionary, and less really significant in their critical judgments, than *L'Art Moderne*. The *Croquis Parisiens*, which, in its first edition, was illustrated by etchings of Forain and Raffaëlli, is simply the attempt to do in words what those artists have done in aquafortis or in pastel. There are the same Parisian types – the omnibus-conductor, the washerwoman, the man who sells hot chestnuts – the same impressions of a sick and sorry landscape. La Bièvre, for preference, in all its desolate and lamentable attraction;[7] there is a marvellously minute series of studies of that typically Parisian music-hall, the Folies-Bergère.[8] Huysmans' faculty of description is here seen at its fullest stretch of agility; precise, suggestive, with all the outline and colour of actual brush-work, it might even be compared with the art of Degas, only there is just that last touch wanting, that breath of palpitating life, which is what we always get in Degas, what we never get in Huysmans.

In *L'Art Moderne*, speaking of the watercolours of Forain, Huysmans attributes to them 'a specious and *cherché* art, demanding, for its appreciation, a certain initiation, a certain special sense.' To realise the full value, the real charm, of *À Rebours*, some such initiation might be deemed necessary. In its fantastic unreality, its exquisite artificiality, it is the natural sequel of *En Ménage* and *À Vau-l'Eau*, which are so much more acutely sordid than the most sordid kind of real life; it is the logical outcome of that hatred and horror of human mediocrity, of the mediocrity of daily existence, which we have seen to be the special form of Huysmans' *névrose*. The motto, taken from a thirteenth-century mystic, Ruysbroeck the Admirable, is a cry for escape, for the 'something in the world that is there in no satisfying measure, or not at all': *Il faut que je me réjouisse au-dessus du temps ... quoique le monde ait horreur de ma joie et que sa grossièreté ne sache pas ce que je veux dire.*[*] And the book is the history of a *Thébaïde raffinée* – a voluntary exile from the world in a new kind of 'Palace of Art.' Des Esseintes, the vague but typical hero, is one of those half-pathological cases which help us to understand the full meaning of the word *décadence*, which they partly represent. The last descendant of an ancient family, his impoverished blood tainted by all sorts of excesses, Des Esseintes finds himself at thirty *sur le chemin, dégrisé, seul, abominablement lassé.*[†] He has already realised that 'the world is divided, in great part, into swaggerers and simpletons.' His one desire is to 'hide himself away, far from the world, in some retreat, where he might deaden the sound of the loud rumbling of inflexible life, as one covers the street with straw, for sick people.' This retreat he discovers, just far enough from Paris to be safe from disturbance, just near enough to be saved from the nostalgia of the unattainable. He succeeds in making his house a paradise of the artificial, choosing the tones of colour that go best with candlelight, for it need scarcely be said that Des Esseintes has effected a simple transposition of night and

---

[*] ['I have to rejoice above our times ... even though the world is horrified by my joy and its vulgarity may not understand what I want to say.']

[†] ['on the road, sober, alone, abominably sad']

day. His disappearance from the world has been complete; it seems to him that the 'comfortable desert' of his exile need never cease to be just such a luxurious solitude; it seems to him that he has attained his desire, that he has attained to happiness.

Disturbing physical symptoms harass him from time to time, but they pass. It is an effect of nerves that now and again he is haunted by remembrance; the recurrence of a perfume, the reading of a book, brings back a period of life when his deliberate perversity was exercised actively in matters of the senses. There are his fantastic banquets, his fantastic amours: the *repas de deuil*, Miss Urania the acrobat, the episode of the ventriloquist-woman and the reincarnation of the Sphinx and the Chimæra of Flaubert, the episode of the boy *chez* Madame Laure. A casual recollection brings up the schooldays of his childhood with the Jesuits, and with that the beliefs of childhood, the fantasies of the Church, the Catholic abnegation of the *Imitatio* joining so strangely with the final philosophy of Schopenhauer. At times his brain is haunted by social theories – his dull hatred of the ordinary in life taking form in the region of ideas. But in the main he feeds himself, with something of the satisfaction of success, on the strange food for the sensations with which he has so laboriously furnished himself. There are his books, and among these a special library of the Latin writers of the Decadence. Exasperated by Virgil, profoundly contemptuous of Horace, he tolerates Lucan (which is surprising), adores Petronius (as well he might), and delights in the neologisms and the exotic novelty of Apuleius. His curiosity extends to the later Christian poets – from the coloured verse of Claudian down to the verse which is scarcely verse of the incoherent ninth century. He is, of course, an amateur of exquisite printing, of beautiful bindings, and possesses an incomparable Baudelaire (*edition tirée à un exemplaire*), a unique Mallarmé. Catholicism being the adopted religion of the Decadence – for its venerable age, valuable in such matters as the age of an old wine, its vague excitation of the senses, its mystical picturesqueness – Des Esseintes has a curious collection of the later Catholic literature, where Lacordaire and the Comte de Falloux, Veuillot and Ozanam, find their place side by side with the half-prophetic, half-ingenious Hello, the amalgam of a monstrous mysticism and a casuistical sensuality, Barbey d'Aurevilly. His collection of 'profane' writers is small, but it is selected for the qualities of exotic charm that have come to be his only

care in art – for the somewhat diseased, or the somewhat artificial
beauty that alone can strike a responsive thrill from his exacting
nerves. 'Considering within himself, he realised that a work of
art, in order to attract him, must come to him with that quality
of strangeness demanded by Edgar Poe; but he fared yet further
along this route, and sought for all the Byzantine flora of the brain,
for complicated deliquescences of style; he required a troubling
indecision over which he could muse, fashioning it after his will
to more of vagueness or of solid form, according to the state of
his mind at the moment. He delighted in a work of art both for
what it was in itself and for what it could lend him; he would fain
go along with it, thanks to it, as though sustained by an adjuvant,
as though borne in a vehicle, into a sphere where his sublimated
sensations would wake in him an unaccustomed stir, the cause of
which he would long and vainly seek to determine.' So he comes
to care supremely for Baudelaire, 'who, more than any other,
possessed the marvellous power of rendering, with a strange sanity
of expression, the most fleeting, the most wavering morbid states
of exhausted minds, of desolate souls.' In Flaubert he prefers *La
Tentation de Saint-Antoine*; in Goncourt, *La Faustin*; in Zola, *La
Faute de l'Abbé Mouret* – the exceptional, the most remote and
recherché outcome of each temperament. And of the three it is the
novel of Goncourt that appeals to him with special intimacy – that
novel which, more than any other, seems to express, in its exquisitely perverse charm, all that decadent civilisation of which Des
Esseintes is the type and symbol. In poetry he has discovered the
fine perfume, the evanescent charm, of Paul Verlaine, and near
that great poet (forgetting, strangely, Arthur Rimbaud) he places
two poets who are curious – the disconcerting, tumultuous Tristan
Corbière, and the painted and bejewelled Théodore Hannon.[9]
With Edgar Poe he has the instinctive sympathy which drew
Baudelaire to the enigmatically perverse Decadent of America;
he delights, sooner than all the world, in the astonishing, unbal-
anced, unachieved genius of Villiers de l'Isle-Adam. Finally, it is in
Stéphane Mallarmé that he finds the incarnation of 'the decadence
of a literature, irreparably affected in its organism, weakened in its
ideas by age, exhausted by the excesses of syntax, sensitive only
to the curiosity which fevers sick people, and yet hastening to
say everything, now at the end, torn by the wish to atone for all

its omissions of enjoyment, to bequeath its subtlest memories of sorrow on its death-bed.'

But it is not on books alone that Des Esseintes nurses his sick and craving fancy. He pushes his delight in the artificial to the last limits, and diverts himself with a bouquet of jewels, a concert of flowers, an orchestra of liqueurs, an orchestra of perfumes. In flowers he prefers the real flowers that imitate artificial ones. It is the monstrosities of nature, the offspring of unnatural adulteries, that he cherishes in the barbarically coloured flowers, the plants with barbaric names, the carnivorous plants of the Antilles – morbid horrors of vegetation, chosen, not for their beauty, but for their strangeness. And his imagination plays harmonies on the sense of taste, like combinations of music, from the flute-like sweetness of anisette, the trumpet-note of kirsch, the eager yet velvety sharpness of curaçao, the clarinet. He combines scents, weaving them into odorous melodies, with effects like those of the refrains of certain poems, employing, for example, the method of Baudelaire in *L'Irréparable* and *Le Balcon*, where the last line of the stanza is the echo of the first, in the languorous progression of the melody. And above all he has his few, carefully chosen pictures, with their diverse notes of strange beauty and strange terror – the two Salomés of Gustave Moreau, the 'Religious Persecutions' of Jan Luyken,[10] the opium-dreams of Odilon Redon. His favourite artist is Gustave Moreau, and it is on this superb and disquieting picture that he cares chiefly to dwell.

A throne, like the high altar of a cathedral, rose beneath innumerable arches springing from columns, thick-set as Roman pillars, enamelled with vari-coloured bricks, set with mosaics, incrusted with lapis lazuli and sardonyx, in a palace like the basilica of an architecture at once Mussulman and Byzantine. In the centre of the tabernacle surmounting the altar, fronted with rows of circular steps, sat the Tetrarch Herod, the tiara on his head, his legs pressed together, his hands on his knees. His face was yellow, parchment-like, annulated with wrinkles, withered with age; his long beard floated like a white cloud on the jewelled stars that constellated the robe of netted gold across his breast. Around this statue, motionless, frozen in the sacred pose of a Hindu god, perfumes burned, throwing out clouds of vapour, pierced, as by the phosphorescent eyes of animals, by the fire of precious stones set in the sides of the throne; then the vapour mounted, unrolling itself beneath arches where the blue smoke mingled with the powdered gold of great sunrays, fallen from the domes.

In the perverse odour of perfumes, in the overheated atmosphere of this church, Salomé, her left arm extended in a gesture of command, her bent right arm holding at the level of the face a great lotus, advances slowly to the sound of a guitar, thrummed by a woman who crouches on the floor.

With collected, solemn, almost august countenance, she begins the lascivious dance that should waken the sleeping senses of the aged Herod; her breasts undulate, become rigid at the contact of the whirling necklets; diamonds sparkle on the dead whiteness of her skin, her bracelets, girdles, rings, shoot sparks; on her triumphal robe, sewn with pearls, flowered with silver, sheeted with gold, the jewelled breastplate, whose every stitch is a precious stone, bursts into flame, scatters in snakes of fire, swarms on the ivory-toned, tea-rose flesh, like splendid insects with dazzling wings, marbled with carmine, dotted with morning gold, diapered with steel-blue, streaked with peacock-green.

....

In the work of Gustave Moreau, conceived on no Scriptural data, Des Esseintes saw at last the realisation of the strange, superhuman Salomé that he had dreamed. She was no more the mere dancing-girl who, with the corrupt torsion of her limbs, tears a cry of desire from an old man; who, with her eddying breasts, her palpitating body, her quivering thighs, breaks the energy, melts the will, of a king; she has become the symbolic deity of indestructible Lust, the goddess of immortal Hysteria, the accursed Beauty, chosen among many by the catalepsy that has stiffened her limbs, that has hardened her muscles; the monstrous, indifferent, irresponsible, insensible Beast, poisoning, like Helen of old, all that go near to her, all that look upon her, all that she touches.[11]

It is in such a 'Palace of Art' that Des Esseintes would recreate his already overwrought body and brain, and the monotony of its seclusion is only once broken by a single excursion into the world without. This one episode of action, this one touch of realism in a book given over to the artificial, confined to a record of sensation, is a projected voyage to London, a voyage that never occurs. Des Esseintes has been reading Dickens, idly, to quiet his nerves, and the violent colours of those ultra-British scenes and characters have imposed themselves upon his imagination. Days of rain and fog complete the picture of that *pays de brume et de boue* [land of fog and mud], and suddenly, stung by the unwonted desire for change, he takes the train to Paris, resolved to distract himself by a visit to London. Arrived in Paris before his time, he takes a cab to the office of *Galignani's Messenger*, fancying himself, as the rain-drops rattle on the roof and the mud splashes against the windows, already in the midst of the immense city, its smoke and dirt. He reaches *Galignani's Messenger* and there, turning over Baedekers and Murrays, loses himself in dreams of an imagined London. He buys a Baedeker, and, to pass the time, enters the 'Bodéga' at the comer of the Rue de Rivoli and the Rue Castiglione. The wine-cellar is crowded with Englishmen: he sees, as he drinks his port, and listens to the unfamiliar accents, all the characters of Dickens – a whole England of caricature; as he drinks his Amontillado, the recollection of Poe puts a new horror into the good-humoured faces about him. Leaving the 'Bodéga' he steps out again into the rain-swept street, regains his cab, and drives to the English tavern of the Rue d'Amsterdam. He has just time for dinner, and he finds a place beside the *insulaires* [islanders], with 'their porcelain eyes, their crimson cheeks,' and orders a heavy English dinner, which he washes down with ale and porter, seasoning his coffee, as he imagines we do in England, with gin. As time passes, and the hour of the train draws near, he begins to reflect vaguely on his project; he recalls the disillusion of the visit he had once paid to Holland. Does not a similar disillusion await him in London? 'Why travel, when one can travel so splendidly in a chair? Was he not at London already, since its odours, its atmos-phere, its inhabitants, its food, its utensils, were all about him?' The train is due, but he does not stir. 'I have felt and seen,' he says to himself, 'what I wanted to feel and see. I have been satu-rated with English life all this time; it would be madness to lose, by a clumsy change of place, these imperishable sensations.' So he gathers together his luggage, and goes home again, resolving never to abandon the 'docile phantasmagoria of the brain' for the mere realities of the actual world. But his nervous malady, one of whose symptoms had driven him forth and brought him back so spasmodically, is on the increase. He is seized by hallucinations, haunted by sounds: the hysteria of Schumann, the morbid exaltation of Berlioz, communicate themselves to him in the music that besieges his brain. Obliged at last to send for a doctor, we find him, at the end of the book, ordered back to Paris, to the normal life, the normal conditions, with just that chance of escape from death or madness. So suggestively, so instructively, closes the record of a strange, attractive folly – in itself partly a serious ideal (which indeed is Huysmans' own), partly the caricature of that ideal. Des Esseintes, though studied from a real man, who is known to those who know a certain kind of society in Paris, is a type rather than a man:[12] he is the offspring of the Decadent art that he adores, and this book a sort of breviary for its worshippers. It has a place of its own in the literature of the day, for it sums up, not only a talent, but a spiritual epoch.

À Rebours is a book that can only be written once, and since that date Huysmans has published a short story, *Un Dilemme* (1887), which is merely a somewhat lengthy anecdote; two novels, *En Rade* (1887) and *Là-Bas* (1891), both of which are interesting experiments, but neither of them an entire success; and a volume of art criticism, *Certains* (1890), notable for a single splendid essay, that on Félicien Rops, the etcher of the fantastically erotic.[13] *En Rade* is a sort of deliberately exaggerated record – vision rather then record – of the disillusions of a country sojourn, as they affect the disordered nerves of a town *névrose*. The narrative is punctuated by nightmares, marvellously woven out of nothing, and with no psychological value – the human part of the book being a sort of picturesque pathology at best, the representation of a series of states of nerves, sharpened by the tragic ennui of the country. There is a cat which becomes interesting in its agonies; but the long boredom of the man and woman is only too faithfully shared with the reader. *Là-Bas* is a more artistic creation, on a more solid foundation. It is a study of Satanism, a dexterous interweaving of the history of Gilles de Retz (the traditional Bluebeard)[14] with the contemporary manifestations of the Black Art. 'The execration of impotence, the hate of the mediocre – that is perhaps one of the most indulgent definitions of Diabolism,' says Huysmans, somewhere in the book, and it is on this side that one finds the link of connection with the others of that series of pessimist studies in life.

Un naturalisme spiritualiste, he defines his own art at this point in its development; and it is in somewhat the 'documentary' manner that he applies himself to the study of these strange problems, half of hysteria, half of a real mystical corruption that does actually exist in our midst. I do not know whether the monstrous tableau of the Black Mass – so marvellously, so revoltingly described in the central episode of the book – is still enacted in our days, but I do know that all but the most horrible practices of the sacrilegious magic of the Middle Ages are yet performed, from time to time, in a secrecy which is all but absolute. The character of Madame Chantelouve is an attempt, probably the first in literature, to diagnose a case of Sadism in a woman. To say that it is successful would be to assume that the thing is possible, which one hesitates to do. The book is even more disquieting, to the normal mind, than *À Rebours*. But it is not, like that, the study of an exception which has become a type. It is the study of an exception which does not profess to be anything but a disease.

Huysmans' place in contemporary literature is not quite easy to estimate. There is a danger of being too much attracted, or too much repelled, by those qualities of deliberate singularity which make his work, sincere expression as it is of his own personality, so artificial and *recherché* in itself. With his pronounced, exceptional characteristics, it would have been impossible for him to write fiction impersonally, or to range himself, for long, in any school, under any master. Interrogated one day as to his opinion of Naturalism, he had but to say in reply:

> Au fond il y a des écrivains qui ont du talent et d'autres qui n'en ont pas, qu'ils soient naturalistes, romantiques, décadents, tout ce que vous voudrez, ça m'est égal! il s'agit pour moi d'avoir du talent, et voilà tout!*

But, as we have seen, he has undergone various influences, he has had his periods. From the first he has had a style of singular pungency, novelty, and colour; and, even in *Le Drageoir à Épices*, we find such daring combinations as this (*Camaïeu Rouge*): *Cette fanfare de rouge étourdissait; cette gamme d'une intensité furieuse, d'une*

---

* ['At bottom, there are writers who have talent and others who have not; let them be Naturalists, Romantics, Decadents, what you will, it is all the same to me: I only want to know if they have talent!' – Symons' translation.[15]]

*violence inouïe, m'aveuglait.** Working upon the foundation of Flaubert and of Goncourt, the two great modern stylists, he has developed an intensely personal style of his own, in which the sense of rhythm is entirely dominated by the sense of colour. He manipulates the French language with a freedom sometimes barbarous, 'dragging his images by the heels or the hair' (in the admirable phrase of Léon Bloy) 'up and down the worm-eaten staircase of terrified syntax,' gaining, certainly, the effects at which he aims.[16] He possesses, in the highest degree, that *style tacheté et faisandé* – high-flavoured and spotted with corruption – that he attributes to Goncourt and Verlaine. And with this audacious and barbaric profusion of words – chosen always for their colour and their vividly expressive quality – he is able to describe the essentially modern aspects of things as no one had ever described them before. No one before him had ever so realised the perverse charm of the sordid, the perverse charm of the artificial. Exceptional always, it is for such qualities as these, rather than for the ordinary qualities of the novelist, that he is remarkable. His stories are without incident, they are constructed to go on until they stop, they are almost without characters. His psychology is a matter of the sensations, and chiefly the visual sensations. The moral nature is ignored, the emotions resolve themselves for the most part into a sordid ennui, rising at times into a rage at existence. The protagonist of every book is not so much a character as a bundle of impressions and sensations – the vague outline of a single consciousness, his own. But it is that single consciousness – in this morbidly personal writer – with which we are concerned. For Huysmans' novels, with all their strangeness, their charm, their repulsion, typical too, as they are, of much beside himself, are certainly the expression of a personality as remarkable as that of any contemporary writer.

1892

---

* ['I was deafened by this fanfare of red; I was blinded by the furious intensity, the incredible violence, of these scales' – the narrator is describing sunlight suddenly filtering through red petals.]

A Note on Zola's Method

The art of Zola is based on certain theories, on a view of humanity which he has adopted as his formula. As a deduction from his formula, he takes many things in human nature for granted, he is content to observe at second-hand; and it is only when he comes to the filling-up of his outlines, the *mise-en-scène*, that his observation becomes personal, minute, and persistent. He has thus succeeded in being at once unreal where reality is most essential, tediously real where a point-by-point reality is sometimes unimportant. The contradiction is an ingenious one, which it may be interesting to examine in a little detail, and from several points of view.

And, first of all, take *L'Assommoir*, no doubt the most characteristic of Zola's novels, and probably the best; and, leaving out for the present the broader question of his general conception of humanity, let us look at Zola's manner of dealing with his material, noting by the way certain differences between his manner and that of Goncourt, of Flaubert, with both of whom he has so often been compared, and with whom he wishes to challenge comparison. Contrast *L'Assommoir* with *Germinie Lacerteux*, which, it must be remembered, was written thirteen years earlier. Goncourt, as he incessantly reminds us, was the first novelist in France to deliberately study the life of the people, after precise documents; and *Germinie Lacerteux* has this distinction, among others, that it was a new thing. And it is done with admirable skill; as a piece of writing, as a work of art, it is far superior to Zola. But, certainly, Zola's work has a mass and bulk, a *fougue*, a *portée* [a fieriness, a breadth], which Goncourt's lacks; and it has a savour of plebeian flesh which all the delicate art of Goncourt could not evoke. Zola sickens you with it; but there it is. As in all his books, but more than in most, there is something greasy, a smear of eating and drinking; the pages, to use his own phrase, *grasses des lichades du lundi* [sticky with Monday's booze]. In *Germinie Lacerteux* you never forget that Goncourt is an aristocrat; in *L'Assommoir* you never forget that Zola is a bourgeois. Whatever Goncourt touches becomes, by the mere magic of his touch, charming, a picture; Zola is totally destitute of charm. But how, in *L'Assommoir*, he drives home to you the horrid realities of these narrow, uncomfortable lives! Zola has made up his mind that he will say everything, without omitting a single item, whatever he has to say; thus, in *L'Assommoir*, there is a great feast which lasts for fifty pages, beginning with the picking of the goose, the day before, and going on to the picking of the goose's bones, by a stray marauding cat, the night after. And, in a sense, he does say everything; and there, certainly, is his novelty, his invention. He observes with immense persistence, but his observation, after all, is only that of the man in the street; it is simply carried into detail, deliberately. And, while Goncourt wanders away sometimes into arabesques, indulges in flourishes, so finely artistic is his sense of words and of the things they represent, so perfectly can he match a sensation or an impression by its figure in speech, Zola, on the contrary, never finds just the right word, and it is his persistent fumbling for it which produces these miles of description; four pages describing how two people went upstairs, from the ground floor to the sixth story, and then two pages afterwards to describe how they came downstairs again. Sometimes, by his prodigious diligence and minuteness, he succeeds in giving you the impression; often, indeed; but at the cost of what *ennui* to writer and reader alike! And so much of it all is purely unnecessary, has no interest in itself and no connection with the story: the precise details of Lorilleux's chain-making, bristling with technical terms: it was *la colonne* that he made, and only that particular kind of chain; Goujet's forge, and the machinery in the shed next door; and just how you cut out zinc with a large pair of scissors. When Goncourt gives you a long description of anything, even if you do not feel that it helps on the story very much, it is such a beautiful thing in itself, his mere way of writing it is so enchanting, that you find yourself wishing it longer, at its longest. But with Zola, there is no literary interest in the writing, apart from its clear and coherent expression of a given thing; and these interminable descriptions have no extraneous, or, if you will, implicit interest, to save them from the charge of irrelevancy; they sink by their own weight. Just as Zola's vision is the vision of the average man, so his vocabulary, with all its technicology, remains mediocre, incapable of expressing subtleties, incapable of a really artistic effect. To find out in a slang dictionary that a filthy idea can be expressed by an ingeniously filthy phrase in *argot*, and to use that phrase, is not a great feat, or, on a purely artistic grounds, altogether desirable. To go to a chainmaker and learn the trade name of the various kinds of chain which he manufactures, and of the instruments with which he manufactures them, is not an elaborate process, or one which can be said to pay you for the little trouble which it no doubt takes. And it is not well to be too certain after all that Zola is always perfectly accurate in his use of all this manifold knowledge. The slang, for example; he went to books for it, in books he found it, and no one will ever find some of it but in books. However, my main contention is that Zola's general use of words is, to be quite frank, somewhat ineffectual. He tries to do what Flaubert did, without Flaubert's tools, and without the craftsman's hand at the back of the tools. His fingers are too thick; they leave a blurred line. If you want merely weight, a certain kind of force, you get it; but no more.

Where a large part of Zola's merit lies, in his persistent attention to detail, one finds also one of his chief defects. He cannot leave well alone; he cannot omit; he will not take the most obvious fact for granted. *Il marcha le premier, elle le suivit*, well, of course, she followed him, if he walked first: why mention the fact? That beginning of a sentence is absolutely typical; it is impossible for him to refer, for the twentieth time, to some unimportant character, without giving name and profession, not one or the other, but both, invariably both. He tells us particularly that a room is composed of four walls, that a table stands on its four legs. And he does not appear to see the difference between doing that and doing as Flaubert does, namely, selecting precisely the detail out of all others which renders or consorts with the scene in hand, and giving that detail with an ingenious exactness. Here, for instance, in *Madame Bovary*, is a characteristic detail in the manner of Flaubert:

> Huit jours après, comme elle étendait du linge dans sa cour, elle fut prise d'un crachement de sang, et le lendemain, tandis que Charles avait le dos tourné pour fermer le rideau de la fenêtre, elle dit: 'Ah! Mon Dieu!' poussa un soupir et s'évanouit. Elle était morte.*

---

* ['Eight days later, as she was hanging out the washing in the courtyard, she started spitting blood, and the next day, whilst Charles had his back turned in order to close the curtain, she said "Ah! My God!" gave a sigh and fainted. She was dead.']

Now that detail, brought in without the slightest emphasis, of the husband turning his back at the very instant that his wife dies, is a detail of immense psychological value; it indicates to us, at the very opening of the book, just the character of the man about whom we are to read so much. Zola would have taken at least two pages to say that, and, after all, he would not have said it. He would have told you the position of the chest of drawers in the room, what wood the chest of drawers was made of, and if it had a little varnish knocked off at the corner of the lower cornice, just where it would naturally be in the way of people's feet as they entered the door. He would have told you how Charles leant against the other corner of the chest of drawers, and that the edge of the upper cornice left a slight dent in his black frock-coat, which remained visible half an hour afterwards. But that one little detail, which Flaubert selects from among a thousand, that, no, he would never have given us that!

And the language in which all this is written, apart from the consideration of language as a medium, is really not literature at all, in any strict sense. I am not, for the moment, complaining of the colloquialism and the slang. Zola has told us that he has, in *L'Assommoir*, used the language of the people in order to render the people with a closer truth. Whether he has done that or not is not the question. The question is, that he does not give one the sense of reading good literature, whether he speaks in Delvau's *langue verte*,[*] or according to the Academy's latest edition of classical French. His sentences have no rhythm; they give no pleasure to the ear; they carry no sensation to the eye. You hear a sentence of Flaubert, and you see a sentence of Goncourt, like living things, with forms and voices. But a page of Zola lies dull and silent before you; it draws you by no charm, it has no meaning until you have read the page that goes before and the page that comes after. It is like cabinet-maker's work, solid, well fitted together, and essentially made to be used.

Yes, there is no doubt that Zola writes very badly, worse than any other French writer of eminence. It is true that Balzac, certainly one of the greatest, does, in a sense, write badly; but his way of writing badly is very different from Zola's, and leaves you with the sense of quite a different result. Balzac is too impatient

---

[*] [Coarse diction – literally 'green tongue'.]

with words; he cannot stay to get them all into proper order, to pick and choose among them. Night, the coffee, the wet towel, and the end of six hours' labour are often too much for him; and his manner of writing his novels on the proof-sheets, altering and expanding as fresh ideas came to him on each re-reading, was not a way of doing things which can possibly result in perfect writing. But Balzac sins from excess, from a feverish haste, the very extravagance of power; and, at all events, he 'sins strongly.' Zola sins meanly, he is penuriously careful, he does the best he possibly can; and he is not aware that his best does not answer all requirements. So long as writing is clear and not ungrammatical, it seems to him sufficient. He has not realised that without charm there can be no fine literature, as there can be no perfect flower without fragrance.

And it is here that I would complain, not as a matter of morals, but as a matter of art, of Zola's obsession by what is grossly, uninterestingly filthy. There is a certain simile in *L'Assommoir*, used in the most innocent connection, in connection with a bonnet, which seems to me the most abjectly dirty phrase which I have ever read. It is one thing to use dirty words to describe dirty things: that may be necessary, and thus unexceptionable. It is another thing again, and this, too, may well be defended on artistic grounds, to be ingeniously and wittily indecent. But I do not think a real man of letters could possibly have used such an expression as the one I am alluding to, or could so meanly succumb to certain kinds of prurience which we find in Zola's work. Such as scene as the one in which Gervaise comes home with Lantier, and finds her husband lying drunk asleep in his own vomit, might certainly be explained and even excused, though few more disagreeable things were ever written, on the ground of the psychological importance which it undoubtedly has, and the overwhelming way in which it drives home the point which it is the writer's business to make. But the worrying way in which *le derrière* [backside] and *le ventre* [womb] are constantly kept in view, without the slightest necessity, is quite another thing. I should not like to say how often the phrase 'sa nudité de jolie fille' [her lovely young naked body] occurs in Zola. Zola's nudities always remind me of those which you can see in the *Foire au pain d'épice* at Vincennes, by paying a penny and looking through a peep-hole.[1] In the laundry scenes, for instance in *L'Assommoir*, he is always reminding you that the laundresses have turned up their sleeves, or undone a button or two of their bodices. His eyes seem eternally fixed on the inch or two of bare flesh that can be seen; and he nudges your elbow at every moment, to make sure that you are looking too. Nothing may be more charming than a frankly sensuous description of things which appeal to the senses; but can one imagine anything less charming, less like art, than this prying eye glued to the peep-hole in the Gingerbread Fair?

Yet, whatever view may be taken of Zola's work in literature, there is no doubt that the life of Zola is a model lesson, and might profitably be told in one of Dr. Smiles's edifying biographies.[2] It may even be brought as a reproach against the writer of these novels, in which there are so many offences against the respectable virtues, that he is too good a bourgeois, too much the incarnation of the respectable virtues, to be a man of genius. If the finest art comes of the intensest living, then Zola has never had even a chance of doing the greatest kind of work. It is his merit and his misfortune to have lived entirely in and for his books, with a heroic devotion to his ideal of literary duty which would merit every praise if we had to consider simply the moral side of the question. So many pages of copy a day, so many hours of study given to mysticism, or Les Halles; Zola has always had his day's work marked out before him, and he has never swerved from it. A recent life of Zola tells us something about his way of getting up a subject.[3] 'Immense preparation had been necessary for the *Faute de l'Abbé Mouret*. Mountains of notebooks were heaped up on his table, and for months Zola was plunged in the study of religious works. All the mystical part of the book, and notably the passages having reference to the cultus of Mary, was taken from the works of the Spanish Jesuits. The *Imitation of Jesus Christ* was largely drawn upon, many passages being copied almost word for word into the novel – much as in *Clarissa Harlowe*, that other great realist, Richardson, copied whole passages from the Psalms. The description of life in a grand seminary was given him by a priest who had been dismissed from ecclesiastical service. The little church of Sainte Marie des Batignolles was regularly visited.'

How commendable all that is, but, surely, how futile! Can one conceive of a more hopeless, a more ridiculous task, than that of setting to work on a novel of ecclesiastical life as if one were cramming for an examination in religious knowledge? Zola apparently imagines that he can master mysticism in a fortnight, as he masters the police regulations of Les Halles. It must be admitted that he does wonders with his second-hand information, alike in regard to mysticism and Les Halles. But he succeeds only to a certain point, and that point lies on the nearer side of what is really meant by success. Is not Zola himself, at his moments, aware of this? A letter written in 1881, and printed in Mr. Sherard's life of Zola, from which I have just quoted, seems to me very significant.

> I continue to work in a good state of mental equilibrium. My novel (*Pot-Bouille*) is certainly only a task requiring precision and clearness. No *bravoura*, not the least lyrical treat. It does not give me any warm satisfaction, but it amuses me like a piece of mechanism with a thousand wheels, of which it is my duty to regulate the movements with the most minute care. I ask myself the question: Is it good policy, when one feels that one has passion in one, to check it, or even to bridle it? If one of my books is destined to become immortal, it will, I am sure, be the most passionate one.

Est-elle en marbre ou non, la Vénus de Milo?* said the Parnassians, priding themselves on their muse with her *peplum bien sculpté*. Zola will describe to you the exact shape and the exact smell of the rags of his naturalistic muse; but has she, under the tatters, really a human heart? In the whole of Zola's works, amid all his exact and impressive descriptions of misery, all his endless annals of the poor, I know only one episode which brings tears to the eyes, the episode of the child-martyr Lalie in *L'Assommoir*. 'A piece of mechanism with a thousand wheels,' that is indeed the image of this immense and wonderful study of human life, evolved out of the brain of a solitary student who knows life only by the report of his documents, his friends, and, above all, his formula.

Zola has defined art, very aptly, as nature seen through a temperament. The art of Zola is nature seen through a formula. This professed realist is a man of theories who studies life with a conviction that he will find there such and such things which he has read about in scientific books. He observes, indeed, with astonishing minuteness, but he observes in support of preconceived ideas. And so powerful is his imagination that he has created a whole world

---

* ['Is the Venus de Milo made of marble or not?' – Paul Verlaine, 'Épilogue III.', in *Poèmes saturniens* (1866).]

which has no existence anywhere but in his own brain, and he has placed there imaginary beings, so much more logical than life, in the midst of surroundings which are themselves so real as to lend almost a semblance of reality to the embodied formulas who inhabit them.

It is the boast of Zola that he has taken up art at the point where Flaubert left it, and that he has developed that art in its logical sequence. But the art of Flaubert, itself a development from Balzac, had carried realism, if not in *Madame Bovary*, at all events in *L'Éducation Sentimentale*, as far as realism can well go without ceasing to be art. In the grey and somewhat sordid history of Frédéric Moreau there is not a touch of romanticism, not so much as a concession to style, a momentary escape of the imprisoned lyrical tendency. Everything is observed, everything is taken straight from life: realism sincere, direct, implacable, reigns from end to end of the book. But with what consummate art all this mass of observation is disintegrated, arranged, composed! with what infinite delicacy it is manipulated in the service of an unerring sense of construction! And Flaubert has no theory, has no prejudices, has only a certain impatience with human imbecility. Zola, too, gathers his documents, heaps up his mass of observation, and then, in this unhappy 'development' of the principles of art which produced *L'Éducation Sentimentale*, flings everything pell-mell into one overflowing *pot-au-feu* [hotpot]. The probabilities of nature and the delicacies of art are alike drowned beneath a flood of turbid observation, and in the end one does not even feel convinced that Zola really knows his subject. I remember once hearing M. Huysmans, with his look and tone of subtle, ironical malice, describe how Zola, when he was writing *La Terre*, took a drive into the country in a victoria, to see the peasants. The English papers once reported an interview in which the author of *Nana*, indiscreetly questioned as to the amount of personal observation he had put into the book, replied that he had lunched with an actress of the Variétés. The reply was generally taken for a joke, but the lunch was a reality, and it was assuredly a rare experience in the life of solitary diligence to which we owe so many impersonal studies in life. Nor did Zola, as he sat silent by the side of Mlle. X., seem to be making much use of the opportunity.[4] The language of the miners in *Germinal*, how much of local colour is there in that? The interminable additions and divisions, the extracts from a financial gazette, in *L'Argent*, how much of the real temper and idiosyncrasy of the financier do they give us? In his description of places, in his *mise-en-scène*, Zola puts down what he sees with his own eyes, and, though it is often done at utterly disproportionate length, it is at all events done with exactitude. But in the far more important observation of men and women, he is content with second-hand knowledge, the knowledge of a man who sees the world through a formula. Zola sees in humanity *la bête humaine*. He sees the beast in all its transformations, but he sees only the beast. He has never looked at life impartially, he has never seen it as it is. His realism is a distorted idealism, and the man who considers himself the first to paint humanity as it really is will be remembered in the future as the most idealistic writer of his time.

1893

Edmond and Jules de Goncourt

My first visit to Edmond de Goncourt was in May, 1892. I remember my immense curiosity about that 'House Beautiful,' at Auteuil, of which I had heard so much, and my excitement as I rang the bell, and was shown at once into the garden, where Goncourt was just saying good-bye to some friends. He was carelessly dressed, without a collar, and with the usual loosely knotted large white scarf rolled round his neck. He was wearing a straw hat, and it was only afterwards that I could see the fine sweep of the white hair, falling across the forehead. I thought him the most distinguished-looking man of letters I had ever seen; for he had at once the distinction of race, of fine breeding, and of that delicate artistic genius which, with him, was so intimately a part of things beautiful and distinguished. He had the eyes of an old eagle; a general air of dignified collectedness; a rare, and a rarely charming, smile, which came out, like a ray of sunshine, in the instinctive pleasure of having said a witty or graceful thing to which one's response had been immediate. When he took me indoors, into that house which was a museum, I noticed the delicacy of his hands, and the tenderness with which he handled his treasures, touching them as if he loved them, with little, unconscious murmurs: *Quel goût! quel goût!* [What taste! What taste!] These rose-coloured rooms, with their embroidered ceilings, were filled with cabinets of beautiful things, Japanese carvings, and prints (the miraculous 'Plongeuses'!), always in perfect condition (*Je cherche le beau* [I seek out beauty]); albums had been made for him in Japan, and in these he inserted prints, mounting others upon silver and gold paper, which formed a sort of frame. He showed me his eighteenth-century designs, among which I remember his pointing out one (a Chardin, I think)[1] as the first he had ever bought; he had been sixteen at the time, and he bought it for twelve francs.

When we came to the study, the room in which he worked, he showed me all of his own first editions, carefully bound, and first editions of Flaubert, Baudelaire, Gautier, with those, less interesting to me, of the men of later generations. He spoke of himself and his brother with a serene pride, which seemed to me perfectly dignified and appropriate; and I remember his speaking (with a parenthetic disdain of the *brouillard scandinave* [Scandinavian fog], in which it seemed to him that France was trying to envelop herself; at the best it would be but *un mauvais brouillard* [a terrible fog]) of the endeavour which he and his brother had made to represent the only thing worth representing, *la vie vécue, la vraie vérité* [life as it is lived, the highest truth]. As in painting, he said, all depends on the way of seeing, *l'optique*: out of twenty-four men who will describe what they have all seen, it is only the twenty-fourth who will find the right way of expressing it. 'There is a true thing I have said in my journal,' he went on. 'The thing is, to find a lorgnette' (and he put up his hands to his eyes, adjusting them carefully) 'through which to see things. My brother and I invented a lorgnette, and the young men have taken it from us.'[2]

How true that is, and how significantly it states just what is most essential in the work of the Goncourts! It is a new way of seeing, literally a new way of seeing, which they have invented; and it is in the invention of this that they have invented that 'new language' of which purists have so long, so vainly, and so thanklessly complained. You remember that saying of Masson, the mask of Gautier, in *Charles Demailly*: 'I am a man for whom the visible world exists.' Well, that is true, also, of the Goncourts; but in a different way.[3]

'The delicacies of fine literature,' that phrase of Pater always comes into my mind when I think of the Goncourts;[4] and indeed Pater seems to me the only English writer who has ever handled language at all in their manner or spirit. I frequently heard Pater refer to certain of their books, to *Madame Gervaisais*, to *L'Art du XVIIIe Siècle*, to *Chérie*; with a passing objection to what he called the 'immodesty' of this last book, and a strong emphasis in the assertion that 'that was how it seemed to him a book should be written.' I repeated this once to Goncourt, trying to give him some idea of what Pater's work was like; and he lamented that his ignorance of English prevented him from what he instinctively realised would be so intimate an enjoyment. Pater was of course far more scrupulous, more limited, in his choice of epithet, less feverish in his variations of cadence; and naturally so, for he dealt with another subject-matter and was careful of another kind of truth. But with both there was that passionately intent preoccupation

with 'the delicacies of fine literature'; both achieved a style of
the most personal sincerity: *tout grand écrivain de tous les temps*, said
Goncourt, *ne se reconnaît absolument qu'à cela, c'est qu'il a une langue
personnelle, une langue dont chaque page, chaque ligne, est signée, pour
le lecteur lettré, comme si son nom était au bas de cette page, de cette
ligne,** and this style, in both, was accused, by the 'literary' criticism of its generation, of being insincere, artificial, and therefore
reprehensible.

It is difficult, in speaking of Edmond de Goncourt, to avoid
attributing to him the whole credit of the work which has so long
borne his name alone. That is an error which he himself would
never have pardoned. *Mon frère et moi* [my brother and I] was the
phrase constantly on his lips, and in his journal, his prefaces, he
has done full justice to the vivid and admirable qualities of that
talent which, all the same, would seem to have been the lesser,
the more subservient, of the two. Jules, I think, had a more active
sense of life, a more generally human curiosity; for the novels
of Edmond, written since his brother's death, have, in even that
excessively specialised world of their common observation, a yet
more specialised choice and direction. But Edmond, there is no
doubt, was in the strictest sense the writer; and it is above all for
the qualities of its writing that the work of the Goncourts will live.
It has been largely concerned with truth – truth to the minute
details of human character, sensation, and circumstance, and also
of the document, the exact words, of the past; but this devotion
to fact, to the curiosities of fact, has been united with an even
more persistent devotion to the curiosities of expression. They
have invented a new language: that was the old reproach against
them; let it be their distinction. Like all writers of an elaborate
carefulness, they have been accused of sacrificing both truth and
beauty to deliberate eccentricity. Deliberate their style certainly
was; eccentric it may, perhaps, sometimes have been; but deliberately eccentric, no. It was their belief that a writer should have a
personal style, a style as peculiar to himself as his handwriting; and

---

* ['Every great writer from across history can only absolutely make himself
  recognised if he has a personal style, a style which signs every page, every
  line, for the literary reader, as if his name was at the bottom of every page and
  every line' – from discussion of the relative merits of Jules Simon and Victor
  Cousin during the Goncourts' salon, recorded in an entry from their *Journals*
  for 27 December 1870.]

indeed I seem to see in the handwriting of Edmond de Goncourt just the characteristics of his style. Every letter is formed carefully, separately, with a certain elegant stiffness; it is beautiful, formal, too regular in the 'continual slight novelty' of its form to be quite clear at a glance: very personal, very distinguished writing.

It may be asserted that the Goncourts are not merely men of genius, but are perhaps the typical men of letters of the close of our century. They have all the curiosities and the acquirements, the new weaknesses and the new powers, that belong to our age; and they sum up in themselves certain theories, aspirations, ways of looking at things, notions of literary duty and artistic conscience, which have only lately become at all actual, and some of which owe to them their very origin. To be not merely novelists (inventing a new kind of novel), but historians; not merely historians, but the historians of a particular century, and of what was intimate and what is unknown in it; to be also discriminating, indeed innovating critics of art, but of a certain section of art, the eighteenth century, in France and in Japan; to collect pictures and *bibelots*, beautiful things, always of the French and Japanese eighteenth century: these excursions in so many directions, with their audacities and their careful limitations, their bold novelty and their scrupulous exactitude in detail, are characteristic of what is the finest in the modern conception of culture and the modern ideal in art. Look, for instance, at the Goncourts' view of history.

Quand les civilisations commencent, quand les peuples se forment, l'histoire est drame ou geste…. Les siècles qui ont précédé notre siècle ne demandaient à l'historien que le personnage de l'homme, et le portrait de son génie…. Le XIXe siècle demande l'homme qui était cet homme d'État, cet homme de guerre, ce poète, ce peintre, ce grand homme de science ou de métier. L'âme qui était en cet acteur, le coeur qui a vécu derrière cet esprit, il les exige et les réclame; et s'il ne peut recueillir tout cet être moral, toute la vie intérieure, il commande du moins qu'on lui en apporte une trace, un jour, un lambeau, une relique.*

* ['When civilisations arise, when a people springs up, history is drama or gesticulation …. The ages which came before our own century only asked the historian for a man's personality and the portrait of his genius…. The nineteenth century wants to know what man this politician was, this warrior,

From this theory, this conviction, came that marvellous series of studies in the eighteenth century in France (*La Femme au XVIIIe Siècle, Portraits intimes du XVIIIe Siècle, La du Barry,* and the others), made entirely out of documents, autograph letters, scraps of costume, engravings, songs, the unconscious self-revelations of the time, forming, as they justly say, *l'histoire intime; c'est ce roman vrai que la postérité appellera peut-être un jour l'histoire humaine.** To be the bookworm and the magician; to give the actual documents, but not to set barren fact by barren fact; to find a soul and a voice in documents, to make them more living and more charming than the charm of life itself: that is what the Goncourts have done. And it is through this conception of history that they have found their way to that new conception of the novel which has revolutionised the entire art of fiction.

Aujourd'hui, they wrote, in 1864, in the preface to *Germinie Lacerteux,*

> que le Roman s'élargit et grandit, qu'il commence à être la grande forme sérieuse, passionnée, vivante, de l'étude littéraire et de l'enquête sociale, qu'il devient, par l'analyse et par la recherche psychologique, l'Histoire morale contemporaine, aujourd'hui que le Roman s'est imposé les devoirs de la science, il peut en revendiquer les libertés et les franchises.†

Le public aime les romans faux [the public loves false novels], is another brave declaration in the same preface; *ce roman est un roman vrai* [this novel is a true novel]. But what, precisely, is it that the Goncourts understood by *un roman vrai*? The old notion of the novel was that it should be an entertaining record of incidents or adventures told

---

this poet, this painter, this great man of science or industry. It demands the soul which lies inside the agent, the heart which beat within the body, and claims them for itself; if it cannot obtain this whole moral being, this entire inner life, it orders us to bring it a trace, a glimpse, a scrap, a relic.' – from the 'Preface' to the first edition of the Goncourts' *Portrait intimes du dix-huitième siècle* (1857–58).]

* ['inner history; it is the true novel which posterity may one day call human history'.]

† ['Today … as the Novel grows bigger and greater, it is becoming the great form – serious, passionate, living – for literary study and social inquiry; it is becoming, through analysis and psychological research, contemporary Moral history, now that the Novel has taken upon itself the duty of science, it can take responsibility for freedoms and franchises.']

for their own sake; a plain, straightforward narrative of facts, the
aim being to produce as nearly as possible an effect of continuity,
of nothing having been omitted, the statement, so to speak, of
a witness on oath; in a word, it is the same as the old notion of
history, *drame ou geste*. That is not how the Goncourts apprehend
life, or how they conceive it should be rendered. As in the study
of history they seek mainly the *inédit* [unpublished], caring only
to record that, so it is the *inédit* of life that they conceive to be the
main concern, the real 'inner history.' And for them the *inédit* of
life consists in the noting of the sensations; it is of the sensations
that they have resolved to be the historians; not of action, nor of
emotion, properly speaking, nor of moral conceptions, but of an
inner life which is all made up of the perceptions of the senses.
It is scarcely too paradoxical to say that they are psychologists
for whom the soul does not exist. One thing, they know, exists:
the sensation flashed through the brain, the image on the mental
retina. Having found that, they bodily omit all the rest as of no
importance, trusting to their instinct of selection, of retaining all
that really matters. It is the painter's method, a selection made
almost visually; the method of the painter who accumulates detail
on detail, in his patient, many-sided observation of his subject, and
then omits everything which is not an essential part of the *ensemble*
which he sees. Thus the new conception of what the real truth of
things consist in has brought with it, inevitably, an entirely new
form, a breaking up of the plain, straightforward narrative into
chapters, which are generally quite disconnected, and sometimes
of less than a page in length. A very apt image of this new, curious
manner of narrative has been found, somewhat maliciously, by
M. Lemaître.

> Un homme qui marche à l'intérieur d'une maison, si nous regar-
> dons du dehors, apparaît successivement à chaque fenêtre, et
> dans les intervalles nous échappe. Ces fenêtres, ce sont les chap-
> itres de MM. de Goncourt. Encore, he adds, y a-t-il plusieurs
> de ces fenêtres où l'homme que nous attendions ne passe point.[*]

---

[*] ['If we are looking from the outside, a man who is walking inside a house
will appear to us successively at each window, and at moments will disappear.
These windows are the chapters in the Goncourts' novels. What's more there
are several windows where the man we're waiting for never appears.' – from

That, certainly, is the danger of the method. No doubt the Goncourts, in their passion for the *inédit*, leave out certain things because they are obvious, even if they are obviously true and obviously important; that is the defect of their quality. To represent life by a series of moments, and to choose these moments for a certain subtlety and rarity in them, is to challenge grave perils. Nor are these the only perils which the Goncourts have constantly before them. There are others, essential to their natures, to their preferences. And, first of all, as we may see on every page of that miraculous *Journal*, which will remain, doubtless, the truest, deepest, most poignant piece of human history that they have ever written, they are sick men, seeing life through the medium of diseased nerves. *Notre oeuvre entier*, writes Edmond de Goncourt,

> repose sur la maladie nerveuse; les peintures de la maladie, nous les avons tirées de nous-mêmes, et, à force de nous disséquer, nous sommes arrivés à une sensitivité supra-aiguë que blessaient les infiniment petits de la vie.*

This unhealthy sensitiveness explains much, the singular merits as well as certain shortcomings or deviations, in their work. The Goncourts' vision of reality might be called an exaggerated sense of the truth of things; such a sense as diseased nerves inflict upon one, sharpening the acuteness of every sensation; or somewhat such a sense as one derives from haschisch, which simply intensifies, yet in a veiled and fragrant way, the charm or the disagreeableness of outward things, the notion of time, the notion of space.[5] What the Goncourts paint is the subtler poetry of reality, its unusual aspects, and they evoke it, fleetingly, like Whistler; they do not render it in hard outline, like Flaubert, like Manet. As in the world of Whistler, so in the world of the Goncourts, we see cities in which there are always fireworks at Cremorne, and fair women reflected beautifully and curiously in mirrors. It is a world which is extraordinarily real; but there is choice, there is curiosity, in the aspect of reality which it presents.

Jules Lemaître's essay 'Edmond et Jules de Goncourt' in *Les Contemporains: études et portraits littéraires 3e series* (1898).]

* ['Our entire oeuvre … rests upon nervous illness; we took these portraits of illness from ourselves, and, by dissecting ourselves, we achieved a highly keen sensitivity which the infinitely small things of life might injure.' – adapted from Edmond de Goncourt's letter to Émile Zola, July 1870.]

Compare the descriptions, which form so large a part of the work of the Goncourts, with those of Théophile Gautier, who may reasonably be said to have introduced the practice of eloquent writing about places, and also the exact description of them. Gautier describes miraculously, but it is, after all, the ordinary observation carried to perfection, or, rather, the ordinary pictorial observation. The Goncourts only tell you the things that Gautier leaves out; they find new, fantastic points of view, discover secrets in things, curiosities of beauty, often acute, distressing, in the aspects of quite ordinary places. They see things as an artist, an ultra-subtle artist of the impressionist kind, might see them; seeing them indeed always very consciously with a deliberate attempt upon them, in just that partial, selecting, creative way in which an artist looks at things for the purpose of painting a picture. In order to arrive at their effects, they shrink from no sacrifice, from no excess; slang, neologism, forced construction, archaism, barbarous epithet, nothing comes amiss to them, so long as it tends to render a sensation. Their unique care is that the phrase should live, should palpitate, should be alert, exactly expressive, super-subtle in expression; and they prefer indeed a certain perversity in their relations with language, which they would have not merely a passionate and sensuous thing, but complex with all the curiosities of a delicately depraved instinct. It is the accusation of the severer sort of French critics that the Goncourts have invented a new language; that the language which they use is no longer the calm and faultless French of the past. It is true; it is their distinction; it is the most wonderful of all their inventions: in order to render new sensations, a new vision of things, they have invented a new language.

1894, 1896

Balzac

I.

The first man who has completely understood Balzac is Rodin, and it has taken Rodin ten years to realise his own conception.[1] France has refused the statue in which a novelist is represented as a dreamer, to whom Paris is not so much Paris as Patmos: 'the most Parisian of our novelists,' Frenchmen assure you. It is more than a hundred years since Balzac was born: a hundred years is a long time in which to be misunderstood with admiration.

In choosing the name of the *Human Comedy* for a series of novels in which as he says, there is at once 'the history and the criticism of society, the analysis of its evils, and the discussion of its principles,' Balzac proposed to do for the modern world what Dante, in his *Divine Comedy*, had done for the world of the Middle Ages. Condemned to write in prose, and finding his opportunity in that restriction, he created for himself a form which is perhaps the nearest equivalent for the epic or the poetic drama, and the only form in which, at all events, the epic is now possible. The world of Dante was materially simple compared with the world of the nineteenth century; the 'visible world' had not yet begun to 'exist,' in its tyrannical modern sense;[2] the complications of the soul interested only the Schoolmen, and were a part of theology; poetry could still represent an age and yet be poetry. But today poetry can no longer represent more than the soul of things; it had taken refuge from the terrible improvements of civilisation in a divine seclusion, where it sings, disregarding the many voices of the street. Prose comes offering its infinite capacity for detail; and it is by the infinity of its detail that the novel, as Balzac created it, has become the modern epic.

There had been great novels, indeed, before Balzac, but no great novelist; and the novels themselves are scarcely what we should today call by that name. The interminable *Astrée* and its companions form a link between the *fabliaux* and the novel,[3] and from them developed the characteristic eighteenth-century *conte*, in narrative, letters, or dialogue, as we see it in Marivaux, Laclos, Crébillon *fils*.[4]

Crébillon's longer works, including *Le Sopha*, with their conventional paraphernalia of Eastern fable, are extremely tedious; but in two short pieces, *La Nuit et le Moment* and *Le Hasard du Coin du Feu*, he created a model of witty, naughty, deplorably natural comedy, which to this day is one of the most characteristic French forms of fiction. Properly, however, it is a form of the drama rather than of the novel. Laclos, in *Les Liaisons Dangereuses*, a masterpiece which scandalised the society that adored Crébillon, because its naked human truth left no room for sentimental excuses, comes much nearer to prefiguring the novel (as Stendhal, for instance, is afterward to conceive it), but still preserves the awkward traditional form of letters. Marivaux had indeed already seemed to suggest the novel of analysis, but in a style which has christened a whole manner of writing that precisely which is least suited to the writing of fiction. Voltaire's *contes*, *La Religieuse* of Diderot, are tracts or satires in which the story is only an excuse for the purpose. Rousseau, too, has his purpose, even in *La Nouvelle Héloïse*, but it is a humanising purpose; and with that book the novel of passion comes into existence, and along with it the descriptive novel.[5] Yet with Rousseau this result is an accident of genius; we cannot call him a novelist; and we find him abandoning the form he has found, for another, more closely personal, which suits him better. Restif de la Bretonne, who followed Rousseau at a distance, not altogether wisely, developed the form of half-imaginary autobiography in *Monsieur Nicolas*, a book of which the most significant part may be compared with Hazlitt's *Liber Amoris*.[6] Morbid and even mawkish as it is, it has a certain uneasy, unwholesome humanity in its confessions, which may seem to have set a fashion only too scrupulously followed by modern French novelists. Meanwhile, the Abbé Prévost's one great story, *Manon Lescaut*, had brought for once a purely objective study, of an incomparable simplicity, into the midst of these analyses of difficult souls;[7] and then we return to the confession, in the works of others not novelists: Benjamin Constant, Mme. De Staël, Chateaubriand, in *Adolphe*, *Corinne*, *René*.[8] At once we are in the Romantic movement, a movement which begins lyrically among poets, and at first with a curious disregard of the more human part of humanity.

Balzac worked contemporaneously with the Romantic movement, but he worked outside it, and its influence upon him is felt only in an occasional pseudo-romanticism, like the episode of the pirate in *La Femme de Trente Ans*. His vision of humanity was essentially a poetic vision, but he was a poet whose dreams were facts. Knowing that, as Mme. Necker has said, 'the novel should be the better world,' he knew also that 'the novel would be nothing if, in that august lie, it were not true in details.'[9] And in the *Human Comedy* he proposed to himself to do for society more than Buffon had done for the animal world.[10]

'There is but one animal,' he declares, in his *Avant-Propos*, with a confidence which Darwin has not yet come to justify. But 'there exists, there will always exist, social species, as there are zoological species.' 'Thus the work to be done will have a triple form: men, women, and things; that is to say, human beings and the material representation which they give to their thought; in short, man and life.' And, studying after nature, 'French society will be the historian, I shall need to be no more than the secretary.' Thus will be written 'the history forgotten by so many historians, the history of manners.' But that is not all, for 'passion is the whole of humanity.' 'In realizing clearly the drift of the composition, it will be seen that I assign to facts, constant, daily, open, or secret, to the acts of individual life, to their causes and principles, as much importance as historians had formerly attached to the events of the public life of nations.' 'Facts gathered together and painted as they are, with passion for element,' is one of his definitions of the task he has undertaken. And in a letter to Mme. de Hanska, he summarises every detail of his scheme.

> The *Études des Moeurs* will represent social effects, without a single situation of life, or physiognomy, or a character of man or woman, or a manner of life, or a profession, or a social zone, or a district of France, or anything pertaining to childhood, old age, or maturity, politics, justice, or war, having been forgotten.
>
> That laid down, the history of the human heart traced link by link, the history of society made in all its details, we have the base. ...
>
> Then, the second stage is the *Études philosophiques*, for after the *effects* come the *causes*. In the *Études des Moeurs* I shall have painted the sentiments and their action, life and the fashion of life. In the *Études philosophiques* I shall say *why the sentiments, on what the life*....
>
> Then, after the *effects* and the *causes*, come the *Études*

analytiques, to which the *Physiologie du mariage* belongs, for, after the *effects* and the *causes*, one should seek the *principles*. …

After having done the poetry, the demonstration, of a whole system, I shall do the science in the *Essai sur les forces humaines*. And, on the bases of this palace I shall have traced the immense arabesque of the *Cent Contes drolatiques*!

Quite all that, as we know, was not carried out; but there, in its intention, is the plan; and after twenty years' work the main part of it, certainly, was carried out. Stated with this precise detail, it has something of a scientific air, as of a too deliberate attempt upon the sources of life by one of those systematic French minds which are so much more logical than facts. But there is one little phrase to be noted: 'La passion est toute l'humanité.'* All Balzac is in that phrase.

Another French novelist, following, as he thought, the example of the *Human Comedy*, has endeavoured to build up a history of his own time with even greater minuteness. But *Les Rougeon-Macquart* is no more than system; Zola has never understood that detail without life is the wardrobe without the man. Trying to outdo Balzac on his own ground, he has made the fatal mistake of taking him only on his systematic side, which in Balzac is subordinate to a great creative intellect, an incessant, burning thought about men and women, a passionate human curiosity for which even his own system has no limits. 'The misfortunes of the *Birotteaus*, the priest and the perfumer,' he says, in his *Avant-Propos*, taking an example at random, 'are, for me, those of humanity.' To Balzac manners are but the vestment of life; it is life that he seeks; and life, to him (it is his own word) is but the vestment of thought. Thought is at the root of all his work, a whole system of thought, in which philosophy is but another form of poetry; and it is from this root of idea that the *Human Comedy* springs.

II.

The two books into which Balzac has put his deepest thought, the two books which he himself cared for the most, are *Séraphita* and *Louis Lambert*. Of *Louis Lambert* he said: 'I write it for myself and a few others'; of *Séraphita*: 'My life is in it.' 'One could write

---

* ['Passion is the whole of humanity' – quoted in translation by Symons, above.]

Goriot any day,' he adds; '*Séraphita* only once in a lifetime.' I have never been able to feel that *Séraphita* is altogether a success. It lacks the breadth of life; it is glacial. True, he aimed at producing very much such an effect; and it is, indeed, full of a strange, glittering beauty, the beauty of its own snows. But I find in it at the same time something a little factitious, a sort of romanesque, not altogether unlike the sentimental romanesque of Novalis;[11] it has not done the impossible, in humanising abstract speculation, in fusing mysticism and the novel. But for the student of Balzac it has extraordinary interest; for it is at once the base and the summit of the *Human Comedy*. In a letter to Mme. de Hanska, written in 1837, four years after *Séraphita* had been begun, he writes: 'I am not orthodox, and I do not believe in the Roman Church. Swedenborgianism, which is but a repetition, in the Christian sense, of ancient ideas, is my religion, with this addition: that I believe in the incomprehensibility of God.' *Séraphita* is a prose poem in which the most abstract part of that mystical system, which Swedenborg perhaps materialised too crudely, is presented in a white light, under a single, superhuman image. In *Louis Lambert* the same fundamental conceptions are worked out in the study of a perfectly human intellect, 'an intelligent gulf,' as he truly calls it; a sober and concise history of ideas in their devouring action upon a feeble physical nature. In these two books we see directly, and not through the coloured veil of human life, the mind in the abstract of a thinker whose power over humanity was the power of abstract thought. They show this novelist, who has invented the description of society, by whom the visible world has been more powerfully felt than by any other novelist, striving to penetrate the correspondences which exist between the human and the celestial existence. He would pursue the soul to its last resting-place before it takes flight from the body; further, on its disembodied flight; he would find out God, as he comes nearer and nearer to finding out the secret of life. And realising, as he does so profoundly, that there is but one substance, but one ever-changing principle of life, 'one vegetable, one animal, but a continual intercourse,' the world is alive with meaning for him, a more intimate meaning than it has for others. 'The least flower is a thought, a life which corresponds to some lineaments of the great whole, of which he has the constant intuition.' And so, in his concerns with the world, he will find spirit everywhere; nothing for him will be inert matter, everything will have its particle of the universal life. One of those divine spies, for whom the world has no secrets, he will be neither pessimist nor optimist; he will accept the world as a man accepts the woman whom he loves, as much for her defects as for her virtues. Loving the world for its own sake, he will find it always beautiful, equally beautiful in all its parts. Now let us look at the programme which he traced for the *Human Comedy*, let us realise it in the light of this philosophy, and we are at the beginning of a conception of what the *Human Comedy* really is.

III.

This visionary, then, who had apprehended for himself an idea of God, set himself to interpret human life more elaborately than any one else. He has been praised for his patient observation; people have thought they praised him in calling him a realist; it has been discussed how far his imitation of life was the literal truth of the photograph. But to Balzac the word realism was an insult. Writing his novels at the rate of eighteen hours a day, in a feverish solitude, he never had the time to observe patiently. It is humanity seen in a mirror, the humanity which comes to the great dreamers, the great poets, humanity as Shakespeare saw it. And so in him, as in all the great artists, there is something more than nature, a divine excess. This something more than nature should be the aim of the artist, not merely the accident which happens to him against his will. We require of him a world like our own, but a world infinitely more vigorous, interesting, profound; more beautiful with that kind of beauty which nature finds of itself for art. It is the quality of great creative art to give us so much life that we are almost overpowered by it, as by an air almost too vigorous to breathe: the exuberance of creation which makes the Sibyl of Michelangelo something more than human, which makes Lear something more than human, in one kind or another of divinity.

Balzac's novels are full of strange problems and great passions. He turned aside from nothing which presented itself in nature; and his mind was always turbulent with the magnificent contrasts and caprices of fate. A devouring passion of thought burned on all the situations by which humanity expresses itself, in its flight from the horror of immobility. To say that the situations which he chose are often romantic is but to say that he followed the soul and the senses faithfully on their strangest errands. Our probable novelists of today are afraid of whatever emotion might be misinterpreted in a gentleman. Believing, as we do now, in nerves and a fatalistic heredity, we have left but little room for the dignity and disturbance of violent emotion. To Balzac, humanity had not changed since the days when Oedipus was blinded and Philoctetes cried in the cave; and equally great miseries were still possible to mortals, though they were French and of the nineteenth century.

And thus he creates, like the poets, a humanity more logical than average life; more typical, more sub-divided among the passions, and having in its veins an energy almost more than human. He realised, as the Greeks did, that human life is made up of elemental passions and necessity; but he was the first to realise that in the modern world the pseudonym of necessity is money. Money and the passions rule the world of his *Human Comedy*.

And, at the root of the passions, determining their action, he saw 'those nervous fluids, or that unknown substance which, in default of another term, we must call the will.' No word returns oftener to his pen. For him the problem is invariable. Man has a given quantity of energy; each man a different quantity: how will he spend it? A novel is the determination in action of that problem. And he is equally interested in every form of energy, in every egoism, so long as it is fiercely itself. This pre-occupation with the force, rather than with any of its manifestations, gives him his singular impartiality, his absolute lack of prejudice; for it gives him the advantage of an abstract point of view, the unchanging fulcrum for a lever which turns in every direction; and as nothing once set vividly in motion by any form of human activity is without interest for him, he makes every point of his vast chronicle of human affairs equally interesting to his readers.

Baudelaire has observed profoundly that every character in the *Human Comedy* has something of Balzac, has genius.[12] To himself, his own genius was entirely expressed in that word 'will.' It recurs constantly in his letters. 'Men of will are rare!' he cries. And, at the time when he had turned night into day for his labour: 'I rise every night with a keener will than that of yesterday.' 'Nothing wearies me,' he says, 'neither waiting nor happiness.' He exhausts the printers, whose fingers can hardly keep pace with his brain; they call him, he reports proudly, 'a man-slayer.' And he tries to express himself: 'I have always had in me something, I know not what,

which made me do differently from others; and, with me, fidelity
is perhaps no more than pride. Having only myself to rely upon,
I have had to strengthen, to build up that self.' There is a scene in
La Cousine Bette which gives precisely Balzac's own sentiment of
the supreme value of energy. The Baron Hulot, ruined on every
side, and by his own fault, goes to Josépha, a mistress who had cast
him off in the time of his prosperity, and asks her to lodge him for
a few days in a garret. She laughs, pities, and then questions him.

> 'Est-ce vrai, vieux,' reprit-elle, 'que tu as tué ton frère et ton
> oncle, ruiné ta famille, surhypothéqué la maison et tes enfants
> et mangé la grenouille du gouvernement en Afrique avec la
> princesse?'
>
> Le Baron inclina tristement la tête.
>
> 'Eh bien, j'aime cela!' s'écria Josépha, qui se leva pleine
> d'enthousiasme. 'C'est un *brûlage* général! c'est sardanapale! c'est
> grand! c'est complet! On est une canaille, mais on a du coeur.'[*]

The cry is Balzac's, and it is a characteristic part of his genius to
have given it that ironical force by uttering it through the mouth
of a Josépha. The joy of the human organism at its highest point of
activity: that is what interests him supremely. How passionate, how
moving he becomes whenever he has to speak of a real passion,
a mania, whether of a lover for his mistress, of a philosopher for
his idea, of a miser for his gold, of a Jew dealer for masterpieces!
His style clarifies, his words become flesh and blood; he is the
lyric poet. And for him every idealism is equal: the gourmandise
of Pons is not less serious, nor less sympathetic, not less perfectly
realised, than the search of Claës after the Absolute. 'The great
and terrible clamour of egoism' is the voice to which he is always
attentive: 'those eloquent faces, proclaiming a soul abandoned
to an idea as to a remorse,' are the faces with whose history he
concerns himself. He drags to light the hidden joys of the *amateur*,
and with especial delight those that are hidden deepest, under the

---

[*] ["'Is it true, old man,' she replied, 'that you killed your brother and your
uncle, ruined your family, mortgaged your house and children and blew the
government's cash on an African scam with the princess?'

The Baron nodded his head sadly.

'Well, I love it!' exclaimed Josépha, standing up in her enthusiasm. 'That
is really *burning your boats*! What a Sardanapalus! It's great! It's the whole thing!
You're a dick, but you've got heart!'"]

most deceptive coverings. He deifies them for their energy, he fashions the world of his *Human Comedy* in their service, as the real world exists, all but passive, to be the pasture of these supreme egoists.

IV.

In all that he writes of life, Balzac seeks the soul, but it is the soul as nervous fluid, the executive soul, not the contemplative soul, that, with rare exceptions, he seeks. He would surprise the motive force of life: that is his *recherche de l'Absolu*; he figures it to himself as almost a substance, and he is the alchemist on its track. 'Can man by thinking find out God?' Or life, he would have added; and he would have answered the question with at least a Perhaps.

And of this visionary, this abstract thinker, it must be said that his thought translates itself always into terms of life. Pose before him a purely mental problem, and he will resolve it by a scene in which the problem literally works itself out. It is the quality proper to the novelist, but no novelist ever employed this quality with such persistent activity, and at the same time subordinated action so constantly to the idea. With him action has always a mental basis, is never suffered to intrude for its own sake. He prefers that an episode should seem in itself tedious rather than it should have an illogical interest.

It may be, for he is a Frenchman, that his episodes are sometimes too logical. There are moments when he becomes unreal because he wishes to be too systematic, that is to be real by measure. He would never have understood the method of Tolstoy, a very stealthy method of surprising life. To Tolstoy life is always the cunning enemy whom one must lull asleep, or noose by an unexpected lasso. He brings in little detail after little detail, seeming to insist on the insignificance of each, in order that it may pass almost unobserved, and be realised only after it has passed. It is his way of disarming the suspiciousness of life.

But Balzac will make no circuit, aims at an open and an unconditional triumph over nature. Thus, when he triumphs, he triumphs signally; and action, in his books, is perpetually crystallising into some phrase, like the single lines of Dante, or some brief scene, in which a whole entanglement comes sharply and suddenly to a luminous point. I will give no instance, for I should have to quote from every volume. I wish rather to remind myself that there are times when the last fine shade of a situation seems to have escaped. Even then, the failure is often more apparent than real, a slight bungling in the machinery of illusion. Look through the phrase, and you will find the truth there, perfectly explicit on the other side of it.

For it cannot be denied, Balzac's style, as style, is imperfect. It has life, and it has an idea, and it has variety; there are moments when it attains a rare and perfectly individual beauty; as when, in *Le Cousin Pons*, we read of

> cette prédisposition aux recherches qui fait faire à un savant germanique cent lieues dans ses guêtres pour trouver une vérité qui le regard en riant, assise à la marge du puits, sous le jasmin de la cour.*

But I am far less sure that a student of Balzac would recognise him in this sentence than that he would recognise the writer of this other: *Des larmes de pudeur qui roulèrent entre les beaux cils de Madame Hulot, arrêtèrent net le garde national.*† It is in such passages that the failure in style is equivalent to a failure in psychology. That his style should lack symmetry, subordination, the formal virtues of form is, in my eyes, a less serious fault. I have often considered whether, in the novel, perfect form is a good, or even a possible thing, if the novel is to be what Balzac made it, history added to poetry. A novelist with style will not look at life with an entirely naked vision. He sees through coloured glasses. Human life and human manners are too various, too moving, to be brought into the fixity of a quite formal order. There will come a moment, constantly, when style must suffer, or the closeness and clearness of narration must be sacrificed, some minute exception of action or psychology must lose its natural place, or its full emphasis. Balzac, with his rapid and accumulating mind, without the patience of selection, and without the desire to select where selection means leaving out something good in itself, if not good in its place, never

---

* ['that predisposition towards inquiry which makes a scholarly Saxon trudge a hundred leagues in his rags to find a truth which is laughing at him, sitting by the side of a well, beneath a flower in a courtyard'.]

† ['Tears of shame rolling from the beautiful lashes of Madame Hulot brought the national guard up short'.]

hesitates, and his parenthesis comes in. And often it is into these parentheses that he puts the profoundest part of his thought.

Yet, ready as Balzac is to neglect the story for the philosophy, whenever it seems to him necessary to do so, he would never have admitted that a form of the novel is possible in which the story shall be no more than an excuse for the philosophy. That was because he was a great creator, and not merely a philosophical thinker; because he dealt in flesh and blood, and knew that the passions in action can teach more to the philosopher, and can justify the artist more fully, than all the unacting intellect in the world. He knew that though life without thought was no more than the portion of a dog, yet thoughtful life was more than lifeless thought, and the dramatist more than the commentator. And I cannot help feeling assured that the latest novelists without a story, whatever other merits they certainly have, are lacking in the power to create characters, to express a philosophy in action; and that the form which they have found, however valuable it may be, is the result of this failure, and not either a great refusal or a new vision.

V.

The novel as Balzac conceived it has created the modern novel, but no modern novelist has followed, for none has been able to follow, Balzac on his own lines. Even those who have tried to follow him most closely have, sooner or later, branched off in one direction or another, most in the direction indicated by Stendhal. Stendhal has written one book which is a masterpiece, unique in its kind, *Le Rouge et le Noir*; a second, which is full of admirable things, *Le Chartreuse de Parme*; a book of profound criticism, *Racine et Shakspeare*; and a cold and penetrating study of the physiology of love, *De l'Amour*, by the side of which Balzac's *Physiologie du Mariage* is a mere *jeu d'esprit*. He discovered for himself, and for others after him, a method of unemotional, minute, slightly ironical analysis, which has fascinated modern minds, partly because it has seemed to dispense with those difficulties of creation, of creation in the block, which the triumphs of Balzac have only accentuated. Goriot, Valérie Marneffe, Pons, Grandet, Madame de Mortsauf even, are called up before us after the same manner as Othello or Don Quixote; their actions express them so significantly that they seem to be independent of their creator; Balzac stakes all upon each creation, and leaves us no choice but to accept or reject each as a whole, precisely as we should a human being. We do not know all the secrets of their consciousness, any more than we know all the secrets of the consciousness of our friends. But we have only to say 'Valérie!' and the woman is before us. Stendhal, on the contrary, undresses Julien's soul in public with a deliberate and fascinating effrontery. There is not a vein of which he does not trace the course, not a wrinkle to which he does not point, not a nerve which he does not touch to the quick. We know everything that passed through his mind, to result probably in some significant inaction. And at the end of the book we know as much about that particular intelligence as the anatomist knows about the body which he has dissected. But meanwhile the life has gone out of the body; and have we, after all, captured a living soul?

I should be the last to say that Julien Sorel is not a creation, but he is not a creation after the order of Balzac; it is a difference of a kind; and if we look carefully at Frédéric Moreau, and Madame Gervaisais, and the Abbé Mouret, we shall see that these also, profoundly different as Flaubert and Goncourt and Zola are from Stendhal, are yet more profoundly, more radically, different from the creations of Balzac. Balzac takes a primary passion, puts it into a human body, and set it to work itself out in visible action. But since Stendhal, novelists have persuaded themselves that the primary passions are a little common, or noisy, or a little heavy to handle, and they have concerned themselves with passions tempered by reflection, and the sensations of elaborate brains. It was Stendhal who substituted the brain for the heart, as the battle-place of the novel; not the brain as Balzac conceived it, a motive-force of action, the mainspring of passion, the force by which a nature directs its accumulated energy; but a sterile sort of brain, set at a great distance from the heart, whose rhythm is too faint to disturb it. We have been intellectualising upon Stendhal ever since, until the persons of the modern novel have come to resemble those diaphanous jelly-fish, with balloon-like heads and the merest tufts of bodies, which float up and down in the Aquarium at Naples.

Thus, coming closer, as it seems, to what is called reality, in this banishment of great emotions, and this attention upon the sensations, modern analytic novelists are really getting further and further from that life which is the one certain thing in the world.

Balzac employs all his detail to call up a tangible world about his men and women, not, perhaps, understanding the full power of detail as psychology, as Flaubert is to understand it; but, after all, his detail is only the background of the picture; and there, stepping out of the canvas, as the sombre people of Velazquez step out of their canvases at the Prado,[13] is the living figure, looking into your eyes with eyes that respond to you like a mirror.

The novels of Balzac are full of electric fluid. To take up one of them is to feel the shock of life, as one feels it on touching certain magnetic hands. To turn over volume after volume is like wandering through the streets of a great city, at that hour of the night when human activity is at its full. There is a particular kind of excitement inherent in the very aspect of a modern city, of London or Paris; in the mere sensation of being in its midst, in the sight of those active and fatigued faces which pass so rapidly; of those long and endless streets, full of houses, each of which is like the body of a multiform soul, looking out through the eyes of many windows. There is something intoxicating in the lights, the movement of shadows under the lights, the vast and billowy sound of that shadowy movement. And there is something more than this mere unconscious action upon the nerves. Every step in a great city is a step into an unknown world. A new future is possible at every street corner. I never know, when I go out into one of those crowded streets, but that the whole course of my life may be changed before I return to the house I have quitted.

I am writing these lines in Madrid, to which I have come suddenly, after a long quiet in Andalusia; and I feel already a new pulse in my blood, a keener consciousness of life, and a sharper human curiosity. Even in Seville I knew that I should see tomorrow, in the same streets, hardly changed since the Middle Ages, the same people that I had seen today. But here there are new possibilities, all the exciting accidents of the modern world, of a population always changing, of a city into which civilisation has brought all its unrest. And as I walk in these broad, windy streets and see these people, whom I hardly recognise for Spaniards, so awake and so hybrid are they, I have felt the sense of Balzac coming back into my veins. At Cordova he was unthinkable; at Cadiz I could realise only his large, universal outlines, vague as the murmur of the sea; here I feel him, he speaks the language I am talking, he sums up the life in whose midst I find myself.

For Balzac is the equivalent of great cities. He is bad reading for solitude, for he fills the minds with the nostalgia of cities. When a man speaks to me familiarly of Balzac I know already something of the man with whom I have to do. 'The physiognomy of women does not begin before the age of thirty,' he has said; and perhaps before that age no one can really understand Balzac. Few young people care for him, for there is nothing in him that appeals to the senses except through the intellect. Not many women care for him supremely, for it is part of his method to express sentiments through facts, and not facts through sentiments. But it is natural that he should be the favourite reading of men of the world, of those men of the world who have the distinction of their kind; for he supplies the key of the enigma which they are studying.

VI.

The life of Balzac was one long labour, in which time, money, and circumstances were all against him. In 1835 he writes: 'I have lately spent twenty-six days in my study without leaving it. I took the air only at that window which dominates Paris, which I mean to dominate.' And he exults in the labour: 'If there is any glory in that, I alone could accomplish such a feat.' He symbolises the course of his life in comparing it to the sea beating against a rock: 'Today one flood, tomorrow another, bears me along with it. I am dashed against a rock, I recover myself and go on to another reef.' 'Sometimes it seems to me that my brain is on fire. I shall die in the trenches of the intellect.'

Balzac, like Scott, died under the weight of his debts;[14] and it would seem, if one took him at his word, that the whole of the *Human Comedy* was written for money. In the modern world, as he himself realised more clearly than any one, money is more often a symbol than an entity, and it can be the symbol of every desire. For Balzac money was the key of his earthly paradise. It meant leisure to visit the woman whom he loved, and at the end it meant the possibility of marrying her.

There were only two women in Balzac's life: one, a woman much older than himself, of whom he wrote, on her death, to the other: 'She was a mother, a friend, a family, a companion, a counsel, she made the writer, she consoled the young man, she formed his taste, she wept like a sister, she laughed, she came every day, like a healing slumber, to put sorrow to sleep.'[15] The other was Mme. de Hanska, whom he married in 1850, three months before his death. He had loved her for twenty years; she was married, and lived in Poland; it was only at rare intervals that he was able to see her, and then very briefly; but his letters to her, published since his death, are a simple, perfectly individual, daily record of a great passion. For twenty years he existed on a divine certainty without a future, and almost without a present. But we see the force of that sentiment passing into his work; *Séraphita* is its ecstasy, everywhere is its human shadow; it refines his strength, it gives him surprising intuitions, it gives him all that was wanting to his genius. Mme. de Hanska is the heroine of the *Human Comedy*, as Beatrice is the heroine of the *Divine Comedy*.

A great lover, to whom love, as well as every other passion and the whole visible world, was an idea, a flaming spiritual perception, Balzac enjoyed the vast happiness of the idealist. Contentedly, joyously, he sacrificed every petty enjoyment to the idea of love, the idea of fame, and to that need of the organism to exercise its forces, which is the only definition of genius. I do not know, among the lives of men of letters, a life better filled, or more appropriate. A young man who, for a short time, was his secretary, declared: 'I would not live your life for the fame of Napoleon and of Byron combined!' The Comte de Gramont did not realise, as the world in general does not realise, that, to the man of creative energy, creation is at once a necessity and a joy, and to the lover, hope in absence is the elixir of life. Balzac tasted more than all earthly pleasures as he sat there in his attic, creating the world over again, that he might lay it at the feet of a woman. Certainly to him there was no tedium in life, for there was no hour without its vivid employment, and no moment in which to perceive the most desolate of all certainties, that hope is in the past. His death was as fortunate as his life; he died at the height of his powers, at the height of his fame, at the moment of the fulfilment of his happiness, and perhaps of the too sudden relief of that delicate burden.

1899

Prosper Mérimée

Stendhal has left us a picture of Mérimée as 'a young man in a grey frock-coat, very ugly, and with a turned-up nose. ... This young man had something insolent and extremely unpleasant about him. His eyes, small and without expression, had always the same look, and this look was ill-natured. ... Such was my first impression of the best of my present friends. I am not too sure of his heart, but I am sure of his talents. It is M. Le Comte Gazul, now so well known; a letter from him, which came to me last week, made me happy for two days. His mother has a good deal of French wit and a superior intelligence. Like her son, it seems to me that she might give way to emotion once a year.'[1] There, painted by a clear-sighted and disinterested friend, is a picture of Mérimée almost from his own point of view, or at least as he would himself have painted the picture. How far is it, in its insistence on the *attendrissement une fois par an*, on the subordination of natural feelings to a somewhat disdainful aloofness, the real Mérimée?

Early in life, Mérimée adopted his theory, fixed his attitude, and to the end of his life he seemed, to those about him, to have walked along the path he had chosen, almost without a deviation. He went to England at the age of twenty-three, to Spain four years later, and might seem to have been drawn naturally to those two countries, to which he was to return so often, by natural affinities of temper and manner. It was the English manner that he liked, that came naturally to him; the correct, unmoved exterior, which is a kind of positive strength, not to be broken by any onslaught of events or emotions; and in Spain he found an equally positive animal acceptance of things as they are, which satisfied his profound, restrained, really Pagan sensuality, Pagan in the hard, eighteenth-century sense. From the beginning he was a student, of art, of history, of human nature, and we find him enjoying, in his deliberate, keen way, the studied diversions of the student; body and soul each kept exactly in its place, each provided for without partiality. He entered upon literature by a mystification, *Le Théâtre de Clara Gazul*, a book of plays supposed to be translated from a living Spanish dramatist; and he followed it by *La*

Guzla, another mystification, a book of prose ballads supposed to be translated from the Illyrian. And these mystifications, like the forgeries of Chatterton, contain perhaps the most sincere, the most undisguised emotion which he ever permitted himself to express; so secure did he feel of the heart behind the pearl necklace of the *décolletée** Spanish actress, who travesties his own face in the frontispiece to the one, and so remote from himself did he feel the bearded gentleman to be, who sits cross-legged on the ground, holding his lyre or *guzla*, in the frontispiece to the other. Then came a historical novel, the *Chronique du Règne de Charles IX*, before he discovered, as if by accident, precisely what it was he was meant to do: the short story. Then he drifted into history, became Inspector of Ancient Monuments, and helped to save Vézelay,[2] among other good deeds towards art, done in his cold, systematic, after all satisfactory manner. He travelled at almost regular intervals, not only in Spain and England, but in Corsica, in Greece and Asia Minor, in Italy, in Hungary, in Bohemia, usually with a definite, scholarly object, and always with an alert attention to everything that came in his way, to the manners of people, their national characters, their differences from one another. An intimate friend of the Countess de Montijo, the mother of the Empress Eugénie, he was a friend, not a courtier, at the court of the Third Empire. He was elected to the Academy, mainly for his *Études sur l'Histoire Romaine*, a piece of dry history, and immediately scandalised his supporters by publishing a story, *Arsène Guillot*, which was taken for a veiled attack on religion and on morals. Soon after, his imagination seemed to flag; he abandoned himself, perhaps a little wearily, more and more to facts, to the facts of history and learning; learned Russian, and translated Pushkin and Turgenev; and died in 1870, at Cannes, perhaps less satisfied with himself than most men who have done, in their lives, far less exactly what they have intended to.

'I have theories about the very smallest things – gloves, boots, and the like,' says Mérimée in one of his letters; *des idées très-arrêtées* [very firm notions], as he adds with emphasis in another. Precise opinions lead easily to prejudices, and Mérimée, who prided himself on the really very logical quality of his mind, put himself somewhat deliberately into the hands of his prejudices. Thus he

---

* [Wearing a low-cut dress.]

hated religion, distrusted priests, would not let himself be carried away by any instinct of admiration, would not let himself do the things which he had the power to do, because his other, critical self came mockingly behind him, suggesting that very few things were altogether worth doing. 'There is nothing I despise and even detest so much as humanity in general,' he confesses in a letter; and it is with a certain self-complacency that he defines the only kind of society in which he found himself at home: '(1) With unpretentious people whom I have known a long time; (2) in a Spanish *venta*, with muleteers and peasant women of Andalusia.' One day, as he finds himself in a pensive mood, dreaming of a woman, he translates for her some lines of Sophocles, into verse, 'English verse, you understand, for I abhor French verse.' The carefulness with which he avoids received opinions shows a certain consciousness of those opinions, which in a more imaginatively independent mind would scarcely have found a place. It is not only for an effect, but more and more genuinely, that he sets his acquirements as a scholar above his accomplishments as an artist. Clearing away, as it seemed to him, every illusion from before his eyes, he forgot the last illusion of positive people: the possibility that one's eyes may be short-sighted.

Mérimée realises a type which we are accustomed to associate almost exclusively with the eighteenth century, but of which our own time can offer us many obscure examples. It is the type of the *esprit fort*: the learned man, the choice, narrow artist, who is at the same time the cultivated sensualist. To such a man the pursuit of women is part of his constant pursuit of human experience, and of the document, which is the summing up of human experience. To Mérimée history itself was a matter of detail. 'In history, I care only for anecdotes,' he says in the preface to the *Chronique du Règne de Charles IX*. And he adds: 'It is not a very noble taste; but I confess to my shame, I would willingly give Thucydides for the authentic memoirs of Aspasia or of a slave of Pericles; for only memoirs, which are the familiar talk of an author with his reader, afford those portraits of *man* which amuse and interest me.' This curiosity of mankind above all things, and mankind at home, or in private actions, not necessarily of any import to the general course of the world, leads the curious searcher naturally to the more privately interesting and the less publicly important half of mankind. Not scrupulous in arriving at any end by the most adaptable means, not disturbed by any illusions as to the physical facts of the universe, a sincere and grateful lover of variety, doubtless an amusing companion with those who amused him, Mérimée found much of his entertainments and instruction, at all events in his younger years, in that 'half world' which he tells us he frequented 'very much out of curiosity, living in it always as in a foreign country.' Here, as elsewhere, Mérimée played the part of the amateur. He liked anecdotes, not great events, in his history; and he was careful to avoid any too serious passions in his search for sensations. There, no doubt, for the sensualist, is happiness, if he can resign himself to it. It is only serious passions which make anybody unhappy; and Mérimée was carefully on the lookout against a possible unhappiness. I can imagine him ending every day with satisfaction, and beginning every fresh day with just enough expectancy to be agreeable, at that period of his life when he was writing the finest of his stories, and dividing the rest of his leisure between the drawing-rooms and the pursuit of uneventful adventures.

Only, though we are *automates autant qu'esprit*,* as Pascal tells us, it is useless to expect that what is automatic in us should remain invariable and unconditioned. If life could be lived on a plan, and for such men on such a plan, if first impulses and profound passions could be kept entirely out of one's own experience, and studied only at a safe distance, then, no doubt, one could go on being happy, in a not too heroic way. But, with Mérimée as with all the rest of the world, the scheme breaks down one day, just when a reasonable solution to things seems to have been arrived at. Mérimée had already entered on a peaceable enough *liaison* when the first letter came to him from the *Inconnue* to whom he was to write so many letters, for nine years without seeing her, and then for thirty years more after he had met her, the last letter being written but two hours before his death.[3] These letters, which we can now read in two volumes, have a delicately insincere sincerity which makes every letter a work of art, not because he tried to make it so, but because he could not help seeing the form simultaneously with the feeling, and writing genuine love-letters with an excellence almost as impersonal as that of his stories. He begins

* ['We are automatons as much as we are mind' – Blaise Pascal, *Pensées* (fragment 252).]

with curiosity, which passes with singular rapidity into a kind of self-willed passion; already in the eighth letter, long before he has seen her, he is speculating which of the two will know best how to torture the other: that is, as he views it, love best. 'We shall never love one another really,' he tells her, as he begins to hope for the contrary. Then he discovers, for the first time, and without practical result, 'that it is better to have illusions than to have none at all.' He confesses himself to her, sometimes reminding her: 'You will never know either all the good or all the evil that I have in me. I have spent my life in being praised for qualities which I do not possess, and calumniated for defects which are not mine.' And, with a strange, weary humility, which is the other side of his contempt for most things and people, he admits: 'To you I am like an old opera, which you are obliged to forget, in order to see it again with any pleasure.' He, who has always distrusted first impulses, finds himself telling her (was she really so like him, or was he arguing with himself?): 'You always fear first impulses; do not you see that they are the only ones which are worth anything and which always succeed?' Does he realise, unable to change the temperament which he has partly made for himself, that just there has been his own failure?

Perhaps of all love-letters, these of Mérimée show us love triumphing over the most carefully guarded personality. Here the obstacle is not duty, nor circumstance, or a rival; but (on her side as on his, it would seem) a carefully trained natural coldness, in which action, and even for the most part feeling, are relinquished to the control of second thoughts. A habit of repressive irony goes deep: Mérimée might well have thought himself secure against the outbreak of an unconditional passion. Yet here we find passion betraying itself, often only by bitterness, together with a shy, surprising tenderness, in this curious lovers' itinerary, marked out with all the customary signposts, and leading, for all its wilful deviations, along the inevitable road.

It is commonly supposed that the artist, by the habit of his profession, has made for himself a sort of cuirass of phrases against the direct attack of emotion, and so will suffer less than most people if he should fall into love, and things should not go altogether well with him. Rather, he is the more laid open to attack, the more helplessly entangled when once the net has been cast over him. He lives through every passionate trouble, not merely with the daily emotions of the crowd, but with the whole of his imagination. Pain is multiplied to him by the force of that faculty by which he conceives delight. What is most torturing in every not quite fortunate love is memory, and the artist becomes an artist by his intensification of memory. Mérimée has himself defined art as exaggeration *à propos*. Well, to the artist his own life is an exaggeration not *à propos*, and every hour dramatises for him its own pain and pleasure, in a tragic comedy of which he is the author and actor and spectator. The practice of art is a sharpening of the sensations, and, the knife once sharpened, does it cut into one's hand less deeply because one is in the act of using it to carve wood?

And so we find Mérimée, the most impersonal of artists, and one of those most critical of the caprices and violences of fate, giving in to an almost obvious temptation, an anonymous correspondence, a mysterious unknown woman, and passing from stage to stage of a finally very genuine love-affair, which kept him in a fluttering agitation for more than thirty years. It is curious to note that the little which we know of this *Inconnue* seems to mark her out as the realisation of a type which had always been Mérimée's type of woman. She has the 'wicked eyes' of all his heroines, from the Mariquita of his first attempt in literature, who haunts the Inquisitor with 'her great black eyes, like the eyes of a young cat, soft and wicked at once.'[4] He finds her at the end of his life, in a novel of Turgenev, 'one of those diabolical creatures, whose coquetry is the more dangerous because it is capable of passion.' Like so many artists, he has invented his ideal before he meets it, and must have seemed almost to have fallen in love with his own creation. It is one of the privileges of art to create nature, as, according to a certain mystical doctrine, you can actualise, by sheer fixity of contemplation, your mental image of a thing into the thing itself. The *Inconnue* was one of a series, the rest imaginary; and her power over Mérimée, we can hardly doubt, came not only from her queer likeness of temperament to his, but from the singular, flattering pleasure which it must have given him to find that he had invented with so much truth to nature.

II.

Mérimée as a writer belongs to the race of Laclos and of Stendhal, a race essentially French; and we find him representing, a little coldly, as it seemed, the claims of mere unimpassioned intellect, at work on passionate problems, among those people of the Romantic period to whom emotion, evident emotion, was everything. In his subjects he is as 'Romantic' as Victor Hugo or Gautier; he adds, even, a peculiar flavour of cruelty to the Romantic ingredients. But he distinguishes sharply, as French writers before him had so well known how to do, between the passion one is recounting and the moved or unmoved way in which one chooses to tell it. To Mérimée art was a very formal thing, almost a part of learning; it was a thing to be done with a clear head, reflectively, with a calm mastery of even the most vivid material. While others, at that time, were intoxicating themselves with strange sensations, hoping that 'nature would take the pen out of their hands and write,'[5] just at the moment when their own thoughts became least coherent, Mérimée went quietly to work over something a little abnormal which he had found in nature, with as disinterested, as scholarly, as mentally reserved an interest as if it were one of those Gothic monuments which he inspected to such good purpose, and, as it has seemed to his biographer, with so little sympathy. His own emotion, so far as it is roused, seems to him an extraneous thing, a thing to be concealed, if not a little ashamed of. It is the thing itself he wishes to give you, not his feelings about it; and his theory is that if the thing itself can only be made to stand and speak before the reader, the reader will supply for himself all the feeling that is needed, all the feeling that would be called out in nature by a perfectly clear sight of just such passions in action. It seems to him bad art to paint the picture, and to write a description of the picture as well.

And his method serves him wonderfully well up to a certain point, and then leaves him, without his being well aware of it, at the moment even when he has convinced himself that he has realised the utmost of his aim. At a time when he had come to consider scholarly dexterity as the most important part of art, Mérimée tells us that *La Vénus d'Ille* seemed to him the best story he had ever written. He has often been taken at his word, but to take him at his word is to do him an injustice. *La Vénus d'Ille* is a

modern setting of the old story of the Ring given to Venus, and
Mérimée has been praised for the ingenuity with which he has
obtained an effect of supernatural terror, while leaving the way
open for a material explanation of the supernatural. What he has
really done is to materialise a myth, by accepting in it precisely
what might be a mere superstition, the form of the thing, and
leaving out the spiritual meaning of which that form was no more
than a temporary expression. The ring which the bridegroom sets
on the finger of Venus, and which the statue's finger closes upon,
accepting it, symbolises the pact between love and sensuality, the
lover's abdication of all but the physical part of love; and the statue
taking its place between husband and wife on the marriage-night,
and crushing life out of him in an inexorable embrace, symbolises
the merely natural destruction which that granted prayer brings
with it, as a merely human Messalina takes her lover on his own
terms, in his abandonment of all to Venus. Mérimée sees a cruel
and fantastic superstition, which he is afraid of seeming to take
too seriously, which he prefers to leave as a story of ghosts or
bogies, a thing at which we are to shiver as at a mere twitch on the
nerves, while our mental confidence in the impossibility of what
we cannot explain is preserved for us by a hint at the muleteer's
vengeance. 'Have I frightened you?' says the man of the world,
with a reassuring smile. 'Think about it no more; I really meant
nothing.'

And yet, does he after all mean nothing? The devil, the old
pagan gods, the spirits of evil incarnated under every form, fascinated him; it gave him a malign pleasure to set them at their evil
work among men, while, all the time, he mocks them and the men
who believed in them. He is a materialist, and yet he believes in
at least a something evil, outside the world, or in the heart of it,
which sets humanity at its strange games, relentlessly. Even then
he will not surrender his doubts, his ironies, his negations. Is he,
perhaps, at times, the atheist who fears that, after all, God may
exist, or at least who realises how much he would fear him if he
did exist?

Mérimée had always delighted in mystifications; he was always
on his guard against being mystified himself, either by nature or
by his fellow creatures. In the early 'Romantic' days he had had a
genuine passion for various things: 'local colour,' for instance. But
even then he had invented it by a kind of trick, and, later on, he

explains what a poor thing 'local colour' is, since it can so easily be invented without leaving one's study. He is full of curiosity, and will go far to satisfy it, regretting 'the decadence,' in our times, 'of energetic passions, in favour of tranquillity and perhaps of happiness.'[6] These energetic passions he will find, indeed, in our own times, in Corsica, in Spain, in Lithuania, really in the midst of a very genuine and profoundly studied 'local colour,' and also, under many disguises, in Parisian drawing-rooms. Mérimée prized happiness, material comfort, the satisfaction of one's immediate desires, very highly, and it was his keen sense of life, of the pleasures of living, that gave him some of his keenness in the realisation of violent death, physical pain, whatever disturbs the equilibrium of things with unusual emphasis. Himself really selfish, he can distinguish the unhappiness of others with a kind of intuition which is not sympathy, but which selfish people often have: a dramatic consciousness of how painful pain must be, whoever feels it. It is not pity, though it communicates itself to us, often enough, as pity. It is the clear-sighted sensitiveness of a man who watches human things closely, bringing them home to himself with the deliberate, essaying art of an actor who has to represent a particular passion in movement.

And always in Mérimée there is this union of curiosity with indifference: the curiosity of the student, the indifference of the man of the world. Indifference in him, as in the man of the world, is partly an attitude, adopted for its form, and influencing the temperament just so much as gesture always influences emotion. The man who forces himself to appear calm under excitement teaches his nerves to follow instinctively the way he has shown them. In time he will not merely seem calm but will be calm, at the moment when he learns that a great disaster has befallen him. But, in Mérimée, was the indifference even as external as it must always be when there is restraint, when, therefore, there is something to restrain? Was there not in him a certain drying up of the sources of emotion, as the man of the world came to accept almost the point of view of society, reading his stories to a little circle of court ladies, when, once in a while, he permitted himself to write a story? And was not this increase of well-bred indifference, now more than ever characteristic, almost the man himself, the chief reason why he abandoned art so early, writing only two or three short stories during the last twenty-five years of his life, and writing these with a labour which by no means conceals itself?

Mérimée had an abstract interest in, almost an enthusiasm for, facts; facts for their meaning, the light they throw on psychology. He declines to consider psychology except through its expression in facts, with an impersonality far more real than that of Flaubert. The document, historical or social, must translate itself into sharp action before he can use it; not that he does not see, and appreciate better than most others, all there is of significance in the document itself; but his theory of art is inexorable. He never allowed himself to write as he pleased, but he wrote always as he considered the artist should write. Thus he made for himself a kind of formula, confining himself, as some thought, within too narrow limits, but, to himself, doing exactly what he set himself to do, with all the satisfaction of one who is convinced of the justice of his aim and confident of his power to attain it.

Look, for instance, at his longest, far from his best work, *La Chronique du Règne de Charles IX*. Like so much of his work, it has something of the air of a *tour de force*, not taken up entirely for its own sake. Mérimée drops into a fashion, half deprecatingly, as if he sees through it, and yet, as with merely mundane elegance, with a resolve to be more scrupulously exact than its devotees. 'Belief,' says someone in this book, as if speaking for Mérimée, 'is a precious gift which has been denied me.' Well, he will do better, without belief, than those who believe. Written under a title which suggests a work of actual history, it is more than possible that the first suggestion of this book really came, as he tells us in the preface, from the reading of 'a large number of memoirs and pamphlets relating to the end of the sixteenth century.' 'I wished to make an epitome of my reading,' he tells us, 'and here is the epitome.' The historical problem attracted him, that never quite explicable Massacre of St. Bartholomew, in which there was precisely the violence of action and uncertainty of motive which he liked to set before him at the beginning of a task in literature. Probable, clearly defined people, in the dress of the period, grew up naturally about this central motive; humour and irony have their part; there are adventures, told with a sword's point of sharpness, and in the fewest possible words; there is one of his cruel and loving women, in whom every sentiment becomes action, by some twisted feminine logic of their own. It is the most artistic, the most clean-cut, of historical novels; and yet this perfect neatness of method suggests a certain indifference on the part of the writer, as if he were more interested in doing the thing well than in doing it.

And that, in all but the very best of his stories (even, perhaps, in *Arsène Guillot* only not in such perfect things as *Carmen*, as *Mateo Falcone*), is what Mérimée just lets us see, underneath an almost faultless skill of narrative. An incident told by Mérimée at his best gathers about it something of the gravity of history, the composed way in which it is told helping to give it the equivalent of remoteness, allowing it not merely to be, but, what is more difficult, to seem classic in its own time. 'Magnificent things, things after my own heart − that is to say, Greek in their truth and simplicity,' he writes in a letter, referring to the tales of Pushkin. The phrase is scarcely too strong to apply to what is best in his own work. Made out of elemental passions, hard, cruel, detached as it were from their own sentiments, the stories that he tells might in other hands become melodramas: *Carmen*, taken thoughtlessly out of his hands, has supplied the libretto to the most popular of modern light operas.[7] And yet, in his severe method of telling, mere outlines, it seems, told with an even stricter watch over what is significantly left out than over what is briefly allowed to be said in words, these stories sum up little separate pieces of the world, each a little world in itself. And each is a little world which he has made his own, with a labour at last its own reward, and taking life partly because he has put into it more of himself than the mere intention of doing it well. Mérimée loved Spain, and *Carmen*, which, by some caprice of popularity, is the symbol of Spain to people in general, is really, to those who know Spain well, the most Spanish thing that has been written since *Gil Blas*.[8] All the little parade of local colour and philology, the appendix on the *Calo* of the gypsies, done to heighten the illusion, has more significance than people sometimes think. In this story all the qualities of Mérimée come into agreement; the student of human passions, the traveller, the observer, the learned man, meet in harmony; and, in addition, there is the *aficionado*, the true *amateur*, in love with Spain and the Spaniards.

It is significant that at the reception of Mérimée at the Académie Française in 1845, M. Étienne thought it already needful to say: 'Do not pause in the midst of your career; rest is not permitted to your talent.'[9] Already Mérimée was giving way to facts, to facts in themselves, as they come into history, into records of scholarship. We find him writing, a little dryly, on Catiline, on Caesar, on Don Pedro the Cruel, learning Russian, and translating from it (yet, while studying the Russians before all the world, never discovering the mystical Russian soul), writing learned articles, writing reports. He looked around on contemporary literature, and found nothing that he could care for. Stendhal was gone, and who else was there to admire? Flaubert, it seemed to him, was 'wasting his talent under the pretence of realism.' Victor Hugo was 'a fellow with the most beautiful figures of speech at his disposal,' who did not take the trouble to think, but intoxicated himself with his own words. Baudelaire made him furious, Renan filled him with pitying scorn.[10] In the midst of his contempt, he may perhaps have imagined that he was being left behind. For whatever reason, weakness or strength, he could not persuade himself that it was worth while to strive for anything any more. He died probably at the moment when he was no longer a fashion, and had not yet become a classic.

1901

Gustave Flaubert

Salammbô is an attempt, as Flaubert, himself his best critic, has told us, to 'perpetuate a mirage by applying to antiquity the methods of the modern novel.'[1] By the modern novel he means the novel as he had reconstructed it; he means *Madame Bovary*. That perfect book is perfect because Flaubert had, for once, found exactly the subject suited to his method, had made his method and his subject one. On his scientific side Flaubert is a realist, but there is another, perhaps a more intimately personal side, on which he is lyrical, lyrical in a large, sweeping way. The lyric poet in him made *La Tentation de Saint-Antoine*, the analyst made *L'Éducation Sentimentale*; but in *Madame Bovary* we find the analyst and the lyric poet in equilibrium. It is the history of a woman, as carefully observed as any story that has ever been written, and observed in surroundings of the most ordinary kind. But Flaubert finds the romantic material which he loved, the materials of beauty, in precisely that temperament which he studies so patiently and so cruelly. Madame Bovary is a little woman, half vulgar and half hysterical, incapable of a fine passion; but her trivial desires, her futile aspirations after second-rate pleasures and second-hand ideals, give to Flaubert all that he wants: the opportunity to create beauty out of reality. What is common in the imagination of Madame Bovary becomes exquisite in Flaubert's rendering of it, and by that counterpoise of a commonness in the subject he is saved from any vague ascents of rhetoric in his rendering of it.

In writing *Salammbô* Flaubert set himself to renew the historical novel, as he had renewed the novel of manners. He would have admitted, doubtless, that perfect success in the historical novel is impossible, by the nature of the case. We are at best only half conscious of the reality of the things about us, only able to translate them approximately into any form of art. How much is left over, in the closest transcription of a mere line of houses in a street, of a passing steamer, of one's next-door neighbour, of the point of view of a foreigner looking along Piccadilly, of one's own state of mind, moment by moment, as one walks from Oxford Circus to the Marble Arch? Think, then, of the attempts to reconstruct no matter what period of the past, to distinguish the difference in the aspect of a world perhaps bossed with castles and ridged with ramparts, to two individualities encased within chain-armour! Flaubert chose his antiquity wisely: a period of which we know too little to confuse us, a city of which no stone is left on another, the minds of Barbarians who have left us no psychological documents. 'Be sure I have made no fantastic Carthage,' he says proudly, pointing to his documents: Ammianus Marcellinus, who has furnished him with 'the *exact* form of a door'; the Bible and Theophrastus, from which he obtains his perfumes and his precious stones; Gesenius, from whom he gets his Punic names; the *Mémoires de l'Académie des Inscriptions*. 'As for the temple of Tanit, I am sure of having reconstructed it as it was, with the treatise of the Syrian Goddess, with the medals of the Duc de Luynes, with what is known of the temple at Jerusalem, with a passage of St. Jerome, quoted by Seldon (*De Diis Syriis*), with a plan of the temple of Gozzo, which is quite Carthaginian, and best of all, with the ruins of the temple of Thugga, which I have seen myself, with my own eyes, and of which no traveller or antiquarian, so far as I know, has ever spoken.' But that, after all, as he admits (when, that is, he has proved point by point his minute accuracy to all that is known of ancient Carthage, his faithfulness to every indication which can serve for his guidance, his patience in grouping rather than his daring in the invention of action and details), that is not the question. 'I care little enough for archaeology! If the colour is not uniform, if the details are out of keeping, if the manners do not spring from the religion and the actions from the passions, if the characters are not consistent, if the costumes are not appropriate to the habits and the architecture to the climate, if, in a word, there is not harmony, I am in error. If not, no.'

And there, precisely, is the definition of the one merit which can give a historical novel the right to exist, and at the same time a definition of the merit which sets *Salammbô* above all other historical novels. Everything in the book is strange, some of it might easily be bewildering, some revolting; but all is in harmony. The harmony is like that of Eastern music, not immediately conveying its charm, or even the secret of its measure, to Western ears; but a monotony coiling perpetually upon itself, after a severe law of its own. Or rather, it is like a fresco, painted gravely in hard, definite colours, firmly detached from a background of burning sky;

a procession of Barbarians, each in the costume of his country, passes across the wall; there are battles, in which elephants fight with men; an army besieges a great city, or rots to death in a defile between mountains; the ground is paved with dead men; crosses, each bearing its living burden, stand against the sky; a few figures of men and women appear again and again, expressing by their gestures the soul of the story.

Flaubert himself has pointed, with his unerring self-criticism, to the main defect of his book: 'The pedestal is too large for the statue.' There should have been, as he says, a hundred pages more about Salammbô. He declares: 'There is not in my book an isolated or gratuitous description; all are useful to my characters, and have an influence, near or remote, on the action.' This is true, and yet, all the same, the pedestal is too large for the statue. Salammbô, 'always surrounded with grave and exquisite things,' has something of the somnambulism which enters into the heroism of Judith; she has a hieratic beauty, and a consciousness as pale and vague as the moon whom she worships. She passes before us, 'her body saturated with perfumes,' encrusted with jewels like an idol, her head turreted with violet hair, the gold chain tinkling between her ankles; and is hardly more than an attitude, a fixed gesture, like the Eastern women whom one sees passing, with oblique eyes and mouths painted into smiles, their faces curiously traced into a work of art, in the languid movements of a pantomimic dance. The soul behind those eyes? the temperament under that at times almost terrifying mask? Salammbô is as inarticulate for us as the serpent, to whose drowsy beauty, capable of such sudden awakenings, hers seems half akin; they move before us in a kind of hieratic pantomime, a coloured, expressive thing, signifying nothing. Mâtho, maddened with love, 'in an invincible stupor, like those who have drunk some draught of which they are to die,' has the same somnambulistic life; the prey of Venus, he has an almost literal insanity, which, as Flaubert reminds us, is true to the ancient view of that passion. He is the only quite vivid person in the book, and he lives with the intensity of a wild beast, a life 'blinded alike' from every inner and outer interruption to one or two fixed ideas. The others have their place in the picture, fall into their attitudes naturally, remain so many coloured outlines for us. The illusion is perfect; these people may not be the real people of history, but at least they have no self-consciousness, no Christian tinge in their minds.

'The metaphors are few, the epithets definite,' Flaubert tells us, of his style in this book, where, as he says, he has sacrificed less 'to the amplitude of the phrase and to the period,' than in *Madame Bovary*. The movement here is in briefer steps, with a more earnest gravity, without any of the engaging weakness of adjectives. The style is never archaic, it is absolutely simple, the precise word being put always for the precise thing; but it obtains a dignity, a historical remoteness, by the large seriousness of its manner, the absence of modern ways of thought, which, in *Madame Bovary*, bring with them an instinctively modern cadence.

Salammbô is written with the severity of history, but Flaubert notes every detail visually, as a painter notes the details of natural things. A slave is being flogged under a tree: Flaubert notes the movement of the thong as it flies, and tells us: 'The thongs, as they whistled through the air, sent the bark of the plane trees flying.' Before the battle of the Macar, the Barbarians are awaiting the approach of the Carthaginian army. First 'the Barbarians were surprised to see the ground undulate in the distance.' Clouds of dust rise and whirl over the desert, through which are seen glimpses of horns, and, as it seems, wings. Are they bulls or birds, or a mirage of the desert? The Barbarians watch intently. 'At last they made out several transverse bars, bristling with uniform points. The bars became denser, larger; dark mounds swayed from side to side; suddenly square bushes came into view; they were elephants and lances. A single shout, "The Carthaginians!" arose.' Observe how all that is seen, as if the eyes, unaided by the intelligence, had found out everything for themselves, taking in one indication after another, instinctively. Flaubert puts himself in the place of his characters, not so much to think for them as to see for them.

Compare the style of Flaubert in each of his books, and you will find that each book has its own rhythm, perfectly appropriate to its subject-matter. The style, which has almost every merit and hardly a fault, becomes what it is by a process very different from that of most writers careful of form. Read Chateaubriand, Gautier, even Baudelaire, and you will find that the aim of these writers has been to construct a style which shall be adaptable to every occasion, but without structural change; the cadence is always the same. The most exquisite word-painting of Gautier can be translated rhythm for rhythm into English, without difficulty; once you have mastered the tune, you have merely to go on; every verse will be the same. But Flaubert is so difficult to translate because he has no fixed rhythm; his prose keeps step with no regular march-music. He invents the rhythm of every sentence, he changes his cadence with every mood for the convenience of every fact. He has no theory of beauty in form apart from what it expresses. For him form is a living thing, the physical body of thought, which it clothes and interprets. 'If I call stones blue, it is because blue is the precise word, believe me,' he replies to Sainte-Beuve's criticism. Beauty comes into his words from the precision with which they express definite things, definite ideas, definite sensations. And in his book, where the material is so hard, apparently so unmalleable, it is a beauty of sheer exactitude which fills it from end to end, a beauty of measure and order, seen equally in the departure of the doves of Carthage at the time of their flight into Sicily, and in the lions feasting on the corpses of the Barbarians, in the defile between the mountains.

1901

Théophile Gautier

Gautier has spoken for himself in a famous passage of *Mademoiselle de Maupin*:

> I am a man of the Homeric age; the world in which I live is not my world, and I understand nothing of the society which surrounds me. For me Christ did not come; I am as much a pagan as Alcibiades or Phidias. I have never plucked on Golgotha the flowers of the Passion, and the deep stream that flows from the side of the Crucified and sets a crimson girdle about the world, has never washed me in its flood; my rebellious body will not acknowledge the supremacy of the soul, and my flesh will not endure to be mortified. I find the earth as beautiful as the sky, and I think that perfection of form is virtue. I have no gift for spirituality; I prefer a statue to a ghost, full noon to twilight. Three things delight me: gold, marble, and purple; brilliance, solidity, colour. ... I have looked on love in the light of antiquity, and as a piece of sculpture more or less perfect. ... All my life I have been concerned with the form of the flagon, never with the quality of its contents.[1]

That is part of a confession of faith, and it is spoken with absolute sincerity. Gautier knew himself, and could tell the truth about himself as simply, as impartially, as if he had been describing a work of art. Or is he not, indeed, describing a work of art? Was not that very state of mind, that finished and limited temperament, a thing which he had collaborated with nature in making, with an effective heightening of what was most natural to him, in the spirit of art?

Gautier saw the world as mineral, as metal, as pigment, as rock, tree, water, as architecture, costume, under sunlight, gas, in all the colours that light can bring out of built or growing things; he saw it as contour, movement; he saw all that a painter sees, when the painter sets himself to copy, not to create. He was the finest copyist who ever used paint with a pen. Nothing that can be expressed in technical terms escaped him; there were no technical terms which he could not reduce to an orderly beauty. But he absorbed all this visible world with the hardly discriminating impartiality of the retina; he had no moods, was not to be distracted by a sentiment, heard no voices, saw nothing but darkness, the negation of day, in night. He was tirelessly attentive, he had no secrets of his own and could keep none of nature's. He could describe every ray of the nine thousand precious stones in the throne of Ivan the Terrible, in the Treasury of the Kremlin; but he could tell you nothing of one of Maeterlinck's bees.[2]

The five senses made Gautier for themselves, that they might become articulate. He speaks for them all with a dreadful unconcern. All his words are in love with matter, and they enjoy their lust and have no recollection. If the body did not dwindle and expand to some ignoble physical conclusion; if wrinkles did not creep yellowing up women's necks, and the fire in a man's blood did not lose its heat; he would always be content. Everything that he cared for in the world was to be had, except, perhaps, rest from striving after it; only, everything would one day come to an end, after a slow spoiling. Decrepit, colourless, uneager things shocked him, and it was with an acute, almost disinterested pity that he watched himself die.

All his life Gautier adored life, and all the processes and forms of life. A pagan, a young Roman, hard and delicate, with something of cruelty in his sympathy with things that could be seen and handled, he would have hated the soul, if he had ever really apprehended it, for its qualifying and disturbing power upon the body. No other modern writer, no writer perhaps, has described nakedness with so abstract a heat of rapture: like d'Albert when he sees Mlle. De Maupin for the first and last time, he is the artist before he is the lover, and he is the lover while he is the artist. It was above all things the human body whose contours and colours he wished to fix for eternity in the 'robust art' of 'verse, marble, onyx, enamel.'[3] And it was not the body as a frail, perishable thing, and a thing to be pitied, that he wanted to perpetuate; it was the beauty of life itself, imperishable at least in its recurrence.

He loved imperishable things: the body, as generation after generation refashions it, the world, as it is restored and rebuilt, and then gems, and hewn stone, and carved ivory, and woven tapestry. He loved verse for its solid, strictly limited, resistant form, which, while prose melts and drifts about it, remains unalterable, indestructible. Words, he knew, can build as strongly as stones, and not merely rise to music, like the walls of Troy, but be themselves music as well as structure. Yet, as in visible things he cared only for hard outline and rich colour, so in words too he had no love of half-tints, and was content to do without that softening of atmosphere which was to be prized by those who came after him as the thing most worth seeking. Even his verse is without mystery; if he meditates, his meditation has all the fixity of a kind of sharp, precise criticism.

What Gautier saw he saw with unparalleled exactitude; he allows himself no poetic license or room for fine phrases; has his eye always on the object, and really uses the words which best describe it, whatever they may be. So his books of travel are guide-books, in addition to being other things; and not by any means 'states of soul' or states of nerves. He is willing to give you information, and able to give it to you without deranging his periods. The little essay on Leonardo is an admirable piece of artistic divination, and it is also a clear, simple, sufficient account of the man, his temperament, and his way of work.[4] The study of Baudelaire, reprinted in the *édition définitive* of the *Fleurs du Mal*, remains the one satisfactory summing up, it is not a solution, of the enigma which Baudelaire personified; and it is almost the most coloured and perfumed thing in words which he ever wrote. He wrote equally well about cities, poets, novelists, painters, or sculptors; he did not understand one better than the other, or feel less sympathy for one than for another. He, the *parfait magicien ès lettres françaises*,[5] to whom faultless words came in faultlessly beautiful order, could realise, against Balzac himself, that Balzac had a style: 'he possesses, though he did not think so, a style, and a very beautiful style, the necessary, inevitable, mathematical style of his ideas.'[6] He appreciated Ingres as justly as he appreciated El Greco; he went through the Louvre, room by room, saying the right thing about each painter in turn. He did not say the final thing; he said nothing which we have to pause and think over before we see the whole of its truth or apprehend the whole of its beauty. Truth, in him, comes to us almost literally through the eyesight, and with the same beautiful clearness as if it were one of those visible things which delighted him most: gold, marble, and purple; brilliance, solidity, colour.

1902

Léon Cladel

I hope that the life of Léon Cladel by his daughter Judith, which Lemerre has brought out in a pleasant volume, will do something for the fame of one of the most original writers of our time.[1] Cladel had the good fortune to be recognised in his lifetime by those whose approval mattered most, beginning with Baudelaire, who discovered him before he had printed his first book, and helped to teach him the craft of letters. But so exceptional an artist could never be popular, though he worked in living stuff and put the whole savour of his countryside into his tragic and passionate stories. A peasant, who writes about peasants and poor people, with a curiosity of style which not only packs his vocabulary with difficult words, old or local, and with unheard of rhythms, chosen to give voice to some never yet articulated emotion, but which drives him into oddities of printing, of punctuation, of the very shape of his accents! A page of Cladel has a certain visible uncouthness, and at first this seems in keeping with his matter; but the uncouthness, when you look into it, turns out to be itself a refinement, and what has seemed a confused whirl, an improvisation, to be the result really of reiterated labour, whose whole aim has been to bring the spontaneity of the first impulse back into the laboriously finished work.

In this just, sensitive, and admirable book, written by one who has inherited a not less passionate curiosity about life, but with more patience in waiting upon it, watching it, noting its surprises, we have a simple and sufficient commentary upon the books and upon the man. The narrative has warmth and reserve, and is at once tender and clear-sighted. *J'entrevois nettement*, she says with truth,

> combien seront précieux pour les futurs historiens de la littérature du XIXe siècle, les mémoires tracés au contact immédiat de l'artiste, exposés de ses faits et gestes particuliers, de ses origines, de la germination de ses croyances et de son talent; ses critiques à venir y trouveront de solides matériaux, ses admirateurs un

aliment à leur piété et les philosophes un des aspects de l'Âme française.*

The man is shown to us, 'les élans de cette âme toujours grondante et fulgurante comme une forge, et les nuances de ce fiévreux visage d'apôtre, brun, fin et sinueux',† and we see the inevitable growth, out of the hard soil of Quercy and out of the fertilising contact of Paris and Baudelaire, of this whole literature, these books no less astonishing than their titles, *Ompdrailles-le-Tombeau-des-Lutteurs*, *Celui de la Croix-aux-Boeufs*, *La Fête Votive de Saint-Bartholomée-Porte-Glaive*. The very titles are an excitement. I can remember how mysterious and alluring they used to seem to me when I first saw them on the cover of what was perhaps his best book, *Les Va-Nu-Pieds*.

It is by one of the stories, and the shortest, in *Les Va-Nu-Pieds*, that I remember Cladel. I read it when I was a boy, and I cannot think of it now without a shiver. It is called *L'Hercule*, and it is about a Sandow of the streets,[2] a professional strong man, who kills himself by an overstrain; it is not a story at all, it is the record of an incident, and there is only the strong man in it and his friend the zany, who makes the jokes while the strong man juggles with bars and cannon-balls. It is all told in a breath, without a pause, as if someone who had just seen it poured it out in a flood of hot words. Such vehemence, such pity, such a sense of the cruelty of the spectacle of a man driven to death like a beast, for a few pence and the pleasure of a few children; such an evocation of the sun and the streets and this sordid tragic thing happening to the sound of drum and cymbals; such a vision in sunlight of a barbarous and ridiculous and horrible accident, lifted by the telling of it into a new and unforgettable beauty, I have never felt or seen in any other story of a like grotesque tragedy. It realises an ideal, it does for once what many artists have tried and failed to do; it wrings the last drop of agony out of that subject which it is so easy to make

---

*   ['I foresee clearly … how precious future historians of nineteenth-century literature will find memoirs derived from immediate contact with the artist, from exposure to his acts, his smallest gestures and his roots, the budding of his beliefs and talent; future critics will find solid material there, admirers will find nourishment for their worship, and philosophers will find one aspect of the French Soul.']

†   ['the ardour of this soul which was rumbling and flashing like a forge, the nuances of his feverish face like an apostle, dark, thin and sinewy'.]

pathetic and effective. Dickens could not have done it, Bret Harte could not have done it,[3] Kipling could not do it: Cladel did it only once, with this perfection.

Something like it he did over and over again, with unflagging vehemence, with splendid variations, in stories of peasants and wrestlers and thieves and prostitutes. They are all, as his daughter says, epic; she calls them Homeric, but there is none of the Homeric simplicity in this tumult of coloured and clotted speech, in which the language is tortured to make it speak. The comparison with Rabelais is nearer. *La recherche du terme vivant, sa mise en valeur et en saveur, la surabondance des vocables puisés à toutes sources … la condensation de l'action autour de ces quelques motifs éternels de l'épopée: combat, ripaille, palabre et luxure,*[*] there, as she sees justly, are links with Rabelais. Goncourt, himself always aiming at an impossible closeness of written to spoken speech, noted with admiration 'la vraie photographie de la parole avec ses tours, ses abbreviations, ses ellipses, son essoufflement presque.'[†] Speech out of breath, this is what Cladel's is always; his words, never the likely ones, do not so much speak as cry, gesticulate, overtake one another. *L'âme de Léon Cladel*, says his daughter, *était dans un constant et flamboyant automne.*[‡] Something of the colour and fever of autumn is in all he wrote. Another writer since Cladel, who has probably never heard of him, has made heroes of peasants and vagabonds. But Maxim Gorki makes heroes of them consciously, with a mental self-assertion, giving them ideas which he has found in Nietzsche. Cladel put into all his people some of his own passionate way of seeing 'scarlet,' to use Barbey d'Aurevilly's epithet: *un rural écarlate.*[4] Vehement and voluminous, he overflowed: his whole aim as an artist, as a pupil of Baudelaire, was to concentrate, to hold himself back; and the effort added impetus to the checked overflow. To the realists he seemed merely extravagant; he saw

---

[*] ['The search for the living epithet, its development and flavour, the over-abundance of meanings taken from all sources … the concentration of action around a few eternal motifs from Epic: fighting, feasting, nattering and desire.']

[†] ['The truly photographic quality of his writing, with its turns of phrase, its abbreviations and ellipses, almost out of breath.' – Judith Cladel quotes Edmond de Goncourt's letter to Léon Cladel (7 December 1873) in her biography.]

[‡] ['Léon Cladel's soul … was in a constant and flamboyant autumnal state'.]

certainly what they could not see; and his romance was always a fruit of the soil. The artist in him, seeming to be in conflict with the peasant, fortified, clarified the peasant, extracted from that hard soil a rare fruit. You see in his face an extraordinary mingling of the peasant, the visionary, and the dandy: the long hair and beard, the sensitive mouth and nose, the fierce brooding eyes, in which wildness and delicacy, strength and a kind of stealthiness, seem to be grafted on an inflexible peasant stock.

1906

Charles Baudelaire

Baudelaire is little known and much misunderstood in England. Only one English writer has ever done him justice, or said anything adequate about him. As long ago as 1862 Swinburne introduced Baudelaire to English readers: in the columns of the *Spectator*, it is amusing to remember. In 1868 he added a few more words of just and subtle praise in his book on Blake, and in the same year wrote the magnificent elegy on his death, *Ave atque Vale*. There have been occasional outbreaks of irrelevant abuse or contempt, and the name of Baudelaire (generally misspelled) is the journalist's handiest brickbat for hurling at random in the name of respectability. Does all this mean that we are waking up, over here, to the consciousness of one of the great literary forces of the age, a force which has been felt in every other country but ours?

It would be a useful influence for us. Baudelaire desired perfection, and we have never realised that perfection is a thing to aim at. He only did what he could do supremely well, and he was in poverty all his life, not because he would not work, but because he would work only at certain things, the things which he could hope to do to his own satisfaction. Of the men of letters of our age he was the most scrupulous. He spent his whole life in writing one book of verse (out of which all French poetry has come since his time), one book of prose in which prose becomes a fine art, some criticism which is the sanest, subtlest, and surest which his generation produced, and a translation which is better than a marvellous original.[1] What would French poetry be today if Baudelaire had never existed? As different a thing from what it is as English poetry would be without Rossetti. Neither of them is quite among the greatest poets, but they are more fascinating than the greatest, they influence more minds. And Baudelaire was an equally great critic. He discovered Poe, Wagner, and Manet. Where even Sainte-Beuve, with his vast materials, his vast general talent for criticism, went wrong in contemporary judgements, Baudelaire was infallibly right. He wrote neither verse nor prose with ease, but he would not permit himself to write either without inspiration. His work is without abundance, but it is without waste. It is made out of his whole intellect and all his nerves. Every poem is a train of thought and every essay is the record of sensation. This 'romantic' had something classic in his moderation, a moderation which becomes at times as terrifying as Poe's logic. To 'cultivate one's hysteria' so calmly,[2] and to affront the reader (*Hypocrite lecteur, mon semblable, mon frère*)* as a judge rather than as a penitent; to be a casuist in confession; to be so much a moralist, with so keen a sense of the ecstasy of evil: that has always bewildered the world, even in his own country, where the artist is allowed to live as experimentally as he writes. Baudelaire lived and died solitary, secret, a confessor of sins who has never told the whole truth, *le mauvais moine* [evil monk] of his own sonnet, an ascetic of passion, a hermit of the brothel.

To understand, not Baudelaire, but what we can of him, we must read, not only the four volumes of his collected works, but every document in Crépet's *Oeuvres Posthumes*, and above all, the letters, and these have only now been collected into a volume, under the care of an editor who has done more for Baudelaire than any one since Crépet.[3] Baudelaire put into his letters only what he cared to reveal of himself at a given moment: he has a different angle to distract the sight of every observer; and let no one think that he knows Baudelaire when he has read the letters to Poulet-Malassis, the friend and publisher, to whom he showed his business side, or the letters to La Présidente, the touchstone of his *spleen et idéal*, his chief experiment in the higher sentiments. Some of his carefully hidden virtues peep out at moments, it is true, but nothing that everybody has not long been aware of. We hear of his ill-luck with money, with proof-sheets, with his own health. The tragedy of the life which he chose, as he chose all things (poetry, Jeanne Duval, the 'artificial paradises') deliberately, is made a little clearer to us; we can moralise over it if we like. But the man remains baffling, and will probably never be discovered.

As it is, much of the value of the book consists in those glimpses into his mind and intentions which he allowed people now and then to see. Writing to Sainte-Beuve, to Flaubert, to Soulary, he sometimes lets out, through mere sensitiveness to an intelligence capable of understanding him, some little interesting secret. Thus

---

* ['Hypocritical reader, my fellow man, my brother' – from the address to the reader at the start of *Fleurs du Mal*.]

it is to Sainte-Beuve that he defines and explains the origin and real meaning of the *Petits Poèmes en Prose*:

> Faire cent bagatelles laborieuses qui exigent une bonne humeur constante (bonne humeur nécessaire, même pour traiter des sujets tristes), une excitation bizarre qui a besoin de spectacles, de foules, de musiques, de réverbères même, voilà ce que j'ai voulu faire!*

And, writing to some obscure person, he will take the trouble to be even more explicit, as in this symbol of the sonnet:

> Avez-vous observé qu'un morceau de ciel aperçu par un soupirail, ou entre deux cheminées, deux rochers, ou par une arcade, donnait une idée plus profonde de l'infini que le grand panorama vu du haut d'une montagne?†

It is to another casual person that he speaks out still more intimately (and the occasion of his writing is some thrill of gratitude towards one who had at last done 'a little justice,' not to himself, but to Manet):

> Eh bien! on m'accuse, moi, d'imiter Edgar Poe! Savez-vous pourquoi j'ai si patiemment traduit Poe? Parce qu'il me resemblait. La première fois que j'ai ouvert un livre de lui, j'ai vu avec épouvante et ravissement, non seulement des sujets rêvés par moi, mais des phrases, pensées par moi, et écrites par lui, vingt ans auparavant.‡

It is in such glimpses as these that we see something of Baudelaire in his letters.

1906

---

* ['To make a hundred laborious trifling things, which demand constant good humour (good humour [is] necessary, even when dealing with sad subjects), a bizarre state of excitement which needs spectacle, crowds, music, even street lamps – that is what I wanted to make!']

† ['Have you noticed that a patch of sky glimpsed through a barred window, or between two chimneys, two rocks, or through an arcade, gives a more profound idea of the infinite than a grand panorama from the top of a mountain?']

‡ ['Well! They accuse me – me! of imitating Edgar Poe! Do you know why I translated Poe so patiently? Because he resembles me. The first time I opened a book by him, I was terrified and ravished to find not only topics I had dreamed of, but phrases, my own thoughts, written by him twenty years before.']

The Decadent Movement in Literature

The latest movement in European literature has been called by
many names, none of them quite exact or comprehensive –
Decadence, Symbolism, Impressionism, for instance. It is easy to
dispute over words, and we shall find that Verlaine objects to
being called a Decadent, Maeterlinck to being called a Symbolist,
Huysmans to being called an Impressionist. These terms, as it
happens, have been adopted as the badge of little separate cliques,
noisy, brainsick young people who haunt the brasseries of the
Boulevard Saint-Michel,[1] and exhaust their ingenuities in theorising over the works they cannot write. But, taken frankly as
epithets which express their own meaning, both Impressionism
and Symbolism convey some notion of that new kind of literature which is perhaps more broadly characterised by the word
Decadence. The most representative literature of the day – the
writing which appeals to, which has done so much to form, the
younger generation – is certainly not classic, nor has it any relation with that old antithesis of the Classic, the Romantic. After a
fashion it is no doubt a decadence; it has all the qualities that mark
the end of great periods, the qualities that we find in the Greek,
the Latin, decadence:[2] an intense self-consciousness, a restless
curiosity in research, an over-subtilising refinement upon refinement, a spiritual and moral perversity. If what we call the classic
is indeed the supreme art – those qualities of perfect simplicity,
perfect sanity, perfect proportion, the supreme qualities – then this
representative literature of today, interesting, beautiful, novel as it
is, is really a new and beautiful and interesting disease.

Healthy we cannot call it, and healthy it does not wish to be
considered. The Goncourts, in their prefaces, in their *Journal*,
are always insisting on their own pet malady, *la névrose* [nervous
disease]. It is in their work, too, that Huysmans notes with delight,
'*le style tacheté et faisandé*' – high-flavoured and spotted with
corruption – which he himself possesses in the highest degree.
'Having desire without light, curiosity without wisdom, seeking

God by strange ways, by ways traced by the hands of men; offering rash incense upon the high places to an unknown God, who is the God of darkness' – that is how Ernest Hello, in one of his apocalyptic moments, characterises the nineteenth century.[3] And this unreason of the soul – of which Hello himself is so curious a victim – this unstable equilibrium, which has overbalanced so many brilliant intelligences into one form or another of spiritual confusion, is but another form of the *maladie fin de siècle*. For its very disease of form, this literature is certainly typical of a civilisation grown over-luxurious, over-inquiring, too languid for the relief of action, too uncertain for any emphasis in opinion or in conduct. It reflects all the moods, all the manners, of a sophisticated society; its very artificiality is a way of being true to nature: simplicity, sanity, proportion – the classic qualities – how much do we possess them in our life, our surroundings, that we should look to find them in our literature – so evidently the literature of a decadence?

Taking the word Decadence, then, as most precisely expressing the general sense of the newest movement in literature, we find that the terms Impressionism and Symbolism define correctly enough the two main branches of that movement. Now Impressionist and Symbolist have more in common than either supposes; both are really working on the same hypothesis, applied in different directions. What both seek is not general truth merely, but *la vérité vraie*, the very essence of truth – the truth of appearances to the senses, of the visible world to the eyes that see it; and the truth of spiritual things to the spiritual vision. The Impressionist, in literature as in painting, would flash upon you in a new, sudden way so exact an image of what you have just seen, just as you have seen it, that you may say, as a young American sculptor, a pupil of Rodin, said to me on seeing for the first time a picture of Whistler's, 'Whistler seems to think his picture upon canvas – and there it is!' Or you may find, with Sainte-Beuve, writing of Goncourt, the 'soul of landscape' – the soul of whatever corner of the visible world has to be realised.[4] The Symbolist, in this new, sudden way, would flash upon you the 'soul' of that which can be apprehended only by the soul – the finer sense of things unseen, the deeper meanings of things evident. And naturally, necessarily, this endeavour after a perfect truth to one's impression, to one's intuition – perhaps an impossible endeavour – has brought with it, in its revolt from ready-made impressions and conclusions, a revolt from the ready-made of language, from the bondage of traditional form, of a form become rigid. In France, where this movement began and has mainly flourished, it is Goncourt who was the first to invent a style in prose really new, impressionistic, a style which was itself almost sensation. It is Verlaine who has invented such another new style in verse.

The work of the brothers De Goncourt – twelve novels, eleven or twelve studies in the history of the eighteenth century, six or seven books about art, the art mainly of the eighteenth century and of Japan, two plays, some volumes of letters and of fragments, and a *Journal* in six volumes – is perhaps, in its intention and its consequences, the most revolutionary of the century. No one has ever tried so deliberately to do something new as the Goncourts; and the final word in the summing up which the survivor has placed at the head of the *Préfaces et Manifestes* is a word which speaks of

> tentatives, enfin, où les deux frères ont cherchés *à faire du neuf*, ont fait leurs efforts pour doter les diverses branches de la litté-rature de quelque chose que n'avaient point songé à trouver leurs prédécesseurs.*

And in the preface to *Chérie*, in that pathetic passage which tells of the two brothers (one mortally stricken, and within a few months of death) taking their daily walk in the Bois de Boulogne, there is a definite demand on posterity. 'The search after *reality* in literature, the resurrection of eighteenth-century art, the triumph of *Japonisme* – are not these,' said Jules, 'the three great literary and artistic movements of the second half of the nineteenth century? And it is we who brought them about, these three movements. Well, when one has done that, it is difficult indeed not to be *some-body* in the future.' Nor, even, is this all. What the Goncourts have done is to specialise vision, so to speak, and to subtilise language to the point of rendering every detail in just the form and colour of the actual impression. M. Edmond de Goncourt once said to me – varying, if I remember rightly, an expression he had put into

---

* ['trials where the two brothers have ultimately tried to *do something new*, have concentrated their efforts in order to endow the various branches of literature with something that their precursors never dreamed of.']

the *Journal* – 'My brother and I have invented an opera-glass: the young people nowadays are taking it out of our hands.'

An opera-glass – a special, unique way of seeing things – that is what the Goncourts have brought to bear upon the common things about us; and it is here that they have done the 'something new,' here more than anywhere. They have never sought 'to see life steadily and see it whole':[5] their vision has always been somewhat feverish, with the diseased sharpness of over-excited nerves. 'We do not hide from ourselves that we have been passionate, nervous creatures, unhealthily impressionable,' confesses the *Journal*. But it is this morbid intensity in seeing and seizing things that has helped to form that marvellous style – 'a style perhaps too ambitious of impossibilities,' as they admit – a style which inherits some of its colour from Gautier, some of its fine outline from Flaubert, but which has brought light and shadow into the colour, which has softened outline in the magic of atmosphere. With them words are not merely colour and sound, they live. That search after '*l'image peinte*,' [the painted image] '*l'épithète rare*,' [the uncommon epithet] is not (as with Flaubert) a search after harmony of phrase for its own sake; it is a desperate endeavour to give sensation, to flash the impression of the moment, to preserve the very heat and motion of life. And so, in analysis as in description, they have found out a way of noting the fine shades; they have broken the outline of the conventional novel in chapters with its continuous story, in order to indicate – sometimes in a chapter of half a page – this and that revealing moment, this or that significant attitude or accident or sensation. For the placid traditions of French prose they have had but little respect; their aim has been but one, that of having (as M. Edmond de Goncourt tells us in the preface to *Chérie*):

> une langue rendant nos idées, nos sensations, nos figurations des hommes et des choses, d'une façon distincte de celui-ci ou de celui-là, une langue personnelle, une langue portant notre signature.*

What Goncourt has done in prose – inventing absolutely a new way of saying things, to correspond with that new way of

---

* ['a language that renders our ideas, our sensations, our representations of men and things, in a distinct fashion from any other language, a personal language, a language that bears our signature.']

seeing things which he has found – Verlaine has done in verse. In a famous poem, 'Art Poétique,' he has himself defined his own ideal of the poetic art:

> Car nous voulons la Nuance encor,
> Pas la Couleur, rien que la Nuance!
> Oh! la Nuance seule fiance
> Le rêve au rêve et la flûte au cor!*

Music first of all and before all, he insists; and then, not colour, but *la nuance*, the last fine shade. Poetry is to be something vague, intangible, evanescent, a winged soul in flight 'toward other skies and other loves.' To express the inexpressible he speaks of beautiful eyes behind a veil, of the palpitating sunlight of noon, of the blue swarm of clear stars in a cool autumn sky; and the verse in which he makes this confession of faith has the exquisite troubled beauty – '*sans rien en lui qui pèse ou qui pose*' ['with nothing in it that poses or poises'] – which he commends as the essential quality of verse. In a later poem of poetical counsel he tells us that art should, first of all, be absolutely clear, absolutely sincere: '*L'art, mes enfants, c'est d'être absolument soi-même.*' ['The art, my children, is to be absolutely oneself.'] The two poems, with their seven years' interval – an interval which means so much in the life of a man like Verlaine – give us all that there is of theory in the work of the least theoretical, the most really instinctive, of poetic innovators. Verlaine's poetry has varied with his life; always in excess – now furiously sensual, now feverishly devout – he has been constant only to himself, to his own self-contradictions. For, with all the violence, turmoil, and disorder of a life which is almost the life of a modern Villon, Paul Verlaine has always retained that childlike simplicity, and, in his verse, which has been his confessional, that fine sincerity, of which Villon may be thought to have set the example in literature.

Beginning his career as a Parnassian with the *Poèmes Saturniens*, Verlaine becomes himself, in his exquisite first manner, in the *Fêtes Galantes*, caprices after Watteau, followed, a year later, by *La Bonne Chanson*, a happy record of too confident a lover's happiness. *Romances sans Paroles*, in which the poetry of Impressionism

---

* ['For we still want nuance, / Not Colour – nothing but Nuance! / Oh! Nuance alone joins / Dream to dream and the flute to the horn!']

reaches its very highest point, is more *tourmenté*, goes deeper, becomes more poignantly personal. It is the poetry of sensation, of evocation; poetry which paints as well as sings, and which paints as Whistler paints, seeming to think the colours and outlines upon the canvas, to think them only, and they are there. The mere magic of words – words which evoke pictures, which recall sensations – can go no further; and in his next book, *Sagesse*, published after seven years' wanderings and sufferings, there is a graver manner of more deeply personal confession – that 'sincerity, and the impression of the moment followed to the letter,' which he has defined in a prose criticism on himself as his main preference in regard to style.[6] 'Sincerity, and the impression of the moment followed to the letter,' mark the rest of Verlaine's work, whether the sentiment be that of passionate friendship, as in *Amour*, of love, human and divine, as in *Bonheur*, of the mere lust of the flesh, as in *Parallèlement* and *Chansons pour Elle*. In his very latest verse the quality of simplicity has become exaggerated, has become, at times, childish; the once exquisite depravity of style has lost some of its distinction; there is no longer the same delicately vivid 'impression of the moment' to render. Yet the very closeness with which it follows a lamentable career gives a curious interest to even the worst of Verlaine's work. And how unique, how unsurpassable in its kind, is the best! '*Et tout le reste est littérature!*' ['And all the rest is literature!'] was the cry, supreme and contemptuous, of that early 'Art Poétique'; and, compared with Verlaine at his best, all other contemporary work in verse seems not yet disenfranchised from mere 'literature.' To fix the last fine shade, the quintessence of things; to fix it fleetingly; to be a disembodied voice, and yet the voice of a human soul: that is the ideal of Decadence, and it is what Paul Verlaine has achieved.

And certainly, so far as achievement goes, no other poet of the actual group in France can be named beside him or near him. But in Stéphane Mallarmé, with his supreme pose as the supreme poet, and his two or three pieces of exquisite verse and delicately artificial prose to show by way of result, we have the prophet and pontiff of the movement, the mystical and theoretical leader of the great emancipation. No one has ever dreamed such beautiful, impossible dreams as Mallarmé; no one has ever so possessed his soul in the contemplation of masterpieces to come. All his life he has been haunted by the desire to create, not so much something new in literature, as a literature which should itself be a new art. He has dreamed of a work into which all the arts should enter, and achieve themselves by a mutual interdependence – a harmonising of all the arts into one supreme art – and he has theorised with infinite subtlety over the possibilities of doing the impossible. Every Tuesday for the last twenty years he has talked more fascinatingly, more suggestively, than any one else has ever done, in that little room in the Rue de Rome, to that little group of eager young poets. 'A seeker after something in the world, that is there in no satisfying measure, or not at all,'[7] he has carried his contempt for the usual, the conventional, beyond the point of literary expression, into the domain of practical affairs. Until the publication, quite recently, of a selection of *Vers et Prose*, it was only possible to get his poems in a limited and expensive edition, lithographed in facsimile of his own clear and elegant handwriting. An aristocrat of letters, Mallarmé has always looked with intense disdain on the indiscriminate accident of universal suffrage. He has wished neither to be read nor to be understood by the bourgeois intelligence, and it is with some deliberateness of intention that he has made both issues impossible. M. Catulle Mendès defines him admirably as 'a difficult author,' and in his latest period he has succeeded in becoming absolutely unintelligible.[8] His early poems, '*L'Après-midi d'un Faune*,' '*Hérodiade*,' for example, and some exquisite sonnets, and one or two fragments of perfectly polished verse, are written in a language which has nothing in common with everyday language – symbol within symbol, image within image; but symbol and image achieve themselves in expression without seeming to call for the necessity of a key. The latest poems (in which punctuation is sometimes entirely suppressed, for our further bewilderment) consist merely of a sequence of symbols, in which every word must be taken in a sense with which its ordinary significance has nothing to do. Mallarmé's contortion of the French language, so far as mere style is concerned, is curiously similar to the kind of depravation which was undergone by the Latin language in its decadence. It is, indeed, in part a reversion to Latin phraseology, to the Latin construction, and it has made, of the clear and flowing French language, something irregular, unquiet, expressive, with sudden surprising felicities, with nervous starts and lapses, with new capacities for the exact noting of sensation. Alike to the ordinary and to the scholarly reader, it is painful, intolerable; a jargon, a massacre. Supremely self-confident, and backed, certainly, by an ardent following of the younger generation, Mallarmé goes on his way, experimenting more and more audaciously, having achieved by this time, at all events, a style wholly his own. Yet the '*chef-d'oeuvre inconnu*' seems no nearer completion, the impossible seems no more likely to be done.[9] The two or three beautiful fragments remain, and we still hear the voice in the Rue de Rome.

Probably it is as a voice, an influence, that Mallarmé will be remembered. His personal magnetism has had a great deal to do with the making of the very newest French literature; few literary beginners in Paris have been able to escape the rewards and punishments of his contact, his suggestion. One of the young poets who form that delightful Tuesday evening coterie said to me the other day, 'We owe much to Mallarmé, but he has kept us all back three years.' That is where the danger of so inspiring, so helping a personality comes in. The work even of M. Henri de Regnier, who is the best of the disciples,[10] has not entirely got clear from the influence that has shown his fine talent the way to develop. Perhaps it is in the verse of men who are not exactly following in the counsel of the master – who might disown him, whom he might disown – that one sees most clearly the outcome of his theories, the actual consequences of his practice. In regard to the construction of verse, Mallarmé has always remained faithful to the traditional syllabic measurement; but the freak or the discovery of 'le vers libre' is certainly the natural consequence of his experiments upon the elasticity of rhythm, upon the power of resistance of the caesura. 'Le vers libre' in the hands of most of the experimenters becomes merely rhymeless irregular prose; in the hands of Gustave Kahn and Édouard Dujardin it has, it must be admitted, attained a certain beauty of its own.[11] I never really understood the charm that may be found in this apparently struc- tureless rhythm until I heard, not long since, M. Dujardin read aloud the as yet unpublished conclusion of a dramatic poem in several parts. It was rhymed, but rhymed with some irregularity, and the rhythm was purely and simply a vocal effect. The rhythm came and went as the spirit moved. You might deny that it was rhythm at all; and yet, read as I heard it read, in a sort of slow chant, it produced on me the effect of really beautiful verse. But M. Dujardin is a poet: '*vers libres*' [*sic*] in the hands of a sciolist are the most intolerably easy and annoying of poetic exercises. Even in the case of *Le Pèlerin Passionné* I cannot see the justification of what is merely regular syllabic verse lengthened or shortened arbitrarily, with the Alexandrine always evident in the background as the foot-rule of the new metre. In this hazardous experiment M. Jean Moréas, whose real talent lies in quite another direction, has brought nothing into literature but an example of deliberate singularity for singularity's sake.[12] I seem to find the measure of the man in a remark I once heard him make in a café, where we were discussing the technique of metre: 'You, Verlaine!' he cried, leaning across the table, 'have only written lines of sixteen syllables; *I* have written lines of twenty syllables!' And turning to me, he asked anxiously if Swinburne had ever done that – had written a line of twenty syllables.

That is indeed the measure of the man, and it points a criticism upon not a few of the busy little *littérateurs* who are founding new *revues* every other week in Paris. These people have nothing to say, but they are resolved to say something, and to say it in the newest mode. They are Impressionists because it is the fashion, Symbolists because it is the vogue, Decadents because Decadence is in the very air of the cafés. And so, in their manner, they are mile-posts on the way of this new movement, telling how far it has gone. But to find a new personality, a new way of seeing things, among the young writers who are starting up on every hand, we must turn from Paris to Brussels – to the so-called Belgian Shakespeare, Maurice Maeterlinck. M. Maeterlinck was discovered to the general French public by M. Octave Mirbeau, in an article in the *Figaro*, August 24, 1890, on the publication of *La Princesse Maleine*.

> M. Maurice Maeterlinck nous a donné l'oeuvre la plus géniale de ce temps, et la plus extraordinaire et la plus naïve aussi, comparable et – oserai-je le dire? – supérieure en beauté à ce qui il y a de plus beau dans Shakespeare. ... plus tragique que *Macbeth*, plus extraordinaire en pensée que *Hamlet*.*

----

* ['M. Maurice Maeterlinck has given us the most pleasant work of the season, it is also the most extraordinary and the most naïve, comparable and – dare I say it? – superior in its beauty to the finest parts of Shakespeare ... more tragic than *Macbeth*; more extraordinary in its thought than *Hamlet*' – Octave Mirabeau, 'Maurice Maeterlinck' [a review of *La Princesse Maleine*], *Le Figaro*, 24 August 1890.]

That is how the enthusiast announced his discovery. In truth, M. Maeterlinck is not a Shakespeare, and the Elizabethan violence of his first play is of the school of Webster and Tourneur rather than of Shakespeare. As a dramatist he has but one note, that of fear; he has but one method, that of repetition. In *La Princesse Maleine* there is a certain amount of action – action which is certainly meant to reinvest the terrors of *Macbeth* and of *Lear*. In *L'Intruse* and *Les Aveugles* the scene is stationary, the action but reflected upon the stage, as if from another plane. In *Les Sept Princesses* the action, such as it is, is 'such stuff as dreams are made of,'[13] and is literally, in great part, seen through a window.

This window, looking out upon the unseen – an open door, as in *L'Intruse*, through which Death, the intruder, may come invisibly – how typical of the new kind of symbolistic and impressionistic drama which M. Maeterlinck has invented! I say invented, a little rashly. The real discoverer of this new kind of drama was that strange, inspiring, incomplete man of genius whom M. Maeterlinck, above all others, delights to honour, Villiers de l'Isle-Adam. Imagine a combination of Swift, of Poe, and of Coleridge, and you will have some idea of the extraordinary, impossible poet and cynic who, after a life of brilliant failure, has left a series of unfinished works in every kind of literature; among the finished achievements one volume of short stories, *Contes Cruels*, which is an absolute masterpiece. Yet, apart from this, it was the misfortune of Villiers never to attain the height of his imaginings, and even *Axël*, the work of a lifetime, is an achievement only half achieved. Only half achieved, or achieved only in the work of others; for, in its mystical intention, its remoteness from any kind of outward reality, *Axël* is undoubtedly the origin of the symbolistic drama. This drama, in Villiers, is of pure symbol, of sheer poetry. It has an exalted eloquence which we find in none of his followers. As M. Maeterlinck has developed it, it is a drama which appeals directly to the sensations – sometimes crudely, sometimes subtly – playing its variations upon the very nerves themselves. The 'vague spiritual fear'[14] which it creates out of our nervous apprehension is unlike anything that has ever been done before, even by Hoffmann, even by Poe. It is an effect of atmosphere – an atmosphere in which outlines change and become mysterious, in which a word quietly uttered makes one start, in which all one's mental activity becomes concentrated on something, one knows not what, something slow, creeping, terrifying, which comes nearer and nearer, an impending nightmare.

La Princesse Maleine, it is said, was written for a theatre of marionettes, and it is certainly with the effect of marionettes that these sudden, exclamatory people come and go. Maleine, Hjalmar, Uglyane - these are no men and women, but a masque of shadows, a dance of silhouettes behind the white sheet of the '*Chat Noir*,' and they have the fantastic charm of these enigmatical semblances, 'luminous, gemlike, ghostlike,'[15] with, also, their somewhat mechanical eeriness. The personages of *L'Intruse*, or *Les Aveugles* – in which the spiritual terror and physical apprehension which are common to all M. Maeterlinck's work have become more interior – are mere abstractions, typifying age, infancy, disaster, but with scarcely a suggestion of individual character. And the style itself is a sort of abstraction, all the capacities of language being deliberately abandoned for a simplicity which, in its calculated repetition is like the drip, drip, of a tiny stream of water. M. Maeterlinck is difficult to quote, but here in English, is a passage from Act I. of *La Princesse Maleine*, which will indicate something of this Biblically monotonous style:

> I cannot see you. Come hither, there is more light here; lean back your head a little towards the sky. You too are strange tonight! It is as though my eyes were opened tonight! It is as though my heart were half opened tonight! But I think you are strangely beautiful! But you are strangely beautiful, Uglyane! It seems to me that I have never looked on you till now! But I think you are strangely beautiful! There is something about you. … Let us go elsewhither – under the light – come!

As an experiment in a new kind of drama, these curious plays do not seem to exactly achieve themselves on the stage; it is difficult to imagine how they could ever be made so impressive, when thus externalised, as they are when all is left to the imagination. *L'Intruse*, for instance, which was given at the Haymarket Theatre on January 27, 1892 – not quite faithfully given, it is true – seemed, as one saw it then, too faint in outline, with too little carrying power for scenic effect. But M. Maeterlinck is by no means anxious to be considered merely or mainly as a dramatist. A brooding poet, a mystic, a contemplative spectator of the comedy of death – that is how he presents himself to us in his work; and the introduction which he has prefixed to his translation of *L'Ornement des Noces Spirituelles*, of Ruysbroeck l'Admirable, shows how deeply he has studied the mystical writers of all ages, and how much akin to theirs is his own temper. Plato and Plotinus, St. Bernard and Jacob Boehme, Coleridge and Novalis – he knows them all, and it is with a sort of reverence that he sets himself to the task of translating the astonishing Flemish mystic of the thirteenth century, known till now only by the fragments translated into French by Ernest Hello from a sixteenth century Latin version. This translation and this introduction help to explain the real character of M. Maeterlinck's dramatic work – dramatic as to form, by a sort of accident, but essentially mystical.

Partly akin to M. Maeterlinck by race, more completely alien from him in temper than it is possible to express, Joris Karl Huysmans demands a prominent place in any record of the Decadent movement. His work, like that of the Goncourts, is largely determined by the *maladie fin de siècle* – the diseased nerves that, in his case, have given a curious personal quality of pessimism to his outlook on the world, his view of life. Part of his work – *Marthe, Les Soeurs Vatard, En Ménage, À Vau-l'Eau* – is a minute and searching study of the minor discomforts, the commonplace miseries of life, as seen by a peevishly disordered vision, delighting, for its own self-torture, in the insistent contemplation of human stupidity, of the sordid in existence. Yet these books do but lead up to the unique masterpiece, the astonishing caprice of *À Rebours*, in which he has concentrated all that is delicately depraved, all that is beautifully, curiously poisonous, in modern art. *À Rebours* is the history of a typical Decadent – a study, indeed, after a real man,[16] but a study which seizes the type rather than the personality. In the sensations and ideas of Des Esseintes we see the sensations and ideas of the effeminate, over-civilised, deliberately abnormal creature who is the last product of our society: partly the father, partly the offspring, of the perverse art that he adores. Des Esseintes creates for his solace, in the wilderness of a barren and profoundly uncomfortable world, an artificial paradise. His Thébaïde raffinée is furnished elaborately for candle-light, equipped with the pictures, the books, that satisfy his sense of the exquisitely abnormal. He delights in the Latin of Apuleius and Petronius,[17] in the French of Baudelaire, Goncourt, Verlaine, Mallarmé, Villiers; in the pictures of Gustave Moreau, the French Burne-Jones, of Odilon Redon, the French Blake.[18] He delights in the beauty of strange, unnatural flowers, in the melodic combination of scents, in the imagined harmonies of the sense of taste. And at last, exhausted by these spiritual and sensory debauches in the delights of the artificial, he is left (as we close the book) with a brief, doubtful choice before him – madness or death, or else a return to nature, to the normal life.

Since *À Rebours*, M. Huysmans has written one other remarkable book, *Là-Bas*, a study in the hysteria and mystical corruption of contemporary Black Magic. But it is on that one exceptional achievement, *À Rebours*, that his fame will rest; it is there that he has expressed not merely himself, but an epoch. And he has done so in a style which carries the modern experiments upon language to their furthest development. Formed upon Goncourt and Flaubert, it has sought for novelty, *l'image peinte*, the exactitude of colour, the forcible precision of epithet, wherever words, images, or epithets are to be found. Barbaric in its profusion, violent in its emphasis, wearying in its splendour, it is – especially in regard to things seen – extraordinarily expressive, with all the shades of a painter's palette. Elaborately and deliberately perverse, it is in its very perversity that Huysmans' work – so fascinating, so repellent, so instinctively artificial – comes to represent, as the work of no other writer can be said to do, the main tendencies, the chief results, of the Decadent movement in literature.

Such, then, is the typical literature of the Decadence – literature which, as we have considered it so far, is entirely French. But those qualities which we find in the work of Goncourt, Verlaine, Huysmans – qualities which have permeated literature much more completely in France than in any other country – are not wanting in the recent literature of other countries. In Holland there is a new school of Sensitivists, as they call themselves, who have done some remarkable work – Couperus, in *Ecstasy*, for example – very much on the lines of the French art of Impressionism.[19] In Italy, Luigi Capuana (in *Giacinta*, for instance) has done some wonderful studies of morbid sensation;[20] Gabriele d'Annunzio, in that marvellous, malarious *Piacere*, has achieved a triumph of exquisite perversity. In Spain, one of the principal novelists, Señora Pardo-Bazan,[21] has formed herself, with some deliberateness, after Goncourt, grafting his method, curiously enough, upon a typically Spanish Catholicism of her own. In Norway, Ibsen has lately developed a personal kind of Impressionism (in *Hedda Gabler*) and of Symbolism (in *The Master-Builder*) – 'opening the door,' in his own phrase, 'to the younger generation.'[22] And in England, too, we find the same influences at work. The prose of Mr. Walter Pater, the verse of Mr. W.E. Henley – to take two prominent examples – are attempts to do with the English language something of what Goncourt and Verlaine have done with the French. Mr. Pater's prose is the most beautiful English prose which is now being written; and, unlike the prose of Goncourt, it has done no violence to language, it has sought after no vivid effects, it has found a large part of mastery in reticence, in knowing what to omit. But how far away from the classic ideals of style is this style in which words have their colour, their music, their perfume, in which there is 'some strangeness in the proportion' of every beauty![23] The *Studies in the Renaissance* have made of criticism a new art – have raised criticism almost to the act of creation. And *Marius the Epicurean*, in its study of 'sensations and ideas' (the conjunction was Goncourt's before it was Mr. Pater's),[24] and the *Imaginary Portraits*, in their evocations of the Middle Ages, the age of Watteau – have they not that morbid curiosity of form, that we have found in the works of the French Decadents? A fastidiousness equal to that of Flaubert has limited Pater's work to six volumes, but in these six volumes there is not a page that is not perfectly finished, with a conscious art of perfection. In its minute elaboration it can be compared only with goldsmith's work – so fine, so delicate is the handling of so delicate, so precious a material.

Mr. Henley's work in verse has none of the characteristics of Mr. Pater's work in prose. Verlaine's definition of his own theory of poetical writing – 'sincerity, and the impression of the moment followed to the letter' – might well be adopted as a definition of Mr. Henley's theory or practice. In *A Book of Verses* and *The Song of the Sword* he has brought into the traditional conventionalities of modern English verse the note of a new personality, the touch of a new method. The poetry of Impressionism can go no further, in one direction, than that series of rhymes and rhythms named *In Hospital*. The ache and throb of the body in its long nights on a tumbled bed, and as it lies on the operating-table awaiting 'the thick, sweet mystery of chloroform,'[25] are brought home to us as nothing else that I know in poetry has ever brought the physical sensations. And for a sharper, closer truth of rendering, Mr. Henley has resorted (after the manner of Heine) to a rhymeless form of lyric verse, which in his hands, certainly, is sensitive and expressive. Whether this kind of *vers libre* can fully compensate, in what it gains of freedom and elasticity, for what it loses of compact form and vocal appeal, is a difficult question. It is one that Mr. Henley's verse is far from solving in the affirmative, for, in his work, the finest things, to my mind, are rhymed. In the purely impressionistic way, do not the *London Voluntaries*, which are rhymed, surpass all the unrhymed vignettes and nocturnes which attempt the same quality of result? They flash before us certain aspects of the poetry of London as only Whistler had ever done, and in another art. Nor is it only the poetry of cities, as here, nor the poetry of the disagreeable, as in *In Hospital*, that Mr. Henley can evoke; he can evoke the magic of personal romance. He has written verse that is exquisitely frivolous, daintily capricious, wayward and fugitive as the winged remembrance of some momentary delight. And, in certain fragments, he has come nearer than any other English singer to what I have called the achievement of Verlaine and the ideal of the Decadence: to be a disembodied voice, and yet the voice of a human soul.

Appendix 2
Translations Added to the 1919 Edition

In his note to the essay on Paul Verlaine in the second edition of
The Symbolist Movement in Literature, Symons remarks: 'A complete
translation of the *Fêtes Galantes*, together with poems from many
other volumes, will be found in a small book which is meant to be
a kind of supplement to this one.' He may be referring to *Knave
of Hearts*, published in 1913 with the subtitle '1894–1908', since it
includes all of his extant translations from Verlaine up to that point,
but these had already been published in an edition of his collected
poems from 1902. The intervention of his mental breakdown in
the summer of 1908 has left his intentions unclear.

Symons started translating Verlaine's poems after their meeting in
1890, adding a selection from *Fêtes galantes* to the second edition of
Silhouettes in 1896. His translation of part of Mallarmé's unfinished
poem in dialogue, *Hérodiade*, appeared prominently in the final
issue of the *Savoy* in December 1896. This appendix reproduces
the translations from Verlaine and Mallarmé that Symons himself
appended to the 1919 edition of *The Symbolist Movement*. Where
I have found significant differences between earlier published
versions of these translations, I have indicated this in a note. In
one case, I have reproduced an alternative version of Symons'
translation of 'L'Amour par terre' because these differences were
so great. I have omitted Symons' translations of 'Soupir' ('Sigh')
and 'Brise-Marine' ('Sea-Wind'), as they can be found in his essay
on Mallarmé (above).

Hérodiade
(Stéphane Mallarmé)

HERODIADE.
To mine own self I am a wilderness.
You know it, amethyst gardens numberless
Enfolded in the flaming, subtle deep,

Strange gold, that through the red earth's heavy sleep
Has cherished ancient brightness like a dream,
Stones whence mine eyes, pure jewels, have their gleam
Of icy and melodious radiance, you,
Metals, which into my young tresses drew
A fatal splendour and their manifold grace!
Thou, woman, born into these evil days
Disastrous to the cavern sibylline,
Who speakest, prophesying not of one divine,
But of a mortal, if from that close sheath,
My robes, rustle the wild enchanted breath
In the white quiver of my nakedness,
In the warm air of summer, O prophetess,
(And woman's body obeys that ancient claim)
Behold me in my shivering starry shame,
I die!
        The horror of my virginity
Delights me, and I would envelop me
In the terror of my tresses, that, by night,
Inviolate reptile, I might feel the white
And glimmering radiance of thy frozen fire,
Thou that art chaste and diest of desire,
White night of ice and of the cruel snow!
Eternal sister, my lone sister, lo
My dreams uplifted before thee! now, apart,
So rare a crystal is my dreaming heart,
I live in a monotonous land alone,
And all about me lives but in mine own
Image, the idolatrous mirror of my pride,
Mirroring this Hérodiade diamond-eyed.
I am indeed alone, O charm and curse!

NURSE.
O lady, would you die then?

HERODIADE.
                No, poor nurse;
Be calm, and leave me; prithee, pardon me,
But, ere thou go, close to the casement; see
How the seraphical blue in the dim glass smiles,

But I abhor the blue of the sky!
Yet miles
On miles of rocking waves! Know'st not a land
Where, in the pestilent sky, men see the hand
Of Venus, and her shadow in dark leaves?
Thither I go.
Light thou the wax that grieves
In the swift flame, and sheds an alien tear
Over the vain gold; wilt not say in mere
Childishness?

NURSE.
Now?

HERODIADE.
Farewell.
You lie, O flower
Of these chill lips!
I wait the unknown hour,
Or, deaf to your crying and that hour supreme,
Utter the lamentation of the dream
Of childhood seeing fall apart in sighs
The icy chaplet of its reveries.

Anguish
(Stéphane Mallarmé)

Tonight I do not come to conquer thee,
O Beast that dost the sins of the whole world bear,
Nor with my kisses' weary misery
Wake a sad tempest in thy wanton hair;
It is that heavy and that dreamless sleep
I ask of the close curtains of thy bed,
Which, after all thy treacheries, folds thee deep,
Who knowest oblivion better than the dead.
For Vice, that gnaws with keener tooth than Time,
Brands me as thee, of barren conquest proud;
But while thou guardest in thy breast of stone
A heart that fears no fang of any crime,

I wander palely, haunted by my shroud,
Fearing to die if I but sleep alone.

From *Fêtes galantes*
(Paul Verlaine)

I. Clair de Lune

Your soul is a sealed garden, and there go
With masque and bergamasque fair companies
Playing on lutes and dancing and as though
Sad under their fantastic fripperies.

Though they in minor keys go carolling
Of love the conqueror and of life the boon
They seem to doubt the happiness they sing
And the song melts into the light of the moon,

The sad light of the moon, so lovely fair
That all the birds dream in the leafy shade
And the slim fountains sob into the air
Among the marble statues in the glade.

II. Pantomime

Pierrot, no sentimental swain,
Washes a pâté down again
With furtive flagons, white and red.

Cassandre, with demure content,
Greets with a tear of sentiment
His nephew disinherited.

That blackguard of a Harlequin
Pirouettes, and plots to win
His Columbine that flits and flies.

Columbine dreams and starts to find

A sad heart sighing in the wind
And in her heart a voice that sighs.

l. 4: Cassandre to chasten his content, [*Silhouettes*, 1896]

III. Sur l'Herbe

The Abbé wanders. – Marquis, now
Set straight your periwig, and speak!
– This Cyprus wine is heavenly, how
Much less, Camargo, than your cheek!

– My goddess ... – Do, mi, sol, la, si.
– Abbé, such treason who'll forgive you?
– May I die, ladies, if there be
A star in heaven I will not give you!

– I'd be my lady's lapdog; then ...
– Shepherdess, kiss your shepherd soon,
Shepherd, come kiss ... – Well, gentlemen?
– Do, mi, so. – Hey, good-night, good moon!

IV. L'Allée

As in the age of shepherd king and queen,
Painted and frail amid her nodding bows,
Under the sombre branches, and between
The green and mossy garden-ways she goes,
With little mincing airs one keeps to pet
A darling and provoking perroquet.
Her long-trained robe is blue, the fan she holds
With fluent fingers girt with heavy rings,
So vaguely hints of vague erotic things
That her eye smiles, musing among its folds.
– Blonde too, a tiny nose, a rosy mouth,
Artful as that sly patch that makes more sly,
In her divine unconscious pride of youth,
The slightly simpering sparkle of the eye.

V. À la Promenade

The sky so pale, and the trees, such frail things
Seem as if smiling on our bright array
That flits so light and gay upon the way
With indolent airs and fluttering as of wings.

The fountain wrinkles under a faint wind.
And all the sifted sunlight falling through
The lime-trees of the shadowy avenue
Comes to us blue and shadowy-pale and thinned.

Faultlessly fickle, and yet fond enough,
With fond hearts not too tender to be free,
We wander whispering deliciously,
And every lover leads a lady-love,

Whose imperceptible and roguish hand
Darts now and then a dainty tap, the lip
Revenges on an extreme finger-tip,
The tip of the left little finger, and,

The deed being so excessive and uncouth,
A duly freezing look deals punishment,
That in the instant of the act is blent
With a shy pity pouting in the mouth.

VI. Dans la Grotte

Stay, let me die, since I am true,
For my distress will not delay,
And the Hyrcanian tigress ravening for prey
Is as a little lamb to you.

Yes, here within, cruel Clymène,
This steel which in how many wars
How many a Cyrus slew, or Scipio, now prepares
To end my life and end my pain.

But nay, what need of steel have I
To haste my passage to the shades?
Did not Love pierce my heart, beyond all mortal aids,
With the first arrow of your eye?

VII. Les Ingénus

High heels and long skirts intercepting them,
So that, according to the wind or way,
An ankle peeped and vanished as in play;
And well we loved the malice of the game.

Sometimes an insect with its jealous sting
Some fair one's whiter neck disquieted,
From which the gleams of sudden whiteness shed
Met in our eyes a frolic welcoming.

The stealthy autumn evening faded out,
And the fair creatures dreaming by our side
Words of such subtle savour to us sighed
That since that time our souls tremble and doubt.

VIII. Cortège

A silver-vested monkey trips
And pirouettes before the face
Of one who twists a kerchief's lace
Between her well-gloved finger-tips.

A little negro, a red elf,
Carries her dropping train, and holds
At arm's length all the heavy folds,
Watching each fold displace itself.

The monkey never lets his eyes
Wander from the fair woman's breast,
White wonder that to be possessed
Would call a god out of the skies.

Sometimes the little negro seems
To lift his sumptuous burden up
Higher than need be, in the hope
Of seeing what all night he dreams.

She goes by corridor and stair,
Still to the insolent appeals
Of her familiar animals
Indifferent or unaware.

IX. Les Coquillages

Each shell incrusted in the grot
Where we two loved each other well
An aspect of its own has got.

The purple of a purple shell
Is our souls' colour when they make
Our burning heart's blood visible.

This pallid shell affects to take
Thy languors, when thy love-tired eyes
Rebuke me for my mockery's sake.

This counterfeits the harmonies
Of thy pink ear, and this might be
Thy plump short nape with rosy dyes.

But one, among these, troubled me.

X. En Patinant

We were the victims, you and I,
Madame, of mutual self deceits;
And that which set our brains awry
May well have been the summer heats.

And the spring too, if I recall,
Contributed to spoil our play,
And yet its share, I think, was small
In leading you and me astray.

For air in springtime is so fresh
That rose-buds Love has surely meant
To match the roses of the flesh
Have odours almost innocent;

And even the lilies that outpour
Their biting odours where the sun
Is new in heaven, do but the more
Enliven and enlighten one,

So stealthily the zephyr blows
A mocking breath that renders back
The heart's rest and the soul's repose
And the flower's aphrodisiac,

And the five senses, peeping out.
Take up their station at the feast.
But, being by themselves, without
Troubling the reason in the least.

That was the time of azure skies,
(Madame, do you remember it?)
And sonnets to my lady's eyes,
And cautious kisses not too sweet.

Free from all passion's idle pother,
Full of mere kindliness, how long,
How well we liked not loved each other,
Without one rapture or one wrong!

Ah, happy hours! But summer came:
Farewell, fresh breezes of the spring!
A wind of pleasure like a flame
Leapt on our senses wondering.

Strange flowers, fair crimson-hearted flowers
Poured their ripe odours over us.
And evil voices of the hours
Whispered above us in the boughs.

We yielded to it all, ah me!
What vertigo of fools held fast
Our senses in its ecstasy
Until the heat of summer passed?

There were vain tears and vainer laughter,
And hands indefinitely pressed,
Moist sadnesses, and swoonings after,
And what vague void within the breast?

But autumn came to our relief,
Its light grown cold, its gusts grown rough,
Came to remind us, sharp and brief,
That we had wantoned long enough,

And led us quickly to recover
The elegance demanded of
Every quite irreproachable lover
And every seemly lady-love.

Now it is winter, and, alas,
Our backers tremble for their stake;
Already other sledges pass
And leave us toiling in their wake.

Put both your hands into your muff,
Sit back, now, steady! off we go.
Fanchon will tell us soon enough
Whatever news there is to know.

XI. Fantoches

Scaramouche waves a threatening hand
To Pulcinella, and they stand,
Two shadows, black against the moon.

The old doctor of Bologna pries
For simples with impassive eyes,
And mutters o'er a magic rune.

The while his daughter, scarce half-dressed,
Glides slyly 'neath the trees, in quest
Of her bold pirate lover's sail;

Her pirate from the Spanish main,
Whose passion thrills her in the pain
Of the loud languorous nightingale.

XII. Cythère

By favourable breezes fanned,
A trellised arbour is at hand
To shield us from the summer airs;

The scent of roses, fainting sweet,
Afloat upon the summer heat,
Blends with the perfume that she wears.

True to the promise her eyes gave,
She ventures all, and her mouth rains
A dainty fever through my veins;

And, Love fulfilling all things, save
Hunger, we 'scape, with sweets and ices,
The folly of Love's sacrifices.

XIII. En bateau

The shepherd's star with trembling glint
Drops in black water; at the hint
The pilot fumbles for his flint.

Now is the time or never, sirs.
No hand that wanders wisely errs:
I touch a hand, and is it hers?

The knightly Atys strikes the strings,
And to the faithless Chloris flings
A look that speaks of many things.

The abbé has absolved again
Eglé, the viscount all in vain
Has given his hasty heart the rein.

Meanwhile the moon is up and streams
Upon the skiff that flies and seems
To float upon a tide of dreams.

XIV. Le Faune

An aged faun of old red clay
Laughs from the grassy bowling-green,
Foretelling doubtless some decay
Of mortal moments so serene

That lead us lightly on our way
(Love's piteous pilgrims have we been!)
To this last hour that runs away
Dancing to the tambourine.

XV. Mandoline

The singers of serenades
Whisper their faded vows
Unto fair listening maids
Under the singing boughs.

Tircis, Aminte, are there,
Clitandre has waited long,
And Damis for many a fair
Tyrant makes many a song.

Their short vests, silken and bright,
Their long pale silken trains,

Their elegance of delight,
Twine soft blue silken chains.

And the mandolines and they,
Faintlier breathing, swoon
Into the rose and grey
Ecstacy of the moon.

l. 6: Clitandre is over-long [*Silhouettes*, 1896; *Savoy*, 1896]
l. 12: Twine soft, blue, shadowy chains. [*Savoy*, 1896]

XVI. À Clymène

Mystical strains unheard,
A song without a word,
Dearest, because thine eyes,
Pale as the skies,

Because thy voice, remote
As the far clouds that float
Veiling for me the whole
Heaven of the soul,

Because the stately scent
Of thy swan's whiteness, blent
With the white lily's bloom
Of thy perfume,

Ah! because thy dear love,
The music breathed above
By angels halo-crowned,
Odour and sound,

Hath, in my subtle heart,
With some mysterious art
Transposed thy harmony,
So let it be!

XVII. Lettre

Far from your sight removed by thankless cares
(The gods are witness when a lover swears)
I languish and I die, Madame, as still
My use is, which I punctually fulfil,
And go, through heavy-hearted woes conveyed,
Attended ever by your lovely shade.
By day in thought, by night in dreams of hell,
And day and night, Madame, adorable!
So that at length my dwindling body lost
In very soul, I too become a ghost,
I too, and in the lamentable stress
Of vain desires remembering happiness,
Remembered kisses, now, alas, unfelt.
My shadow shall into your shadow melt.

Meanwhile, dearest, your most obedient slave.

How does the sweet society behave,
Thy cat, thy dog, thy parrot? and is she
Still, as of old, the black-eyed Silvanie
(I had loved black eyes if thine had not been blue)
Who ogled me at moments, palsambleu!
Thy tender friend and thy sweet confidant?
One dream there is, Madame, long wont to haunt
This too impatient heart: to pour the earth
And all its treasures (of how little worth!)
Before your feet as tokens of a love
Equal to the most famous flames that move
The hearts of men to conquer all but death.
Cleopatra was less loved, yes, on my faith,
By Antony or Caesar than you are,
Madame, by me, who truly would by far
Out-do the deeds of Caesar for a smile,
O Cleopatra, queen of word and wile.
Or, for a kiss, take flight with Antony

With this, farewell, dear, and no more from me;
How can the time it takes to read it, quite
Be worth the trouble that it took to write?

XVIII. Les Indolents

Bah! spite of Fate, that says us nay,
Suppose we die together, eh?
– A rare conclusion you discover!

– What's rare is good. Let us die so,
Like lovers in Boccaccio.
– Ha! ha! ha! you fantastic lover!

– Nay, not fantastic. If you will,
Fond, surely irreproachable.
Suppose, then, that we die together?

– Good sir, your jests are fitlier told
Than when you speak of love or gold.
Why speak at all, in this glad weather?

Whereat, behold them once again,
Tircis beside his Dorimène,
Not far from two blithe rustic rovers,

For some caprice of idle breath
Deferring a delicious death.
Ha! ha! ha! what fantastic lovers!

XIX. Colombine

The foolish Leander,
Cape-covered Cassander,
And which
Is Pierrot? 'tis he
With the hop of a flea
Leaps the ditch;

And Harlequin who
Rehearses anew
His sly task,
With his dress that's a wonder.

And eyes shining under
His mask;

Mi, sol, mi, fa, do!
How gaily they go,
And they sing
And they laugh and they twirl
Round the feet of a girl
Like the Spring,

Whose eyes are as green
As a cat's are, and keen
As its claws.
And her eyes without frown
Bid all newcomers: Down
With your paws!

On they go with the force
Of the stars in their course,
And the speed:
O tell me toward what
Disaster unthought,
Without heed

The implacable fair,
A rose in her hair,
Holding up
Her skirts as she runs
Leads this dance of the dunce
And the dupe?

XX. L'Amour par Terre

The other night a sudden wind laid low
The Love, shooting an arrow at a mark,
In the mysterious corner of the park,
Whose smile disquieted us long ago.

The wind has overthrown him, and above

His scattered dust, how sad it is to spell
The artist's name still faintly visible
Upon the pedestal without its Love,

How sad it is to see the pedestal
Still standing! as in dream I seem to hear
Prophetic voices whisper in my ear
The lonely and despairing end of all.

How sad it is! Why, even you have found
A tear for it, although your frivolous eye
Laughs at the gold and purple butterfly
Poised on the piteous litter on the ground.

L'Amour par Terre
[alternative version from *Silhouettes*, 1896]

The wind the other evening overthrew
        The little Love who smiled so mockingly
        Down that mysterious alley, so that we,
Remembering, mused thereon a whole day through.

The wind has overthrown him! The poor stone
        Lies scattered to the breezes. It is sad
        To see the lonely pedestal, that had
The artist's name, scarce visible, alone,

Oh! it is sad to see the pedestal
        Left lonely! and in a dream I seem to hear
        Prophetic voices whisper in my ear
The lonely and despairing end of all.

Oh! It is sad! And thou, hast thou not found
        One heart-throb for the pity, though thine eye
        Lights at the gold and purple butterfly
Brightening the littered leaves upon the ground?

XXI. En Sourdine

Calm where twilight leaves have stilled
With their shadow light and sound,
Let our silent love be filled
With a silence as profound.

Let our ravished senses blend
Heart and spirit, thine and mine,
With vague languors that descend
From the branches of the pine.

Close thine eyes against the day,
Fold thine arms across thy breast,
And for ever turn away
All desire of all but rest.

Let the lulling breaths that pass
In soft wrinkles at thy feet,
Tossing all the tawny grass,
This and only this repeat.

And when solemn evening
Dims the forest's dusky air.
Then the nightingale shall sing
The delight of our despair.

XXII. Colloque Sentimental

In the old park, solitary and vast.
Over the frozen ground two forms once passed.

Their lips were languid and their eyes were dead,
And hardly could be heard the words they said.

In the old park, solitary and vast,
Two ghosts once met to summon up the past.

– Do you remember our old ecstasy?
– Why would you bring it back again to me?

– Do you still dream as you dreamed long ago?
Does your heart beat to my heart's beating? – No.

– Ah, those old days, what joys have those days seen
When your lips met my lips! – It may have been.

– How blue the sky was, and our hope how light!
– Hope has flown helpless back into the night.

They walked through weeds withered and grasses dead,
And only the night heard the words they said.

From *Poèmes saturniens*
(Paul Verlaine)

I. Soleils couchants

Pale dawn delicately
Over earth has spun
The sad melancholy
Of the setting sun.
Sad melancholy
Brings oblivion
In sad songs to me
With the setting sun.
And the strangest dreams,
Dreams like suns that set
On the banks of the streams,
Ghost and glory met,
To my sense it seems.
Pass, and without let,
Like great suns that set
On the banks of streams.

II. Chanson d'automne

When a sighing begins
In the violins
Of the autumn-song,
My heart is drowned
In the slow sound
Languorous and long.

Pale as with pain,
Breath fails me when
The hour tolls deep.
My thoughts recover
The days that are over,
And I weep.

And I go
Where the winds know,
Broken and brief,
To and fro,
As the winds blow
A dead leaf.

III. Femme et Chatte

They were at play, she and her cat,
And it was marvellous to mark
The white paw and the white hand pat
Each other in the deepening dark.

The stealthy little lady hid
Under her mittens' silken sheath
Her deadly agate nails that thrid
The silk-like dagger-points of death.

The cat purred primly and drew in
Her claws that were of steel filed thin:
The devil was in it all the same.

And in the boudoir, while a shout
Of laughter in the air rang out,
Four sparks of phosphor shone like flame.

From *La Bonne chanson*
(Paul Verlaine)

I.
The white moon sits
And seems to brood
Where a swift voice flits
From each branch in the wood
That the tree-tops cover...

O lover, my lover!

The pool in the meadows
Like a looking-glass
Casts back the shadows
That over it pass
Of the willow-bower...

Let us dream: 'tis the hour...

A tender and vast
Lull of content
Like a cloud is cast
From the firmament
Where one planet is bright...

'Tis the hour of delight.

II.
The fireside, the lamp's little narrow light;
The dream with head on hand, and the delight
Of eyes that lose themselves in loving looks;
The hour of steaming tea and of shut books;
The solace to know evening almost gone;

The dainty weariness of waiting on
The nuptial shadow and night's softest bliss;
Ah, it is this that without respite, this
That without stay, my tender fancy seeks,
Mad with the months and furious with the weeks.

From *Romances sans Paroles*
(Paul Verlaine)

I.
'Tis the ecstasy of repose,
'Tis love when tired lids close,
'Tis the wood's long shuddering
In the embrace of the wind,
'Tis, where grey boughs are thinned,
Little voices that sing.

O fresh and frail is the sound
That twitters above, around,
Like the sweet tiny sigh
That lies in the shaken grass;
Or the sound when waters pass
And the pebbles shrink and cry.

What soul is this that complains
Over the sleeping plains,
And what is it that it saith?
Is it mine, is it thine,
This lowly hymn I divine
In the warm night, low as a breath?

II.
I divine, through the veil of a murmuring,
The subtle contour of voices gone,
And I see, in the glimmering lights that sing,
The promise, pale love, of a future dawn.

And my soul and my heart in trouble
What are they but an eye that sees.
As through a mist an eye sees double,
Airs forgotten of songs like these?

O to die of no other dying,
Love, than this that computes the showers
Of old hours and of new hours flying:
O to die of the swing of the hours!

III.
Tears in my heart that weeps,
Like the rain upon the town.
What drowsy languor steeps
In tears my heart that weeps?

O sweet sound of the rain
On earth and on the roofs!
For a heart's weary pain
O the song of the rain!

Vain tears, vain tears, my heart!
What, none hath done thee wrong?
Tears without reason start,
From my disheartened heart.

This is the weariest woe,
O heart, of love and hate
Too weary, not to know
Why thou hast all this woe.

IV.
A frail hand in the rose-grey evening
Kisses the shining keys that hardly stir,
While, with the light, small flutter of a wing,
An old song, like an old tired wanderer,
Goes very softly, as if trembling,
About the room long redolent of Her.

What lullaby is this that comes again
To dandle my poor being with its breath?
What wouldst thou have of me, gay laughing strain?
What hadst thou, desultory faint refrain
That now into the garden to thy death
Floatest through the half-opened window-pane?

V.
O sad, sad was my soul, alas!
For a woman, a woman's sake it was.

I have had no comfort since that day.
Although my heart went its way,

Although my heart and my soul went
From the woman into banishment.

I have had no comfort since that day,
Although my heart went its way.

And my heart, being sore in me,
Said to my soul: How can this be,

How can this be or have been thus,
This proud, sad banishment of us?

My soul said to my heart: Do I
Know what snare we are tangled by,

Seeing that, banished, we know not whether
We are divided or together?

VI.
Wearily the plain's
Endless length expands;
The snow shines like grains
Of the shifting sands.

Light of day is none,
Brazen is the sky;
Overhead the moon
Seems to live and die.

Where the woods are seen,
Grey the oak-trees lift
Through the vaporous screen
Like the clouds that drift.

Light of day is none,
Brazen is the sky;
Overhead the moon
Seems to live and die.

Broken-winded crow,
And you, lean wolves, when
The sharp north-winds blow,
What do you do then?

Wearily the plain's
Endless length expands;
The snow shines like grains
Of the shifting sands.

VII.
There's a flight of green and red
In the hurry of hills and rails,
Through the shadowy twilight shed
By the lamps as daylight pales.

Dim gold light flushes to blood
In humble hollows far down;
Birds sing low from a wood
Of barren trees without crown.

Scarcely more to be felt
Than that autumn is gone;
Languors, lulled in me, melt
In the still air's monotone.

VIII. Spleen

The roses were all red,
The ivy was all black:
Dear, if you turn your head,
All my despairs come back.

The sky was too blue, too kind,
The sea too green, and the air
Too calm: and I know in my mind
I shall wake and not find you there.

I am tired of the box-tree's shine
And the holly's, that never will pass,
And the plain's unending line,
And of all but you, alas!

IX. Streets

Dance the jig!

I loved best her pretty eyes
Clearer than stars in any skies,
I loved her eyes for their dear lies.

Dance the jig!

And ah! the ways, the ways she had
Of driving a poor lover mad:
It made a man's heart sad and glad.

Dance the jig!

But now I find the old kisses shed
From her flower-mouth a rarer red
Now that her heart to mine is dead.

Dance the jig!

And I recall, now I recall
Old days and hours, and ever shall,
And that is best, and best of all.

Dance the jig!

From *Jadis et naguère*
(Paul Verlaine)

I. Art poétique

Music first and foremost of all!
Choose your measure of odd not even,
Let it melt in the air of heaven,
Pose not, poise not, but rise and fall.

Choose your words, but think not whether
Each to other of old belong:
What so dear as the dim grey song
Where clear and vague are joined together?

'Tis veils of beauty for beautiful eyes,
'Tis the trembling light of the naked noon,
'Tis a medley of blue and gold, the moon
And stars in the cool of autumn skies.

Let every shape of its shade be born;
Colour, away! come to me, shade!
Only of shade can the marriage be made
Of dream with dream and of flute with horn.

Shun the Point, lest death with it come,
Unholy laughter and cruel wit
(For the eyes of the angels weep at it)
And all the garbage of scullery-scum.

Take Eloquence, and wring the neck of him!
You had better, by force, from time to time,
Put a little sense in the head of Rhyme:
If you watch him not, you will be at the beck of him.

O, who shall tell us the wrongs of Rhyme?
What witless savage or what deaf boy
Has made for us this twopenny toy
Whose bells ring hollow and out of time?

Music always and music still!
Let your verse be the wandering thing
That flutters in flight from a soul on the wing
Towards other skies at a new whim's will.

Let your verse be the luck of the lure
Afloat on the winds that at morning hint
Of the odours of thyme and the savour of mint ...
And all the rest is literature.

II. Mezzetin chantant

Go, and with never a care
But the care to keep happiness!
Crumple a silken dress
And snatch a song in the air.

Hear the moral of all the wise
In a world where happy folly
Is wiser than melancholy:
Forget the hour as it flies!

The one thing needful on earth, it
Is not to be whimpering.
Is life after all a thing
Real enough to be worth it?

From *Sagesse*
(Paul Verlaine)

I.
The little hands that once were mine,
The hands I loved, the lovely hands.

After the roadways and the strands,
And realms and kingdoms once divine,

And mortal loss of all that seems
Lost with the old sad pagan things.
Royal as in the days of kings
The dear hands open to me dreams.

Hands of dream, hands of holy flame
Upon my soul in blessing laid.
What is it that these hands have said
That my soul hears and swoons to them?

Is it a phantom, this pure sight
Of mother's love made tenderer,
Of spirit with spirit linked to share
The mutual kinship of delight?

Good sorrow, dear remorse, and ye,
Blest dreams, O hands ordained of heaven
To tell me if I am forgiven.
Make but the sign that pardons me!

II.
O my God, thou hast wounded me with love,
Behold the wound, that is still vibrating,
O my God, thou hast wounded me with love.

O my God, thy fear hath fallen upon me,
Behold the burn is there, and it throbs aloud,
O my God, thy fear hath fallen upon me.

O my God, I have known that all is vile
And that thy glory hath stationed itself in me,
O my God, I have known that all is vile.

Drown my soul in floods, floods of thy wine,
Mingle my life with the body of thy bread.
Drown my soul in floods, floods of thy wine.

Take my blood, that I have not poured out.
Take my flesh, unworthy of suffering.
Take my blood, that I have not poured out.

Take my brow, that has only learned to blush.
To be the footstool of thine adorable feet,
Take my brow, that has only learned to blush.

Take my hands, because they have laboured not
For coals of fire and for rare frankincense,
Take my hands, because they have laboured not.

Take my heart, that has beaten for vain things,
To throb under the thorns of Calvary,
Take my heart that has beaten for vain things.

Take my feet, frivolous travellers,
That they may run to the crying of thy grace,
Take my feet, frivolous travellers.

Take my voice, a harsh and a lying noise,
For the reproaches of thy Penitence,
Take my voice, a harsh and a lying noise.

Take mine eyes, luminaries of deceit,
That they may be extinguished in the tears of prayer,
Take mine eyes, luminaries of deceit.

Alas, thou, God of pardon and promises,
What is the pit of mine ingratitude,
Alas, thou, God of pardon and promises.

God of terror and God of holiness,
Alas, my sinfulness is a black abyss,
God of terror and God of holiness.

Thou, God of peace, of joy and delight,
All my tears, all my ignorances.
Thou, God of peace, of joy and delight.

Thou, O God, knowest all this, all this,
How poor I am, poorer than any man,
Thou, O God, knowest all this, all this.

And what I have, my God, I give to thee.

III.
Slumber dark and deep
Falls across my life;
I will put to sleep
Hope, desire, and strife.

All things pass away.
Good and evil seem
To my soul today
Nothing but a dream;

I a cradle laid
In a hollow cave,
By a great hand swayed:
Silence, like the grave.

IV.
The body's sadness and the languor thereof
Melt and bow me with pity till I could weep,
Ah! when the dark hours break it down in sleep
And the bedclothes score the skin and the hot hands move;
Alert for a little with the fever of day,
Damp still with the heavy sweat of the night that has thinned,
Like a bird that trembles on a roof in the wind:
And the feet that are sorrowful because of the way,

And the breast that a hand has scarred with a double blow.
And the mouth that as an open wound is red,
And the flesh that shivers and is a painted show,
And the eyes, poor eyes so lovely with tears unshed
For the sorrow of seeing this also over and done:
Sad body, how weak and how punished under the sun!

V.
Fairer is the sea
Than the minster high,
Faithful nurse is she,
And last lullaby,
And the Virgin prays
Over the sea's ways.

Gifts of grief and guerdons
From her bounty come,
And I hear her pardons
Chide her angers home;
Nothing in her is
Unforgivingness.

She is piteous,
She the perilous!
Friendly things to us
The wave sings to us:
You whose hope is past,
Here is peace at last.

And beneath the skies,
Brighter-hued than they
She has azure dyes,
Rose and green and grey.
Better is the sea
Than all fair things or we.

From *Parallèlement*: **Impression fausse**
(Paul Verlaine)

Little lady mouse,
Black upon the grey of light;
Little lady mouse,
Grey upon the night.

Now they ring the bell,
All good prisoners slumber deep;

Now they ring the bell,
Nothing now but sleep.

Only pleasant dreams.
Love's enough for thinking of;
Only pleasant dreams.
Long live love!

Moonlight over all,
Someone snoring heavily;
Moonlight over all
In reality.

Now there comes a cloud,
It is dark as midnight here;
Now there comes a cloud,
Dawn begins to peer.

Little lady mouse,
Rosy in a ray of blue,
Little lady mouse:
Up now, all of you!

From *Chansons pour elle*
(Paul Verlaine)

You believe that there may be
Luck in strangers in the tea:
I believe only in your eyes.

You believe in fairy-tales,
Days one wins and days one fails:
I believe only in your lies.

You believe in heavenly powers,
In some saint to whom one prays
Or in some Ave that one says.

I believe only in the hours,
Coloured with the rosy lights
You rain for me on sleepless nights.

And so firmly I receive
These for truth, that I believe
That only for your sake I live.

From *Epigrammes*
(Paul Verlaine)

When we go together, if I may see her again,
Into the dark wood and the rain;

When we are drunken with air and the sun's delight
At the brink of the river of light;

When we are homeless at last, for a moment's space
Without city or abiding-place;

And if the slow good-will of the world still seem
To cradle us in a dream;

Then, let us sleep the last sleep with no leave-taking,
And God will see to the waking.

Notes

Further information about names or concepts in bold can be found in the Glossary. Editorial annotations are given after Symons' own bibliographical notes. He prefaced these with the announcement:

The essays contained in this book are not intended to give information. They are concerned with ideas rather than with facts; each is a study of a problem, only in part a literary one, in which I have endeavoured to consider writers as personalities under the action of spiritual forces, or as themselves so many forces. But it has seemed to me that readers have a right to demand information in regard to writers who are so often likely to be unfamiliar to them. I have therefore given a bibliography of the works of each writer with whom I have dealt, and I have added a number of notes, giving particulars which I think are likely to be useful in fixing more definitely the personal characteristics of these writers.

Dedication

1. Symons would omit this dedication to **W.B. Yeats** from the second American edition of 1919 as part of a coolness between the two writers, following his mental breakdown in 1908. Symons' friendship with Yeats and its influence on *The Symbolist Movement* is discussed in my introduction.
2. AE was the pen name of the poet George William Russell (1867–1935). With Yeats, AE was a key member of the Literary Revival movement in Ireland. As well as being steeped in Irish mythology, his poetry is characterised by his strong spiritualist beliefs and interests in mysticism.
3. Between 1894 and 1895 the Russian poet and writer Valery Yakovlevich Bryusov published three slim anthologies under the title *Russkie Simvolisty* (Russian Symbolists), placing translations of the French Symbolists alongside original Russian works. With Konstantin Balmont (1867–1942), Bryusov helped to establish Symbolism as a significant force within Russian literature.
4. Symons is not explicit about which Dutch writers he has in mind here, but in 'The Decadent Movement in Literature' he mentions Louis

Couperus (1863–1923), citing his novel *Extaze* [Ecstasy] (1890).

5. The Portuguese poet Eugenio de Castro (1869–1944) published *Oaristos* [Intimate Conversations] in 1890, incorporating his own Symbolist manifesto. It helped to establish a small school of young poets around him. In 1895 he was elected to the Academy of Sciences of Lisbon. Other important Symbolist poets in Portugal include Camilo Pessanha (1867–1926) and Roberto de Mesquita (1871–1923).

6. Symons published an essay on the Spanish poet Ramon de Campoamor in *Harper's Monthly Magazine* during December 1901, reprinting it in *Studies in Prose and Verse* (1904). He compares Campoamor with Verlaine and singles out the shorter poems published as *Doloras* for particular praise.

Introduction

1. *Sartor Resartus* is the only published novel by the historian, biographer and essayist Thomas Carlyle (1795–1881). The passages quoted from Book Three, Chapter Three are clearly attributed to a fictitious character, a German Professor Teufelsdröckh ('Devil's shit'), although Symons treats them as Carlyle's own views. Other major works by Carlyle include *On Heroes and Hero-Worship* (1841), *Chartism* (1839) and *Past and Present* (1843).

2. Symons quotes twice from the 'Author's Preface' to the English translation of *The Migration of Symbols* (1894), by Eugène Felicien Albert, Comte Goblet d'Alviella (1846–1925). D'Alviella takes a comparativist approach, arguing that where cultures and societies across history seem to share the same symbols, it betrays hidden material and historical links between them.

Gérard de Nerval

Derived, with minor revisions, from 'The Problem of Gérard de Nerval', *Fortnightly Review* 63 (January 1898), pp. 81–91.

Symons' note

Napoléon et la France Guerrière, élégies nationales, 1826; *La mort de Talma*, 1826; *L'Académie, ou les Membres Introuvables, comédie satirique en vers*, 1826; *Napoléon et Talma, élégies nationales nouvelles*, 1826; *M. Dentscourt, ou le Cuisinier Grand Homme*, 1826; *Élégies Nationales et Satires Politiques*, 1827; *Faust, tragédie de Goethe*, 1828 (suivi du second *Faust*, 1840); *Couronne Poétique de Béranger*, 1828; *Le Peuple, ode*, 1830; *Poésies Allemandes, Morçeaux choisis et traduits*, 1830; *Choix de Poésies de Ronsard et de Regnier*,

1830; *Nos Adieux à la Chambre de Députés de l'an 1830*, 1831; *Lénore, traduite de Burger*, 1835; *Piquilo, opéra comique* (with Dumas), 1837; *L'Alchimiste, drame en vers* (with Dumas), 1839; *Léo Burckhardt, drame en prose* (with Dumas), 1839; *Scènes de la Vie Orientale*, 2 vols., 1848–1850; *Les Monténégrins, opéra comique* (with Alboize), 1849; *Le Chariot d'Enfant, drame en vers* (with Méry), 1850; *Les Nuits du Ramazan*, 1850; *Voyage en Orient*, 1851; *L'Imagier de Harlem, légende en prose et en vers* (with Méry and Bernard Lopez), 1852; *Contes et Facéties*, 1852; *Lorely, souvenirs d'Allemagne*, 1852; *Les Illuminés*, 1852; *Petits Châteaux de Bohême*, 1853; *Les Filles du Feu*, 1854; *Misanthropie et Repentir, drame de Kotzebue*, 1855; *La Bohême galante*, 1855; *Le Rêve et la Vie: Aurélia*, 1855; *Le Marquis de Fayolle* (with E. Gorges), 1856; *Oeuvres Complètes*, 6 vols (1, *Les Deux Faust de Goethe*; 2, 3, *Voyage en Orient*; 4, *Les Illuminés, Les Faux Saulniers*; 5. *Le Rêve et la Vie, Les Filles du Feu, La Bohême galante*; 6, *Poésies Complètes*), 1867.

The sonnets, written at different periods and published for the first time in the collection of 1854, 'Les Filles du Feu,' which also contains 'Sylvie,' were reprinted in the volume of *Poésies Complètes*, where they are imbedded in the midst of deplorable juvenilia. All, or almost all, of the verse worth preserving was collected, in 1897, by that delicate amateur of the curiosities of beauty, M. Remy de Gourmont, in a tiny volume called *Les Chimères*, which contains the six sonnets of 'Les Chimères,' the sonnet called 'Vers Dorés,' the five sonnets of 'Le Christ aux Oliviers,' and, in facsimile of the autograph, the lyric called 'Les Cydalises.' The true facts of the life of Gérard have been told for the first time, from original documents, by Mme. Arvède Barine, in two excellent articles in the *Revue des Deux Mondes*, October 15 and November 1, 1897, since reprinted in *Les Nevrosés*, 1898; and, later, by M. G. Labrunie de Ferrières, in *La Vie et l'Oeuvre de Gérard de Nerval*, 1906.

Annotations

1. Nerval committed suicide before he had completed the serial publication of *Aurélia*. Symons quotes here from a posthumous collection of Nerval's writings put together by **Théophile Gautier** and Arsène Houssaye, entitled *Le Rêve et la vie* (1855). At this point in Nerval's manuscript, the text contains a gap which his editors decided to fill by including the fragments of letters Nerval apparently wrote to a lover. Subsequent scholarship suggests, however, that these texts may be fictional rather than autobiographical.

2. Symons translates here from an article by Nerval entitled 'Paradoxe et Verité' published in *L'Artiste*, 2 June 1844. Parts of this article were re-published in 1865 as Nerval's *Pensées*, although not, apparently, this remark. Symons probably found it in the account of Nerval's life

given by Arvède Barine cited in his notes (above).

3. Having declared himself Emperor of France in 1804, Napoleon Bonaparte (1769–1821) assembled a *Grande Armée* defeating the combined Russian and Austrian armies at the Battle of Austerlitz in December 1805 (although failing in his attempt to invade England). His forces retained this name during subsequent campaigns until his forced abdication in 1814.

4. Symons translates here from 'Introduction. XIV – Le Songe de Polyphile', in *Voyage en Orient* (1851).

5. Originating with Nerval's friend, **Théophile Gautier**, Symons probably found this famous anecdote in Barine. The Palais Royal is an arcade of shops and booths along the edges of a large courtyard near to the Louvre in the centre of Paris. For a detailed social and cultural history see Eric Hazan, *The Invention of Paris*, trans. David Fernbach (London: Verso, 2011).

6. 'Sylvie' is the second story in Nerval's *Les Filles du Feu* (1854), a collection of seven short stories, each weaving autobiography, history and fiction around a central female figure. The first edition also included Nerval's sonnets, *Les Chimères*, and a preface addressed to Alexandre Dumas, explaining the origin of *Les Filles du Feu* and taking Dumas to task for printing Nerval's sonnet 'El Desdichado' without permission while he was detained in a mental asylum.

7. Madame de Maintenon was the second wife of Louis XIV. She established a convent school for girls in 1686 at Saint-Cyr, near Versailles, and commissioned the French playwright Jean Racine (1639–99) to write the plays from biblical sources, *Esther* (1689) and *Athalie* (1691). Both plays were first performed by girls at the school.

8. **Dante Gabriel Rossetti** translated two old French poems ('My Father's Close' and 'John of Tours') in his *Poems* (1870), based upon texts reproduced by Nerval in 1842.

9. Situated on the right bank of the Seine in Paris, close to the Palais du Louvre, the Place du Carrousel was part of an intricate warren of small, dirty backstreets during Nerval's lifetime, inhabited by bohemians. Slowly torn down from the 1840s onwards, its destruction was completed in the 1850s under Napoleon III, prompting Baudelaire to remark that 'the shape of a town / Changes more quickly, alas, than the heart of a man', in his poem 'Le Cygne' [The Swan]. Nerval describes living in a squat on the Rue du Doyenné in *Petits Châteaux de Bohême* (1852).

10. Vindice from Cyril Tourneur's play *The Revenger's Tragedy* (1606): 'Joy's a subtle elf; / I think man's happiest when he forgets himself' (IV.iv.83–83). In the 1898 version of this essay, Symons misattributed the line to Webster's *Duchess of Malfi*.

11. A short novel by French writer and translator Antoine-François Prévost (1697–1763), *L'Histoire du chevalier des Grieux et de Manon Lescaut* (1731) begins as a story of the forbidden and unrequited love of a young aristocrat for a serving-girl (Manon) who cheats on him for wealthy men. Eventually they are exiled to America but Manon's death cuts short their chances of happiness.

12. In *De l'amour* (1822) **Stendhal** describes the imaginative transformation love performs upon its object as 'crystallisation […] a certain fever of the imagination that makes the most ordinary of objects unrecognisable and sets them apart from everything else' – *On Love*, trans. Sophie Lewis; intr. A.C. Grayling (London: Hesperus, 2009).

13. The New Testament: 'And from the days of John the Baptist until now the kingdom of heaven suffereth violence, and the violent take it by force' (Matthew 11:12).

14. Pico della Mirandola (1463–96) was an Italian humanist whose motto was reputed to be '*De omni re scibili*' ('of all things knowable'). Jan Meursius (1579–1639) was a Dutch philologist and the author of a commentary on Lycophron, reputed to be the most obscure of Greek authors. Nicholas of Cusa (1401–64) was known for his polymathic command of languages, philosophy, theology and mathematics.

15. Nerval's friend and colleague **Théophile Gautier** describes him in these terms in the preface to *Le Rêve et la vie*.

16. As well as laying the foundations for modern trigonometry, Greek philosopher and mathematician Pythagoras (c.580–500 BC) is associated with the doctrine of the transmigration of souls whereby the soul is immortal and passes from body to body in search of perfection. He was interested in the mathematical bases of music and saw mathematics as a tool for uncovering various forms of symbolic harmony within the universe.

17. The *Tabula Smaragdine* (1541) was a medieval Latin treatise on alchemy, attributed to Hermes Trismegistus, a Hellenised form of the Egyptian god of writing, Thoth. Bridging Greek, Egyptian and Christian sources, this text was highly influential upon the development of Hermetic mysticism from the seventeenth century onwards. **W.B. Yeats** also cites it at the head of his essay, 'Symbolism in Painting' (1898).

18. In an interview with Jules Huret, Stéphane Mallarmé famously remarked that the aim of poetry was not to 'name' things but to 'suggest' them. Symons develops this in more detail in his essay on Mallarmé.

Villiers de l'Isle-Adam

First published as 'Villiers de l'Isle Adam', *Fortnightly Review* 66 (August 1899), pp. 197–204.

Symons' note

Premières Poésies, 1859; *Isis*, 1862; *Elën*, 1864; *Morgane*, 1865; *Claire Lenoir* (in the *Revue des Lettres et des Arts*), 1867; *L'Evasion*, 1870; *La Révolte*, 1870; *Azraël*, 1878; *Le Nouveau Monde*, 1880; *Contes Cruels*, 1880; *L'Eve Future*, 1886; *Akëdysséril*, 1886; *L'Amour Suprême*, 1886; *Tribulat Bonhomet*, 1887; *Histoires Insolites*, 1888; *Nouveaux Contes Cruels*, 1889; *Axël*, 1890; *Chez les Passants*, 1890; *Propos d'Au-delà*, 1893; *Histoires Souveraines*, 1899 (a selection). Among works announced, but never published, it may be interesting to mention: *Seid, William de Strally, Faust, Poésies Nouvelles (Intermèdes; Gog; Ave, Mater Victa; Poésies diverses), La Tentation sur la Montagne, Le Vieux de la Montagne, L'Adoration des Mages, Méditations Littéraires, Mélanges, Théâtre* (2 vols.), *Documents sur les Règnes de Charles VI. et de Charles VII., L'Illusionisme, De la Connaissance de l'Utile, L'Exégèse Divine*.

A sympathetic, but slightly vague, Life of Villiers was written by his cousin, Vicomte Robert du Pontavice de Heussey: *Villiers de l'Isle-Adam*, 1893; it was translated by Lady Mary Lloyd, 1894. See Verlaine's *Poètes Maudits*, 1884, and his biography of Villiers in *Les Hommes d'Aujourd'hui*, the series of penny biographies, with caricature portraits, published by Vanier; also Mallarmé's *Villiers de l'Isle-Adam*, the reprint of a lecture given at Brussels a few months after Villiers' death. *La Révolte* was translated by Mrs Theresa Barclay in the *Fortnightly Review*, December 1897, and acted in London by the New Stage Club in 1906. I have translated a little poem, *Aveu*, from the interlude of verse in the *Contes Cruels* called *Chant d'Amour*, in *Days and Nights*, 1889. An article of mine, the first, I believe, to be written on Villiers in English, appeared in the *Woman's World* in 1889; another in the *Illustrated London News* in 1891.

Annotations

1. Idealism is a philosophical doctrine, which tends to hold that mind or spirit constitutes the most basic reality in the universe and that the physical world exists only as an expression of mind. It is most strongly associated with the German philosophers Immanuel Kant (1724–1804) and Georg Wilhelm Hegel (1770–1831). Idealism is philosophically opposed to realism and naturalism, which hold that values emerge from material things and processes. Note that these philosophical doctrines should not be confused with literary movements of the same name.

2. This note translates Verlaine's remarks in his essay 'Villiers de l'Isle Adam', from the collection *Les Hommes d'Aujourd'hui* (1885–93), cited in Symons' note above.

3. Villiers wrote and re-wrote *Axël* throughout his life, publishing parts and fragments in 1872, 1882 and 1884. An incomplete version was published posthumously by his friends Mallarmé and Huysmans in 1890. This incorporates four 'parts':

> Part I – Le Monde Religieux [The Religious World]: Sara is a novitiate in a nunnery. The Archdeacon and Abbess plan to make her join the convent and give over her inherited wealth to the order. Her attachment to another nun, Sister Aloyse, and her fascination with Rosicrucian occult books give the Archdeacon and the Abbess cause for concern. At the critical moment, Sara refuses and escapes from the monastery.

> Part II – Le Monde Tragique [The Tragic World]: Commander Kaspar of Auërsperg is visiting his nephew Axël in a secluded castle in the Black Forest. An aged attendant, Zacharias, reveals that a fortune in gold and jewels belonging to the German state is hidden somewhere on the castle's estate. When Kaspar urges Axël to seek out the treasure, he is challenged to a duel: Axël disdains Kaspar's worldly materialist concerns, rejects the claims of the state and perceives an insult to his family's honour. To his surprise, Kaspar is killed in the duel; as the body is taken away a mysterious figure appears, Axël's mentor, Maître Janus.

> Part III – Le Monde Occult [The Occult World]: In this shortest section of the play, Axël rejects Maître Janus's appeal for him to turn away from the world towards an occult initiation and resolves to abandon his estate.

> Part IV – Le Monde Passionel [The Passionate World] Sara arrives at Auërsperg, having learned of the hidden treasure from a secret manuscript at the cloister. She is discovered by Axël as she opens the treasure vault; they fight and he is wounded. They fall in love. Axël persuades Sara to join him in suicide, because the world holds nothing as good as the delights they have imagined together in the first raptures of their love. They swallow poison and die.

The patchwork of quotations in Symons' essay is translated freely and out of sequence from dialogue between Axël and Maître Janus in Part Three, Section One 'Au Seuil' [At the Threshold], where they describe and debate the possibility of transcending the material world by occult means.

4. From Act I, Scene V of *Elën*: high-minded student Samuel Wissler

rejects the worldly pleasures espoused by his companion Goetz. In the course of the play, Samuel is seduced by Elën, a beautiful but capricious Italian courtesan incapable of true love. Samuel later tells Goetz he has found an ideal love in 'Marie'. Elën is murdered at the instigation of a former lover and when Samuel learns of her true identity he leaves for self-imposed exile. *Elën* was Villiers' first play; privately published in 1865, it only became more widely available in 1896.

5. **Henrik Ibsen**'s *A Doll's House* (1879) depicts the marriage of Nora and Torvald Helmer. During the course of the play, Nora comes to realise that her defenceless personality is an act and that she needs to realise her own desires and ambitions outside of the constraints of marriage. Early audiences were shocked by this apparently frank treatment of marital unhappiness, the faults of marriage as an institution and Nora's final decision to leave her husband.

6. The opening description of the two locations in which *Axël* is set. Part I takes place in 'a Monastery housing Trinitarian Nuns, the Cloister of Saint Apollodora, located at the shoreline of old French Flanders'; the other three parts are set in 'a very old castle, the feudal residence of the Margraves of Auërsperg, isolated in the middle of the Black Forest'.

7. Sara doesn't speak at all during the first part of *Axël* until Part I Section II Scene VI ('La Renonciatrice') when she answers 'No' in response to the Archdeacon's question 'Do you accept the Light, the Hope and the Life?' as part of the ritual for imposing orders upon her.

8. Alexandre Dumas, *fils* (1824–95), French playwright and son of Alexandre Dumas, *père* (1802–70), was most famous for the novel *La Dame aux camélias* (1848). This was turned into a play of the same name in 1852, which became the basis for Giuseppe Verdi's opera *La Traviata* (1853).

9. One of the oldest surviving roads in Paris, the rue des Martyrs runs north-south between the eighteenth and ninth arrondissements in Paris. Villiers lived on this street in 1879 and was known to frequent the Brasserie des Martyrs. The area was known as an impoverished artists' quarter and borders on the red light district, Pigalle.

10. Written by Alfred de Musset (1810–57) in 1834 but not performed until 1866, the play *Fantasio* depicts the exploits of a young cynic, who masquerades as a jester at the court of Bavaria in order to escape from his creditors. Fantasio's interventions produce various kinds of chaos and disruption. De Musset's play was subsequently adapted into operatic form in 1872 by Jacques Offenbach (1819–80).

11. Symons translates Axel's words ('Vivre? les serviteurs feront cela

pour nous') in the last scene of *Axël*. W.B. Yeats used this translation as an epigraph to *The Secret Rose* (1897).
12. A slight abbreviation from **Walter Pater**'s description of Leonardo da Vinci in *The Renaissance* as 'so possessed by his genius that he passes unmoved through the most tragic events, overwhelming his country and friends, like one who comes across them by chance on some secret errand'.

Arthur Rimbaud

First published as 'Arthur Rimbaud', *Saturday Review* (28 May 1898), pp. 706–707.

Symons' note
Une Saison en Enfer, 1873; *Les Illuminations*, 1886; *Reliquaire*, 1891 (containing several poems falsely attributed to Rimbaud); *Les Illuminations*: *Un Saison en Enfer*, 1892; *Poésies Complètes*, 1895; *Oeuvres*, 1898.

See also Paterne Berrichon, *La Vie de Jean-Arthur Rimbaud*, 1898, and *Lettres de Jean-Arthur Rimbaud*, 1899; Paul Verlaine, *Les Poètes Maudits*, 1884, and the biography by Verlaine in *Les Hommes d'Aujourd'hui*. Mr. George Moore was the first to write about Rimbaud in 'Two Unknown Poets' (Rimbaud and Laforgue) in *Impressions and Opinions*, 1891. In Mr. John Gray's *Silverpoints*, 1893, there are translations of 'Charleville' and 'Sensation.' The latter, and 'Les Chercheuses de Poux,' are translated by Mr. T. Sturge Moore in *The Vinedresser, and other Poems*, 1899.

Annotations
1. Poet, painter and editor Pierre-Eugène Dufour (1855–1922) published under the name 'Paterne Berrichon'. He married Rimbaud's sister Isabelle in 1897 and became his first biographer. *La vie de Jean-Arthur Rimbaud* (1897) first appeared as a series of articles in *La Revue Blanche* between August 1896 and September 1897. It concludes by quoting a long letter by Isabelle Rimbaud describing the last months of her brother's life, from which Symons translates here.
2. Described by Graham Robb as 'the flagship of the French penal system', the Mazas was the main prison in Paris during the nineteenth century. Built in 1841 and destroyed in 1900, it was located near to the Gare de Lyon. Rimbaud was imprisoned there for vagrancy during several days at the beginning of September 1870.
3. André Gill [Louis-Alexandre Gosset de Guînes] (1840–85) was a French artist, illustrator and caricaturist, best known for his satirical cartoons of French writers and literary figures in periodicals such as *La Lune* and *L'Éclipse*.

4. Verlaine abandoned his wife and young child to travel with Rimbaud through England and Belgium. In July 1873 Verlaine was arrested in Brussels for shooting and wounding Rimbaud in the wrist during a violent row. Although Rimbaud withdrew charges, Verlaine was sentenced to two years' imprisonment for his disorderly conduct.

5. Étienne Marchand (1755–93) was a French explorer who circumnavigated the globe on the ship *Solide* between 1790 and 1792.

6. Another quotation from Isabelle Rimbaud's letters in *La vie de Jean-Arthur Rimbaud* (1897); this description of Rimbaud's final words concludes a paragraph in which Isabelle describes her brother as 'un saint, un martyr, un élu' (a saint, a martyr, one of the elect).

7. Verlaine wrote 'Crimen Amoris' (The Crime of Love) in Brussels during his imprisonment in 1873 and later published it in *Jadis et Naguère* (1884). It describes a visionary scene in which a Satanic figure (clearly inspired by Rimbaud) offers to reconcile virtue and vice, by sacrificing Hell. The offer is rejected with a cataclysmic thunderbolt from the heavens.

Paul Verlaine

This essay draws upon Symons' obituary article, 'Paul Verlaine', *Saturday Review* (11 January 1896), pp. 34–35, and incorporates material from his review of an exhibition by William Rothenstein in 'The Portraits of Verlaine', *Saturday Review* 85 (5 March 1898), pp. 319–20.

Symons' note
Poèmes Saturniens, 1866; *Fêtes Galantes*, 1869; *La Bonne Chanson*, 1870; *Romances sans Paroles*, 1874; *Sagesse*, 1881; *Les Poètes Maudits*, 1884; *Jadis et Naguère*, 1884; *Les Mémoires d'un Veuf*, 1886; *Louise Leclerq* (suivi de *Le Poteau, Pierre Duchatelet, Madame Aubin*), 1887; *Amour*, 1888; *Parallèlement*, 1889; *Dédicaces*, 1890; *Bonheur*, 1891; *Mes Hôpitaux*, 1891; *Chansons pour Elle*, 1891; *Liturgies Intimes*, 1892; *Mes Prisons*, 1893; *Odes en son Honneur*, 1893; *Elégies*, 1893; *Quinze Jours en Hollande*, 1894; *Dans les Limbes*, 1894; *Epigrammes*, 1894; *Confessions*, 1895; *Chair*, 1896; *Invectives*, 1896; *Voyage en France d'un Français* (posthumous), 1907.

The complete works of Verlaine are now published in six volumes at the Librairie Léon Vanier (now Messein); the text is very incorrectly printed, and it is still necessary to refer to the earlier editions in separate volumes. *A Choix de Poèsies*, 1891, with a preface by François Coppée and a reproduction of Carrière's admirable portrait, is published in one volume by Charpentier; the series of *Hommes d'Aujourd'hui* contains twenty-seven biographical notices by Verlaine; and a considerable number of poems and prose articles exists, scattered in various magazines, some of them English, such as the *Senate*; in some cases the articles themselves are translated into English, such as 'My Visit to London,' in the *Savoy* for April 1896, and 'Notes on England: Myself as a French Master,' and 'Shakespeare and Racine,' in the *Fortnightly Review* for July 1894 and September 1894. The first English translation in verse from Verlaine is Arthur O'Shaughnessy's rendering of 'Clair de Lune' in *Fêtes Galantes*, under the title 'Pastel,' in *Songs of a Worker*, 1881. A volume of translations in verse, *Poems of Verlaine*, by Gertrude Hall, was published in America in 1895. In Mr. John Gray's *Silverpoints*, 1893, there are translations of 'Parsifal,' 'A Crucifix,' 'Le Chevalier Malheur,' 'Spleen,' 'Clair de Lune,' 'Mon Dieu m'a dit,' and 'Green.' A complete translation of the *Fêtes Galantes*, together with poems from many other volumes, will be found in a small book which is meant to be a kind of supplement to this one.

As I have mentioned, there have been many portraits of Verlaine. The three portraits drawn on lithographic paper by Mr. Rothenstein, and published in 1898, are but the latest, if also among the best, of a long series, of which Mr. Rothenstein himself has done two or three others, one of which was reproduced in the *Pall Mall Gazette* in 1894, when Verlaine was in London. M. F. A. Cazals, a young artist who was one of Verlaine's most intimate friends, has done I should not like to say how many portraits, some of which he has gathered together in a little book, *Paul Verlaine: ses Portraits*, 1898. There are portraits in nine of Verlaine's own books, several of them by M. Cazals (roughly jotted, expressive notes of moments), one by M. Anquetin (a strong piece of thinking flesh and blood), and in the *Choix de Poésies* there is a reproduction of the cloudy, inspired poet of Eugène Carrière's painting. Another portrait, which I have not seen, but which Verlaine himself calls, in the *Dédicaces*, *un portrait enfin reposé* [a finally relaxed portrait], was done by M. Aman-Jean. M. Niederhausern has done a bust in bronze, Mr. Rothenstein a portrait medallion. A new edition of the *Confessions*, 1899, contains a number of sketches; *Verlaine Dessinateur*, 1896, many more; and there are yet others in the extremely objectionable book of M. Charles Donos, *Verlaine Intime* 1898. The *Hommes d'Aujourd'hui* contains a caricature-portrait, many other portraits have appeared in French and English and German and Italian magazines, and there is yet another portrait in the admirable little book of Charles Morice, *Paul Verlaine*, 1888, which contains by far the best study that has ever been made of Verlaine as a poet. I believe Mr. George Moore's article, 'A Great Poet,' reprinted in *Impressions and Opinions*, 1891, was the first that was written on Verlaine in England; my own article in the *National Review* in 1892 was, I believe, the first detailed study of the whole of his work up to that date. At last, in the *Vie de Paul Verlaine* of Edmund Lepelletier, there has come the authentic record.

Annotations

1. Having learned of his death sentence, the narrator of **Victor Hugo**'s short novel, *Le dernier jour d'un condamné* [Last day of a condemned man] (1829) cites this as a proverbial phrase at the start of chapter three. A version of the same phrase is quoted by **Walter Pater** in his conclusion to *The Renaissance* (1873).

2. In November 1894 Verlaine travelled to England to give a lecture at Oxford; he stayed with Symons in his lodgings at Fountaincourt en route and gave a talk at Barnard's Inn on French verse. Symons published his translation of Verlaine's account of this visit in the *Savoy* 2 (April 1896). Verlaine had previously lived in London between September 1872 and March 1873, sharing lodgings with his lover, Rimbaud.

3. Having studied at the Académie Julian in Paris, the English artist William Rothenstein (1872–1945) became associated with the New English Art Club, established in 1866 to counteract the influence of the Royal Academy. Rothenstein was famous for his literary connections and his associations with Paris.

4. Writing as 'Karl Mohr', Charles Morice published a hostile response to Verlaine's verse statement of his aesthetics, 'Art Poétique', in *La Nouvelle Rive Gauche*, 8 December 1882. Verlaine's reply (in the same paper) on 15 December converted Morice into an admirer, prompting him to write the first full-length study of his work in French (quoted here), *Paul Verlaine* (1888). When Verlaine published 'Art Poétique' in the collection *Jadis et naguère*, he dedicated it to Morice.

5. The most important French poet of the sixteenth century, Pierre de Ronsard (1524–85) is sometimes known as the Prince of Poets and led an influential group of humanist poets known as the Pléiade. He was neglected during the eighteenth century and rediscovered by the critic Sainte-Beuve during the nineteenth century.

6. Hamlet tells the actors visiting Elsinore that the aim of acting (and by extension, art) is 'to hold, as 'twere, the mirror up to nature' (III. ii.20–21).

7. In 'The School of Giorgione', **Walter Pater** famously observed that 'All art constantly aspires towards the condition of music.' This essay was first published in the *Fortnightly Review* in 1877, then added to the third edition of *The Renaissance* in 1888.

8. Oscar Wilde was fond of quoting this phrase: it appears in *The Picture of Dorian Gray* (1890), attributed to **Théophile Gautier**, and can be traced to the journals of **Jules and Edmond Goncourt** (1 May 1857), where Gautier is said to have remarked 'je suis un homme pour qui le monde visible existe' ['I am a man for whom the visible

world exists'] in defence of his literary achievements.

9. The Belgian poet Émile Verhaeren made these remarks in 'Paul Verlaine', *La Revue Blanche* (15 April 1897).

10. Symons quotes from the opening lines and the last line of the fifth poem in 'Lucien Létinois', from *Amour* (1888). This sequence of poems is dedicated to the memory of one of Verlaine's pupils at the college de Rethel, who died of typhoid fever in 1883, aged 22.

11. **Alfred Tennyson** started writing *In Memoriam* during the 1830s but did not publish it until 1850. This long poem in 132 sections describes his response to the death of his best friend Arthur Hallam in 1832 and the gradual accommodation of his grief with his religious views.

12. A misquotation from *Sagesse* (1880) – the child should be clothed in linen ('lin'), not wool ('laine').

13. These phrases ('mystical rose, tower of ivory, gate of heaven') are all taken from the Catholic litany for the Virgin Mary.

14. Verlaine included an essay about his own life and career in the second volume of *Poètes maudits* (1888), using the name 'Pauvre Lelian' (an anagram of his own name).

Jules Laforgue

First published as 'Jules Laforgue', *Saturday Review* 86 (3 September 1898), pp. 305–306.

Symons' note

Les Complaintes, 1885; *L'Imitation de Notre-Dame la Lune*, 1886; *Le Concile Féerique*, 1886; *Moralités Légendaires*, 1887; *Derniers Vers*, 1890 (a privately printed volume, containing *Des Fleurs de Bonne Volonté*, *Le Concile Féerique*, and *Derniers Vers*); *Poésies Complètes* 1894, *Oeuvres Complètes*, *Poésies*, *Moralités Légendaires*, *Mélanges Posthumes* (3 vols.), 1902, 1903.

An edition of the *Moralités Légendaires* in two volumes was published in 1897, under the care of M. Lucien Pissarro, at the Sign of the Dial; it is printed in Mr. Ricketts' admirable type, and makes one of the most beautiful books issued in French during this century. In 1896 M. Camille Mauclair, with his supple instinct for contemporary values, wrote a study, or rather an eulogy, of Laforgue, to which M. Maeterlinck contributed a few searching and delicate words by way of preface.

Annotations

1. Edgar Degas (1834–1917) was one of the most important French Impressionist artists, best known for his paintings of urban scenes of washerwomen and his fine studies of young ballet dancers. He was

friends with Stéphane Mallarmé and Paul Valéry and had some small literary pretensions of his own.

2. Maeterlinck offered this observation in his 'Introduction' to Camille Mauclair, *Jules Laforgue* (1896).

3. *René* (1802) by François-René de Chateaubriand (1768–1848) is a short novella about a passionate, sensitive young nobleman and his unhappy experiences in Louisana. Werther is the protagonist in **Johann Wolfgang von Goethe**'s epistolary novel *The Sorrows of Young Werther* (1774), which tells of the unhappy love of an impassioned and impoverished young artist and his eventual suicide.

4. Tannucio describes himself in these terms in Act II of Villiers de l'Isle-Adam's play *Elën* (1866).

Stéphane Mallarmé

First published as 'Stéphane Mallarmé', in *Fortnightly Review* 64 (November 1898), pp. 677–85, this essay also incorporates material from 'Mallarmé's Divagations' in *The Saturday Review* (30 January 1897), pp. 109–10.

Symons' note

Le Corbeau (traduit de Poe), 1875; *La Dernière Mode*, 1875; *L'Après-Midi d'un Faune*, 1876; *Le Vathek de Beckford*, 1876; *Petite Philologie à l'Usage des Classes et du Monde: Les Mots Anglais*, 1877; *Poésies Complètes* (photogravées sur le manuscrit), 1887; *Les Poèmes de Poe*, 1888; *Le Ten o'Clock de M. Whistler*, 1888; *Pages*, 1891; *Les Miens: Villiers de l'Isle Adam*, 1892; *Vers et Prose*, 1892; *La Musique et les Lettres* (Oxford, Cambridge), 1894; *Divagations*, 1897; *Poésies*, 1899.

See, on this difficult subject, Edmund Gosse, *Questions at Issue*, 1893, in which will be found the first study of Mallarmé that appeared in English; and Vittorio Pica, *Letteratura d'Eccezione*, 1899, which contains a carefully-documented study of more than a hundred pages. There is a translation of the poem called 'Fleurs' in Mr. John Gray's *Silverpoints*, 1893, and translations of 'Hérodiade' and three shorter poems will be found in the first volume of my collected poems. Several of the poems in prose have been translated into English; my translation of the 'Plainte d'Automne,' contained in this volume, was made in momentary forgetfulness that the same poem in prose had already been translated by Mr. George Moore in *Confessions of a Young Man*. Mr. Moore also translated 'Le Phénomène Futur' in the *Savoy*, July 1896.

Annotations

1. **Catulle Mendès** described Mallarmé as 'a difficult writer' in his

autobiographical reflections upon the **Parnassian** movement, *La Legende de Parnasse Contemporain* (1884).

2. Symons translates and paraphrases here from Mallarmé's defence of linguistic beauty over clarity of meaning in 'Le mystère dans les lettres' in the collection *Divagations*. This essay was first published in *La Revue blanche* in September 1896 and was written in response to Marcel Proust's essay 'Against Obscurity' published in July within the same journal.

3. Shakespeare's Sonnet 110, which begins with the poet accusing himself of putting himself, his art and his feelings too much on display.

4. Lines 69–70 of **Dante Gabriel Rossetti**'s 'Soothsay'. **Walter Pater** described this poem, which urges the reader to 'gaze onward' without hope, while refraining from looking 'backward' with regret, as a 'monumental gnomic piece'.

5. In 1875 Mallarmé moved into a small apartment on the fourth floor of 87 rue de Rome. During the 1880s, he began convening weekly evening literary salons in his apartment in Paris between 9pm and midnight. They were attended by aspiring poets, including his protégé Paul Valéry, and established literary figures, such as the **Goncourt brothers** and Alphonse Daudet. Symons first attended Mallarmé's Tuesdays with Havelock Ellis on his second visit to Paris in 1890.

6. The French Impressionist painter Édouard Manet (1832–83) is probably best known for *Le déjeuner sur l'herbe* (1863), showing two naked women in a bucolic picnic scene, with two male companions.

7. The Taverne Lorraine and Café d'Harcourt were located on the Boulevard Saint-Michel near to the Sorbonne university at the heart of the Latin Quarter of Paris on the left bank of the Seine. Although frequented by prostitutes and students, the paper and pens available there also made them good places for writers to ply their trade.

8. This remark is commonly associated with Mallarmé's essay 'Crise de vers' from *Divagations*. Although this critical prose poem includes the general statement that 'literature is here undergoing an exquisite and fundamental crisis', crucially it does not contain the words Symons cites. Prince André Poniatowski, however, recorded in his memoirs that Mallarmé told him 'poetry … is the language of crisis', so it is likely that Symons is recalling a remark from one of the poet's Tuesday salons in the Rue de Rome.

9. Verlaine used this phrase about Mallarmé in *Les Poètes maudits* (1884), his collection of essays about contemporary 'cursed' poets. Clarity, says Verlaine, came second to beauty and musicality for Mallarmé.

10. English critic and man of letters Sir Edmund William Gosse

(1849–1928) occupied a central place within the English literary establishment from the 1870s until his death. Gosse knew Mallarmé personally and they corresponded. Symons' own translation from parts of 'Hérodiade' can be found in Appendix 2.

11. These terms are translated from **Wagner**'s 'Lettre sur la musique', an open letter to Fréderic Villot published as an introduction to French prose translations of Wagner's collected libretti in 1860. Reference to 'the most complete work of the poet' echoes his concept of the *Gesamtkunstwerk* (the complete or ideal work of art), articulated in two essays from 1849, 'Art and Revolution' and 'The Artwork of the Future'.

12. Symons quotes from three separate places (slightly out of sequence) in 'L'Action restraint', from 'Quant au Livre' [As for the Book], in *Divagations*.

13. English novelist and poet George Meredith (1828–1909) enjoyed a reputation as a difficult writer. Symons may have in mind his collection of sonnets, *Modern Love* (1862), in which the narrator painfully discovers and confronts his wife's infidelity.

14. Symons alludes here to famous remarks by Mallarmé recorded in an interview with Jules Huret, published in *L'Écho de Paris* during March 1891. Mallarmé approved the text of this article, which quotes him as claiming that 'to *name* an object is to banish three quarters of the poem's enjoyment which derives from a process of gradual revelation: *suggestion*, that is the dream'.

15. The Greek philosopher Aristotle (384–322 BC) described 'the soul' as 'the actuality of a body' in Book II, Chapter 1 of *De Anima*, trans. Hugh Lawson-Tancred (Harmondsworth: Penguin, 1986), p. 158.

16. This paragraph translates several passages from 'Crise de vers', quoting them out of sequence.

17. These are the concluding words of **Walter Pater**'s essay ('A Prince of Court Painters') on the eighteenth-century French painter Antoine Watteau (1684–1721) in *Imaginary Portraits* (London: Macmillan, 1887). This essay was originally published in *Macmillan's Magazine* during 1885.

18. At the start of his essay 'The Poetic Principle', **Edgar Allan Poe** pronounces: 'I hold that a long poem does not exist. I maintain that the phrase, "a long poem," is simply flat contradiction in terms' (*Selected Writings*, ed. David Galloway (Harmondsworth: Penguin, 1967), p. 499).

The Later Huysmans

In the first edition of *The Symbolist Movement in Literature*, the essay 'Huysmans as a Symbolist' consisted mostly of material from 'M. Huysmans' New Novel', *Saturday Review* 85 (12 February 1898), pp. 199–200. For the second edition in 1908, Symons revised this essay, changing the title to 'The Later Huysmans'. He added material from an unsigned review of Huysmans' *De Tout* (1902) in the *Athenaeum* (16 August 1902), p. 215, and from 'M. Huysmans as Mystic', *Saturday Review* 79 (9 March 1895), pp. 312–13, although he had already published this separately in *Studies in Two Literatures* (1897). For the third edition of *The Symbolist Movement in Literature* in 1919, Symons reprinted 'The Later Huysmans' but inserted another essay, 'Joris-Karl Huysmans', before it (see Section II).

Symons' note

Le Drageoir à Épices, 1874; *Marthe, Histoire d'une Fille*, 1876; *Les Soeurs Vatard*, 1879; *Croquis Parisiens*, 1880; *En Ménage*, 1881; *À Vau-l'Eau*, 1882; *L'Art Moderne*, 1883; *À Rebours*, 1884; *Un Dilemme*, 1887; *En Rade*, 1887; *Certains*, 1889; *La Bièvre*, 1890; *Là-Bas*, 1891; *En Route*, 1895; *La Cathédrale*, 1898; *La Bièvre et Saint-Séverin*, 1898; *Pages Catholiques*, 1900; *Sainte Lydwine de Schiedam*, 1901; *De Tout*, 1902; *L'Oblat*, 1903; *Trois Primitifs*, 1905; *Les Foules de Lourdes*, 1906. See also the short story, *Sac au Dos*, in the *Soirées de Medan*, 1880, and the pantomime, *Pierrot Sceptique*, 1881, in collaboration with Léon Hennique. *En Route* was translated into English by Mr. Kegan Paul, in 1896; and *La Cathédrale* by Miss Clara Bell, in 1898.

I have been concerned here only with Huysmans under his latest aspect, but I may preserve, from an article in the *Fortnightly Review* of March 1892, as not perhaps without some psychological interest, a personal impression of the man, which I made at the time when he was writing *Là-Bas*.

'To realise how faithfully and how completely Huysmans has revealed himself in all he has written, it is necessary to know the man. "He gave me the impression of a cat," some interviewer once wrote of him; "courteous, perfectly polite, almost amiable, but all nerves, ready to shoot out his claws at the least word." And, indeed, there is something of his favourite animal about him. The face is grey, wearily alert, with a look of benevolent malice. At first sight it is commonplace, the features are ordinary, one seems to have seen it at the Bourse or the Stock Exchange. But gradually that strange, unvarying expression, that look of benevolent malice, grows upon you, as the influence of the man makes itself felt. I have seen Huysmans in his office: he was formerly an employé ("Sous-chef de bureau à la direction de la sûreté générale') in the Ministry of Foreign Affairs, and a model employé; I have seen him in a café, in various houses; but I always see him in memory as I used to see him at the house of the bizarre Madame X. He leans back on the sofa, rolling a cigarette between his thin, expressive fingers, looking at no one and at nothing, whilst Madame X. moves about with solid vivacity in the midst of her extraordinary menagerie of *bric-à-brac*. The spoils of all the world are there, in that incredibly tiny *salon*; they lie underfoot, they climb up walls, they cling to screens, brackets, and tables; one of your elbows menaces a Japanese toy, the other a Dresden china shepherdess; all the colours of the rainbow clash in a barbaric discord of notes. And in a corner of this fantastic room, Huysmans lies back indifferently on the sofa, with the air of one perfectly resigned to the boredom of life. Something is said by my learned friend who is to write for the new periodical, or perhaps it is the young editor of the new periodical who speaks, or (if that were not impossible) the taciturn Englishman who accompanies me; and Huysmans, without looking up, and without taking the trouble to speak very distinctly, picks up the phrase, transforms it, more likely transpierces it, in a perfectly turned sentence, a phrase of impromptu elaboration. Perhaps it is only a stupid book that some one has mentioned, or a stupid woman; as he speaks, the book looms up before one, becomes monstrous in its dulness, a masterpiece and miracle of imbecility; the unimportant little woman grows into a slow horror before your eyes. It is always the unpleasant aspect of things that he seizes, but the intensity of his revolt from that unpleasantness brings a touch of the sublime into the very expression of his disgust. Every sentence is an epigram, and every epigram slaughters a reputation or an idea. He speaks with an accent as of pained surprise, an amused look of contempt, so profound that it becomes almost pity, for human imbecility.'

Annotations

1. These words were attributed to Huysmans in an article by 'A. Meunier', published in an issue of *Les Hommes d'Aujourd'hui* (1885), dedicated to his life and work. In fact, Huysmans wrote the article himself.

2. Symons was fond of this phrase, which has been attributed to **Théophile Gautier**. He quotes it in the essay on Verlaine, alludes to it in the essay on **Balzac** and quotes it again in the essay on the **Goncourt brothers** (see Section II).

3. Swiss historian, political theorist and novelist Henri-Benjamin de Constant de Rebecque (1767–1830) published his most famous novel, *Adolphe*, in 1816. This semi-autobiographical work tells of

an unhappy love affair between a young man (Adolphe) and an older woman, Ellénore, who is also mistress to an aristocrat. **Stendhal** published his most famous novel *Le Rouge et le noir* in 1830, relating the love affairs and social rise of Julien Sorel, a carpenter's son.

4. English poet and political pamphleteer John Milton (1608–74) published his epic poem *Paradise Lost* in 1667. In twelve books, it retells the biblical story of humankind's fall from grace. Theologian and philosopher Saint Augustine of Hippo (354–430) gave an account of his early (sinful) life and conversion to Christianity in his *Confessions* (c. 398).

5. Claude Monet (1840–1926) is probably the most famous painter associated with Impressionism. Among his best known works are his studies of the effects of atmospheric conditions on our perceptions of the world, achieved through painting series representing the same subjects (Rouen Cathedral, the Thames, haystacks) at different times of day. His late studies on oversized canvases of waterlilies in the ponds at his garden in Giverny, now at the Orangerie Galleries in the centre of Paris, verge upon an absorbing, luminous abstraction.

Maeterlinck as a Mystic

First published as 'Maeterlinck as a Mystic' in *Contemporary Review* (September 1897), pp. 349–54.

Symons' note

Serres Chaudes, 1889; *La Princesse Maleine*, 1890; *Les Aveugles* (*L'Intruse*, *Les Aveugles*), 1890; *L'Ornement des Noces Spirituelles, de Ruysbroeck l'Admirable*, 1891; *Les Sept Princesses*, 1891; *Pelléas et Mélisande*, 1892; *Alladine et Palomides, Intérieur, La Mort de Tintagiles*, 1894; *Annabella de John Ford*, 1895; *Les Disciples à Saïs et les Fragments de Novalis*, 1895; *Le Trésor des Humbles*, 1896; *Douze Chansons*, 1896; *Aglavaine et Sélysette*, 1896; *La Sagesse et la Destinée*, 1898; *Théâtre*, 1901 (3 vols.); *La Vie des Abeilles*, 1901; *Monna Vanna*, 1902; *Le Temple Enseveli*, 1902; *Joyzelle*, 1903; *Le Double Jardin*, 1904; *L'Intelligence des Fleurs*, 1907.

Maeterlinck has had the good or bad fortune to be more promptly, and more violently, praised at the beginning of his career than at all events any other writer of whom I have spoken in this volume. His fame in France was made by a flaming article of M. Octave Mirbeau in the *Figaro* of August 24, 1890. M. Mirbeau greated him as the 'Belgian Shakespeare,' and expressed his opinion of *La Princesse Maleine* by saying 'M. Maeterlinck has given us the greatest work of genius that has been produced in our time, and the most extraordinary and the most naïve too, comparable (dare I say?) superior in beauty to what is most beautiful in Shakespeare … more tragic than *Macbeth*, more extraordinary in thought than *Hamlet*.' Mr. William Archer introduced Maeterlinck to England in an article called 'A Pessimist Playwright' in the *Fortnightly Review*, September 1891. Less enthusiastic than M. Mirbeau, he defined the author of *La Princesse Maleine* as 'a Webster who had read Alfred de Musset.' A freely adapted version of *L'Intruse* was given by Mr. Tree at the Haymarket Theatre, January 27, 1892, and since that time many of Maeterlinck's plays have been acted, without cuts, or with but few cuts, at various London theatres. The earliest of his books to be translated into English were: *The Princess Maleine* (by Gerard Harry) and *The Intruder* (by William Wilson), 1892; *Pelleas and Melisanda* and *The Sightless* (by Laurence Alma-Tadema), 1892; *Ruysbroeck and the Mystics* (by J.T. Stoddart), 1894; *The Treasure of the Humble* (by A. Sutro), 1897; *Aglavaine and Selysette* (by A. Sutro), 1897; *Wisdom and Destiny* (by A. Sutro), 1898; *Alladine and Palomides* (by A. Sutro), *Interior* (by William Archer), and *The Death of Tintagiles* (by A. Sutro), 1899. The later plays and essays have all been translated into English, for the most part simultaneously with their appearance in French.

I have spoken, in this volume, chiefly of Maeterinck's essays, and but little of his plays, and I have said all that I had to say without special reference to the second volume of essays, *La Sagesse et la Destinée*. Like *Le Trésor des Humbles*, that book is a message, a doctrine, even more than it is a piece of literature. It is a treatise on wisdom and happiness, on the search for happiness because it is wisdom, not for wisdom because it is happiness. It is a book of patient and resigned philosophy, a very Flemish philosophy, more resigned than even *Le Trésor des Humbles*. In a sense it seems to aim less high. An ecstatic mysticism has given way to a kind of prudence. Is this coming nearer to the earth really an intellectual ascent or descent? At least it is a divergence, and it probably indicates a divergence in art as well as in meditation. Yet, while it is quite possible to at least indicate Maeterlinck's position as a philosopher, it seems to me premature to attempt to define his position as a dramatist. Interesting as his dramatic work has always been, there is, in the later dramas, so singular an advance in all the qualities that go to make great art, that I find it impossible, at this stage of his development, to treat his dramatic work as in any sense the final expression of a personality. What the next stage of his development may be it is impossible to say. He will not write more beautiful dramas than he has written in *Aglavaine et Sélysette* and in *Pélleas et Mélisande*. But he may, and he probably will, write something which will move the general world more profoundly, touching it more closely, in the manner of the great writers, in whom beauty has not been more beautiful than in writers less great, but has come to men with a more splendid energy.

Was I when I wrote that, anticipating *Monna Vanna*?

Annotations

1. An allusion to the famous beginning of Jaques' speech in *As You Like It* (1599): 'All the world's a stage / And all the men and women merely players' (II.vii.139–40).

2. Inspired by Celtic myth and Wagner's Arthurian opera of infidelity, *Tristan und Isolde*, Maeterlinck's Symbolist drama tells of the adulterous passion between Pelléas and his adoptive step-sister, Mélisande, the wife of King Golaud. They discover their love for each other while meeting by a fountain into which Mélisande accidentally drops her wedding ring.

3. An allusion to line 70 of 'Guinevere', from *The Idylls of the Kings* by **Alfred Tennyson**. This part of Tennyson's Arthurian cycle concerns courtly infidelity and the phrase describes Guinevere's apprehension that her relationship with Sir Lancelot will be uncovered by the evil Modred and revealed to her husband, King Arthur.

4. I have been unable to trace the exact source of this quotation. In Franz Hartmann's *The Life and Doctrines of Jacob Boehme* (Boston: Occult Publishing, 1891), Boehme's answer to the question 'But what is it that prevents man from recognising God within his own self?' is quoted as 'if you keep quiet, and desist from thinking and feeling with your own personal selfhood, then will the eternal hearing, seeing, and speaking become revealed to you, and God will see and hear and perceive through you' (p. 41). Symons probably discussed Boehme with Yeats, who consulted this book for his edition of William Blake in 1893, while they were sharing accommodation at Fountain Court. Yeats quotes the same remark from Boehme in *A Vision*.

5. Maeterlinck remarks how 'étonnant' (astonishing) the simple fact of living is at the start of 'Le Tragique Quotidien' (The Tragedy of the Everyday), an essay in *Le Trésor des humbles*.

6. This phrase is used by the mystic figure of 'Aherne' in 'The Tables of the Law' by **W.B. Yeats** as a simile to describe the creative and destructive effects of 'the beautiful arts'. Yeats' short story was first published in the *Savoy* by Symons in 1896.

Conclusion

1. A passage from 'On Providence' by the Neoplatonic philosopher Plotinus (204–270). The wording matches an eighteenth-century translation by Thomas Taylor, *Five Books of Plotinus* (London: Edward Jeffrey, 1798).

Joris-Karl Huysmans

First published as 'J.K. Huysmans', *Fortnightly Review* (March 1892), pp. 402–14, then reprinted in *Figures of Several Centuries* (1916). Symons quotes from this essay in his notes to Huysmans in the first two editions of *The Symbolist Movement in Literature*. He added this essay to the 1919 edition of the book, placing it before 'The Later Huysmans'.

1. The Faubourg St-Germain is an aristocratic district in the seventh arrondissement of Paris on the Left Bank.
2. **Émile Zola**'s dictum that 'a work of art is a corner of creation seen through a temperament' can be found twice in his collection of essays about art and literature, *Mes Haines* (1866), and elsewhere in his correspondence.
3. Havelock Ellis describes his visit to Paris with Symons in 1890 in *My Life* (1939), where he mentions that 'we spent an evening with [Huysmans] in Madame Courrière's tiny salon crammed with small bibelots'. Caroline Louise Victoire Courrière (1852–1916) was a fashionable Parisian literary lady and the lover of the critic and novelist Rémy de Gourmont, who depicted her in fictional form in *Sixtine* (1890) and *Fantôme* (1893).
4. The rue de Sèvres runs south-west through the Left Bank of Paris. Huysmans' parents bought a bookbindery there in the 1850s and in *Les Soeurs Vatard* he describes two characters taking an evening walk past the religious goods shops that line parts of the street.
5. Symons also refers to the annual *Foire du pain d'épice* (Gingerbread Fair) in the twelfth arrondissement in his essay on **Zola** below.
6. French painter Jean-François Raffaëlli (1850–1924) turned towards realism in the 1870s, was adopted by Huysmans and fellow painter Edgar Degas in the 1880s and evolved his own theory of realism, called 'caracterisme', in the 1890s. He is best known for his depictions of Paris street life in *Les Types de Paris* (1889). French painter and illustrator Jean-Louis Forain (1852–1931) moved in Parisian literary and cultural circles, associating with Rimbaud, Verlaine, Manet and Degas. Stylistically he is most strongly associated with Impressionism. He supplied illustrations to Huysmans' works *Marthe* (1876) and *Croquis parisiens* (1880).
7. The Bièvre is a river that flows into the Seine on the Left Bank of Paris. Since the fifteenth century it has been known for high levels of industrial pollution, a consequence of the tanneries and dye-manufactures along its banks. In 1886, Huysmans published an account of the impoverished lives of workers along its course in the Dutch periodical *De Nieuwe Gids*, which he later reprinted as a

pamphlet in its own right, *La Bièvre* (1890).

8. Established in 1869, the Folies Bergère is a music-hall in the ninth arrondissement of Paris, famous for its scantily clad female dancers and their supposedly loose morals.

9. Huysmans praised Belgian poet Théodore Hannon (1851–1916) in *À Rebours* but his work remains relatively obscure. Breton Symbolist poet Tristan Corbière (1845–75) published only one collection, *Les Amours jaunes* (1873), before his premature death. His works were largely overlooked until Verlaine wrote about him in *Les Poètes maudits* (1884). T.S. Eliot thought highly of Corbière and criticised Symons for omitting him from *The Symbolist Movement*.

10. Jan Luyken (1649–1712) belonged to a renowned family of Dutch illustrators. Huysmans' uncle owned a collection of his engravings.

11. Symons quotes extensively here from the description of **Gustave Moreau**'s painting of Salomé in Chapter 6 of *À Rebours*.

12. The central character of Des Esseintes in Huysmans' novel *À Rebours* is based on that of the aristocratic dandy and Symbolist poet Robert de Montesquiou.

13. Belgian printmaker Félicien Rops (1833–98) started his career as a political caricaturist but eventually made a name for himself as an engraver, supplying a frontispiece for Baudelaire's *Les Épaves* (1866).

14. Gilles de Retz, sometimes Gilles de Rais (c. 1404–40), was a soldier, paedophile and sadist who fought alongside Joan of Arc and became a marshal of France until he was executed for heresy and sorcery. He is often identified as the inspiration for Charles Perrault's folktale 'Bluebeard' about an aristocrat who murders his wives.

15. Symons quotes an article pertaining to be an interview with Huysmans by A. Meunier in *Les Hommes d'Aujourd'hui* (1885). In fact, the whole thing was written by Huysmans himself.

16. Symons here translates from comments made by French novelist and critic Léon Bloy (1846–1917) in a review of *À Rebours* for *Le Chat noir* (14 June 1884). Bloy incorporated the same remarks into his posthumous tribute *Sur la tombe de Huysmans* [On Huysmans' Tomb] (1913).

A Note on Zola's Method

This essay was first published in *Studies in Two Literatures* (1897) using material from Symons' unsigned review of Ernest Vizetelly's translation *Doctor Pascal, or Life and Heredity* in the *Athenaeum* (5 August 1893), his unsigned review of Robert Sherard's biography of Zola in the *Athenaeum* (18 November 1893) and the preface to his own translation of Zola, *L'Assommoir* (London: Lutetian Society, 1894). Symons then reprinted it in *Studies in Prose and Verse* (1904) before adding it to the 1919 edition of *The Symbolist Movement in Literature*.

1. The *Foire au pain d'épice* or Gingerbread Fair (now known as the *Foire du Trône*) has been held during Eastertime in the twelfth arrondissement of Paris since 957, when monks were granted leave to sell spiced bread. Over time it transformed into a carnival and funfair. During August 1896, Symons published 'The Gingerbread Fair at Vincennes: A Colour Study' in the fourth issue of the *Savoy* (August 1896). It describes events at the fair over the course of a day, dwelling in particular upon the erotic appeal of female performers used to advertise circus events. In 'Joris-Karl Huysmans', Symons alludes to another literary description of the fair in Huysmans' novel *Les Soeurs Vatard* (1879).

2. Samuel Smiles (1812–1904) first published *Self Help* in 1859; it contains improving stories about the social and financial success of individuals from different walks of life and in different fields of endeavour.

3. Symons incorporated parts of his review of Robert Sherard's *Émile Zola: A Biographical and Critical Study* (1893) into this essay.

4. In fact, as Graham Robb recounts in *Parisians* (London: Picador, 2010), pp. 174–94, Zola had an affair with his servant, Jeanne Rozerot, late in life and fathered two illegitimate children.

Edmond and Jules de Goncourt

For his essay 'The Goncourts' in *Figures of Several Centuries*, Symons stitched together three previously printed articles: 'A Literary Causerie: On Edmond de Goncourt', *Savoy* 5 (1896), pp. 85–87, an obituary – 'M. Edmond de Goncourt', *Athenaeum* (25 July 1896), p. 129, and 'The Goncourts', *Saturday Review* 78 (29 December 1894), pp. 701–702. He then added this to *The Symbolist Movement in Literature* for the 1919 edition.

1. Eighteenth-century French painter Jean-Siméon Chardin (1699-1779) is renowned for his skill at still life and his genre paintings. Neglected after his death, the enthusiasm of the **Goncourt brothers** for the realism of his finely detailed studies helped to recuperate his reputation.

2. A translation from the entry in the **Goncourts**' journal for the end of April, 1874. Symons alludes to the same entry in his essay on 'The Decadent Movement in Literature'.

3. Symons quotes this same remark in his essay on Verlaine and may

allude to it in his essay on **Balzac**. It can be traced, through the **Goncourt brothers**' journals, directly to **Théophile Gautier**, but is also attributed to the character of Masson in their novel *Les Hommes de lettres* [Men of Letters] (1860), later called *Charles Demailly* (1868). As Symons points out, Masson is fairly transparently based upon Gautier.

4.   'For it is with the delicacies of fine literature especially, its gradations of expression, its fine judgment, its pure sense of words, of vocabulary – things, alas! dying out in the English literature of the present, together with the appreciation of them in our literature of the past – that his literary mission is chiefly concerned': from **Walter Pater**'s essay 'Charles Lamb', in *Appreciations* (1889), first published in *The Fortnightly Review* (October 1878).

5.   Symons took hashish in the form of pellets (ingested orally) with **W.B. Yeats** in Paris during December 1896.

Balzac

First published as 'Balzac', *Fortnightly Review* 65 (May 1899), pp. 745–47, then reprinted in *Studies in Prose and Verse* (1904) and added to *The Symbolist Movement in Literature* in 1919.

1.   France's foremost sculptor, Auguste Rodin (1840–1917), laboured for six years over his monument to Balzac, but its imposing mass and fluid forms were so far from the public's taste that it was rejected when it was unveiled in 1897.

2.   Symons may be alluding here to **Gautier**'s remark 'I am a man for whom the visible world exists', which he quotes directly in his essay on Paul Verlaine and in his essay on the **Goncourts**.

3.   *L'Astrée* by Honoré d'Urfé (1567–1625) is a seventeenth-century historical pastoral novel, set in fifth-century Gaul, about love, infidelity and jealousy. The *fabliaux* were short comic narratives, a form which (as Symons indicates) preceded the development of the novel in France.

4.   Pierre Marivaux (1688–1763), Choderlos de Laclos (1741–1803), and Claude-Prosper Jolyot de Crébillon (1707–77) – known as Crébillon *fils* – were all eighteenth-century French novelists, using (as Symons points out) dialogue or epistolary forms for their works.

5.   Denis Diderot (1713–84), Voltaire [François-Marie Arouet] (1694–1778), Jean-Jacques Rousseau (1712–78), and Nicolas-Edmé Restif de la Bretonne (1734–1806) were eighteenth-century French writers and philosophers who turned to fictional forms in order to express some of their ideas. For example, written in 1760 but not published

until 1780, Diderot's *La Religieuse* [The Nun] dramatises the adverse conditions in religious houses and convents; Rousseau's tale of frustrated love *Julie, or La Nouvelle Héloïse* (1761) couches protest against social convention in the form of an epistolary novel.

6. Combining fiction and autobiography, *Liber Amoris* by the English literary critic and essayist William Hazlitt (1778–1830) tells the story of his failed marriage to Sarah Walker and her infidelity through dialogues and letters.

7. Antoine-François Prévost (1697–1763) is best known for *Manon Lescaut* (1731), a short novel describing the unhappy and initially unreciprocated passion of a young aristocrat for a serving girl, but in addition to writing novels, Prévost was also a translator, whose works include a version of Samuel Richardson's *Clarissa – Lettres Anglaises* (1751).

8. *Adolphe* (1816), by the Swiss-French politician and novelist Benjamin Constant (1767–1830), describes the hero's unhappy affair with an older married woman; *René* (1802) by François-René Chateaubriand (1768–1848) describes the lonely life of the title character and his self-imposed exile to avoid an incestuous passion for his sister Amélie; *Corinne ou l'Italie* (1807), by French novelist and thinker Germaine de Staël (1766–1817) recounts the doomed love of poetess Corinne for a Scottish lord. Elements of autobiography have been read into the melancholy presentation of all of these novels, which may explain why Symons labels them as 'confessions'.

9. Suzanne Curchod (1737–94), known by her married name, Madame Necker, hosted a brilliant salon in Paris for writers and politicians. She was also the mother of Madame de Staël. Symons quotes remarks attributed to her by **Balzac** in his preface to the *Comédie humaine*.

10. An encyclopaedic and comprehensive *Natural History* by George-Louis Leclerc, the Comte de Buffon (1707–88), appeared in in thirty-six volumes between 1749 and 1804. He is also known for his 'Discourse on Style', an address given to the Académie française in 1753.

11. In addition to his fragmentary reflections upon aesthetics, the Romantic German philosopher Novalis [Georg Philipp Friedrich Freiherr von Hardenberg] (1772–1801) left behind two unfinished novels and a prose poem at his untimely death. Symons also lists his works among the mystic texts familiar to Maeterlinck in 'The Decadent Movement in Literature', alongside **Jacob Boehme**, Coleridge and the neo-Platonists.

12. **Charles Baudelaire** praised **Balzac**, in passing, as 'this great genius' in a review of the *Exposition universelle* which first appeared in *Le Pays* in 26 May 1855.

13. Portraits by the Spanish painter Diego Velázquez (c. 1599–1660) were highly celebrated across Europe in the seventeenth century for their verisimilitude. The Prado is the Spanish national art gallery in Madrid where Velázquez's best works hang.

14. The prolific Scottish novelist and poet Sir Walter Scott (1771–1832) laboured under debt and the threat of bankruptcy at several points in his life. A severe economic recession in 1825 crippled his publishers Archibald Constable and Co. and the printing company he had established with friends, John Ballantyne & Co., leaving Scott with such great debts that they were not paid off until the realisation of his life insurance and the sale of his copyrights in 1833 after his death.

15. **Balzac** had a number of affairs before his late marriage to the Russian countess Evelyn de Hanska. Symons probably has in mind Balzac's relationship with Laure de Berny, who was twenty-two years older than him and took a motherly interest in his career as a writer.

Prosper Mérimée

This essay was first published as a critical introduction to Lady Mary Loyd's translation of *Columbia and Carmen* (London: William Heinemann, 1901) in Edmund Gosse's 'A Century of French Romance' series. Symons reprinted it in *Studies in Prose and Verse* (1904) and then added it to *The Symbolist Movement in Literature* in 1919.

1. From **Stendhal**'s essay on Mérimée in *Souvenirs d'egotisme*, ed. Casimir Stryienski (written 1832; published 1892).

2. Vézelay Abbey is a Benedictine monastery in the Burgundy region of France. Mérimée wrote to the French Minister of the Interior in 1834 urging him to save this Romanesque masterpiece from dilapidation.

3. Mérimée's *Lettres à une inconnue* was published posthumously in 1874. Purporting to be an impassioned correspondence between himself and an unknown lady between 1841 and 1870, it prompted much speculation about the identity of his correspondent, who turned out to be one Jeanne-Françoise (Jenny) Daquin. A translation was rapidly published in the same year by Richard Stodard as *Letters to an Incognita*.

4. Mérimée's first literary production was the play *Une femme est un diable* [A Woman is a Devil] (1825); Symons quotes here from a description of the character Mariquita by the Inquisitor Antonio.

5. In his essay 'Byron' from *Essays in Criticism, Second Series* (1888), Matthew Arnold enthused: 'When [Byron] warms to his work, when he is inspired, Nature herself seems to take the pen from him

as she took from Wordsworth, and to write for him as she wrote for Wordsworth, though in a different fashion, with her own penetrating simplicity.'

6. In his essay 'Prosper Mérimée', in *Miscellaneous Studies* (1895), **Walter Pater** wrote: 'Comparing that favourite century of the French Renaissance with our own, he notes a decadence of the more energetic passions in the interest of general tranquillity, and perhaps (only perhaps!) of general happiness.' This essay was first delivered as a lecture at Oxford in 1890, which Symons attended, and it was published in the *Fortnightly Review* that year.

7. George Bizet's operatic adaptation of Mérimée's short story 'Carmen' was first performed in March 1875. Bizet died shortly afterwards, ignorant of its success.

8. Breton novelist, dramatist and translator Alain-René Lesage (1668–1747) published his novel *Gil Blas* in instalments between 1715 and 1735. It relates the fictional rise of a Spanish everyman, from humble origins to prime minister of Spain.

9. Mérimée was elected to the the Académie française in March 1844; Symons quotes from the speech given by dramatist and politician Charles-Guillaume Étienne (1778–1845) at his inauguration in 1845.

10. Symons here translates Mérimée's verdict upon **Victor Hugo** and **Gustave Flaubert** from letters sent to Jenny Daquin, dated September 1862 and January 1863, respectively. These letters were published in *Lettres à une inconnue* (discussed above).

Gustave Flaubert

First published as the introduction to J.W. Matthews' translation of *Salammbô*, published by Grant Richards in London in 1901 in the series 'French Novels of the Nineteenth Century' under the editorship of A.R. Waller, this essay was reprinted in *Figures of Several Centuries* (1916) and then again in the 1919 edition of *The Symbolist Movement in Literature*.

1. Here and throughout the essay, Symons quotes **Flaubert**'s defensive reply to a negative review of *Salammbô* by the influential critic Sainte-Beuve, in a letter of 23–24 December 1862.

Théophile Gautier

This essay draws upon an unsigned review of F.C. Sumichrast's translation of the works of **Théophile Gautier** in 24 volumes: 'Gautier in

English', *Saturday Review* (15 February 1902), pp. iii–iv, which Symons partially reprinted in *Studies in Prose and Verse* (1904) before adding it to the 1919 edition of *The Symbolist Movement in Literature*.

1. There are grounds for doubting Symons' confidence that **Gautier** speaks 'for himself' in the passage quoted from this gender-bending novel of cross-dressing and ambiguous sexual identities, since it is taken from chapter nine in which the protagonist, the Chevalier d'Albert, writes to his friend Silvio in an attempt to come to terms with the fact that he has fallen in love with a man. In fact, he is mistaken and the object of his affection, 'Théodore', is the eponymous Mademoiselle de Maupin in disguise.

2. Maurice Maeterlinck (see above) published his account of apiculture, *La Vie des abeilles* [The Life of the Bee], in 1901.

3. Symons translates the fourth line of **Gautier**'s poem 'L'Art' in *Émaux et Camées* (1852), which celebrates the difficulties of poetic form by comparing it with these intractable materials.

4. **Gautier** first published his essay on Leonardo da Vinci in *L'Artiste* in 1858, then reprinted it in *The Gods and Demi-Gods of Painting* (1863), before adding it to his guidebook *Le Musée du Louvre* in 1867.

5. **Baudelaire** dedicated *Les Fleurs du Mal* (1857) to **Gautier** using this phrase ('French literature's perfect magician').

6. Symons translates **Gautier**'s verdict on **Balzac** in his study *Honoré de Balzac* (1858).

Léon Cladel

First published as 'Léon Cladel', *Saturday Review* 102 (1 September 1906), pp. 264–65; Symons reprinted this essay in *Figures of Several Centuries* (1916) and added it to the 1919 edition of *The Symbolist Movement in Literature*.

1. Judith Cladel, *La vie de Léon Cladel: suivie de Léon Cladel en Belgique* (Paris: Alphonse Lemerre, 1905). Symons' hope proved unfounded: I have been unable to find English translations of Cladel's work for this volume, nor does the reception of his work seem to have entered the critical mainstream.

2. Eugene Sandow (1867–1925) was a famous nineteenth-century strongman. As well as performing feats of strength, he published a self-help fitness book, *Strength and How to Obtain It* (1897).

3. American writer Bret Harte (1836–1902) became famous for his stories about mining life in California during the Gold Rush.

4. French novelist and critic Jules Barbey d'Aurevilly (1808–89)

published an article on Cladel, 'Un Rural Écarlate', in *Le Figaro* 4 May 1872 in response to his novel, *La Fête votive*. Cladel wasn't 'a red', d'Aurevilly claimed, but 'a rural scarlet' – a republican who lived in the countryside.

Charles Baudelaire

First published as 'Baudelaire in His Letters', 103 *Saturday Review* (26 January 1907), pp. 107–108, then reprinted in *Figures of Several Centuries* (1916), before it was added to the 1919 edition of *The Symbolist Movement in Literature*. Symons reused parts of this essay as the preface to an edition of his translations of **Baudelaire**'s *Prose and Poetry* in 1927.

1. Symons alludes respectively to *Les Fleurs du Mal* (1857), *Le Spleen de Paris* (1869) and **Baudelaire**'s translations of the *Tales* of **Edgar Allan Poe**.
2. **Baudelaire** wrote about having 'cultivated his hysteria with joy and terror' in his intimate journals, published posthumously as *Mon Coeur mis à nu* [My Heart Stripped Naked] in 1897. In his review of Symons' translations from Baudelaire, T.S. Eliot was particularly exercised by the liberties he felt Symons took when quoting this phrase.
3. The French critic Eugène Crépet (1827–92) published a posthumous edition of **Baudelaire**'s works with some of his letters in 1887. The occasion for Symons' essay seems to have been the publication of the first full edition of Baudelaire's correspondence by the Société du Mercure de France in 1906.

The Decadent Movement in Literature

'The Decadent Movement in Literature' was first published in *Harper's New Monthly Magazine* 87 (November 1893), pp. 858–68. Symons reprinted it with alterations (omitting sections on the British writers, Walter Pater and W.E. Henley) in the *London Quarterly Review* 129 (January 1918) and *Living Age* (20 April 1918) and in his collection of essays *Dramatis Personae* (1923).

1. Created by Baron Haussmann in the 1860s, the Boulevard Saint-Michel runs south through the left bank of Paris from the Pont St Michel to the Jardins de Luxembourg. It is the heart of the student quarter of Paris and its bars and cafés have always been the favourite haunts of aspiring writers.

2. The analogy between modern Decadent writing, contemporary history and periods of decline in Greek and Roman classical history and literature is common. As Symons points out below, it was given prominent exposition in the description of Des Esseintes' literary tastes in Huysmans' *À Rebours* (1884).

3. This passage collapses quotations from two parts of an essay on the German writer E.T.A. Hoffmann by the French Catholic novelist Ernest Hello (1828–85) in *Les Plateaux de la balance* (1880), pp. 288 and 302. The first part of the quotation summarises Hello's response to the nineteenth century; the second part is from his concluding verdict upon Hoffmann.

4. In a preface to the second edition of their poorly received first novel, *En 18...* (1851; 1884), **Edmond de Goncourt** recorded Sainte-Beuve's criticism of their over-ambitious style, that they aimed to 'render "the soul of landscapes"'.

5. From Matthew Arnold's sonnet 'To a Friend' (1849), line 12. Probably addressed to Arthur Clough, this line identifies the Greek dramatist Sophocles as a 'prop' for Arnold's mind.

6. Verlaine makes this comment writing about a reprint of his first volume of poetry, 'Critique des *Poèmes Saturniens*', published in *La Revue d'aujourd'hui* 3 (15 March 1890).

7. The same quotation from the conclusion to **Walter Pater**'s essay on Watteau, 'A Prince of Court Painters', in *Imaginary Portraits* is applied to Mallarmé in *The Symbolist Movement in Literature*.

8. The same phrase from **Catulle Mendès**, *La Legende de Parnasse Contemporain* (1884), is applied to Mallarmé at the start of 'Stéphane Mallarmé' in *The Symbolist Movement*.

9. Throughout his life, Mallarmé referred to 'l'oeuvre', a grand literary 'work', to epitomise his theories on art. On some occasions he would describe his plan to complete this work with a particular poem, such as 'L'Après-midi d'un faune'; on others he would describe 'l'oeuvre' as a project filling up to five volumes and likely to take twenty years to complete. Symons refers to this by alluding to a short story by **Balzac** about an artist who spends his lifetime re-working his exemplary masterpiece in a search for perfection before this impossible pursuit drives him mad.

10. As Symons' remarks indicate, Henri de Regnier (1864–1936) was a Symbolist poet who experimented with a mixture of *vers libre* and traditional forms. Contrary to Symons' judgment, some critics have described him as the foremost French poet of the early twentieth century, and he was elected to the Académie française in 1911.

11. French novelist and poet Édouard Dujardin (1861–1949) played an important role in the development of Symbolism through his

editorship of *La Revue wagnérienne* and as drama critic for *La Revue independent*. Symons' description of a 'dramatic poem in several parts' may refer to *La Légende d'Antonia*, a trilogy based in part upon **Wagner**'s *Parsifal*. Dujardin subsequently became famous for inventing the 'interior monologue' in his novel *Les Lauriers sont coupés* (1888), which James Joyce credited as a source for *Ulysses*.

12. The author of a Symbolist manifesto, published in *Le Figaro* on 18 September 1888, Jean Moréas [Iannis Papadiamantopoulous] (1856–1910) had already founded an alternative 'École Romane' by 1891, the same year he published his collection of poems, *Le Pèlerin passionné*. This inconstancy may explain some of the disdain Symons expresses towards him here.

13. From Prospero's speech in Act IV Scene 1 of *The Tempest*: 'We are such stuff / As dreams are made on; and our little life / Is rounded with a sleep.'

14. An allusion to these same words from line 70 of 'Guinevere', from *The Idylls of the Kings* by **Tennyson**, can be found in the essay on Maeterlinck in *The Symbolist Movement*.

15. From Part I Section III of **Tennyson**'s *Maud* (1855); the speaker describes the vision of Maud's face which interrupts his sleep as 'luminous, gemlike, ghostlike, deathlike'.

16. The central character of Des Esseintes in Huysmans' novel *À Rebours* is based upon that of the aristocratic dandy and Symbolist poet Robert de Montesquiou.

17. Roman politician in the court of Nero, Gaius Petronius (c. 27–66) wrote one of the earliest surviving precursors to the novel, *The Satyricon*. Stylistically, it mixes classical Latin with more specialised and demotic forms of vocabulary in a manner supposed to be characteristic of this 'decadent' period of Latin literature. Roman poet and philosopher Apuleius (c. 125–c. 170) is best known for his comic novel *The Golden Ass*. His writing is also full of unusual diction, combining poetic and archaic words with apparent neologisms.

18. As Symons points out, both **Gustave Moreau** and **Odilon Redon** feature in chapter six of Huysmans' *À Rebours*, which contains an elaborate description of Moreau's painting *Salome Dancing before Herod*. Huysmans' protagonist Des Esseintes also collects Redon's curious and slightly fantastic works inspired by the stories of **Edgar Allan Poe**. Symons compares Moreau with the English painter and designer Sir Edward Burne-Jones (1833–98), who was closely associated with the Pre-Raphaelite Brotherhood and tended to favour subjects from medieval literature and Arthurian legend.

19. Dutch novelist Louis Couperus (1863–1923) became well known in the English-speaking world through the translations of Alexander

Teixera de Mattos, whose version of *Ecstasy: A Study of Happiness* was published in 1897. In his introduction to this translation, John Gray describes Sensitivism as characterised by 'exact observation' and a commitment to representing 'exactly' what an observer sees, 'not what his intellect, going upon his past experience, would tell him he saw'. The novel concerns a passionate but unconsummated affair between two members of Dutch high society.

20. Sicilian novelist, critic and dramatist Luigi Capuana (1839–1915) was the leading proponent of 'verismo' – the Italian equivalent of **Naturalism**. His novel *Giacinta* (1879, revised 1886) is a study in 'moral pathology' depicting the arduous life of a young countess, forced to act outside the bounds of conventional marriage after a sexual scandal in her youth.

21. The early novels of Spanish writer Emila Pardo-Bazan (1851–1921), such as *Insolación* [Sunstroke] (1889) or her best-known novel *Los Pazos de Ulloa* [The House of Ulloa] (1886), are clearly influenced by the **Naturalism** of **Émile Zola**, in whose defence she wrote in her essay 'La cuestión palpitante' [The Burning Question]. She is now widely recognised as an early feminist.

22. In **Henrik Ibsen**'s play *Hedda Gabler* (1890) the headstrong eponymous female lead returns to her home town after her loveless marriage to an aspiring academic, George Tesman. A moral, sexual and intellectual tangle ensues between Hedda, Tesman and his academic rival Eilert Lövborg, which culminates in Hedda's death by suicide.

    In *The Master Builder* (1892) the central character, Bygmester Solness, repeatedly expresses the concern that he will be overtaken by a 'younger generation' knocking at his door; Symons quotes the advice given him by his young love interest, Hilde, that he should open the door when they do. The play was first translated into English by William Archer and Edmund Gosse in 1893.

23. Francis Bacon observes that 'there is no excellent beauty that hath not some strangeness in the proportion' in his essay 'Of Beauty', in his *Essays* (1625).

24. The subtitle of **Walter Pater**'s *Marius the Epicurean* (1885) is 'his sensations and ideas'. It is a historical novel, about a young Roman boy growing up in the century after Christ's death.

25. In his poem 'Before', in the collection *In Hospital*, Henley describes the feelings of a patient immediately prior to an operation, as he anticipates 'the thick, sweet mystery of chloroform, / the drunken dark, the little death-in-life' (lines 3–4).

Glossary

Balzac, Honoré de (1799–1850), prolific French novelist who wrote over 90 novels and short stories between 1829 and 1840. Balzac turned to literature having trained as a lawyer in the 1830s; during the 1840s he evolved an ambitious project of thematically linked novels, with recurring characters, the *Comédie humaine*. Although Balzac's human comedy aimed to take in 'scenes' from across French society ('provincial life', 'political life' etc.), his most famous novels are probably those depicting life in Paris, such as *Le Père Goriot* (1835) and *La Cousine Bette* (1847) and *Illusions perdues* (1837–1843). Balzac's writings are **realist** in style and focus on the materialism of the French middle classes in the years after the French revolution.

Baudelaire, Charles (1821–67), one of the pre-eminent poets of French literature. His collection of poems *Les Fleurs du mal* (1857) contains his most famous work, but his essays on art (particularly 'The Painter of Modern Life') have been highly influential, as have his prose poems and his translations from the American author **Edgar Allan Poe**. The world of Baudelaire's poetry revels in sensual experience while revolting from its corruption. Symons translated a great deal of Baudelaire's prose and poetry in the early years of the twentieth century, but his efforts were later excoriated by T.S. Eliot as 'fumbled'.

Boehme, Jacob (1575–1624), German shoemaker turned mystic visionary and author of books on theology, philosophy and cosmology. His best known works are *Mysterium Magnum* (The Great Mystery) (1623), *Aurora* (1612) and *De rerum signatura* (1622), in which he maintained that 'the whole outward visible world with all its being is a signature, or figure of the inward spiritual world' (Ch. IX).

D'Annunzio, Gabriele (1863–1938), charismatic Italian novelist, playwright, poet and politician. D'Annunzio published his first collection of poetry, *Primo vere*, in 1879, aged 16. Among his most famous works is his novel *Il Fuoco* (1900), which alludes to his affair with the actress Eleonora Duse between 1895 and 1898. D'Annunzio's novel *Il Piacere* (1889) has been compared to J.-K. Huysmans' notorious novel of **Decadence**, *À Rebours* (1884), in form and content, although some critics maintain that his work displays sufficient interest in transcendent concerns to count as Symbolist. Symons met D'Annunzio (and Duse) in Paris during 1896 and translated several of his works, including *The Dead City* (1900), *La Gioconda* (1901) and *Francesca da Rimini* (1902).

Decadence. While Decadence was an important influence on literature across Europe at the close of the nineteeenth century, it is worth noting that different groups of writers in different countries came to align themselves in different ways with the term. In France, *le décadence* is traced back to literary expressions of discontent with the bourgeois consensus after the suppression of the Paris commune in 1871. However, it soon became associated with the poetry of Verlaine and the literary style of Huysmans, the **Goncourt** brothers and Mallarmé, modelled in part upon the syntax and exotic vocabulary of late Latin literature. Their work came to express a rejection of the philosophy and aesthetics of **Positivism** and **Naturalism**. In this respect, Decadence is a clear precursor of and influence on Symbolism.

In England during the 1880s and 1890s, the term came to be inseparable from a group of writers associated with the *Yellow Book* magazine: Oscar Wilde, Aubrey Beardsley, and Arthur Symons himself, who wrote 'The Decadent Movement in Literature' (see Appendix 1). See the introduction for a discussion of this problematic term in relation to Symons' conception of the Symbolist movement.

De Quincey, Thomas (1785–1859), English journalist and author of *Confessions of an Opium Eater* (1822), an account of his own experiences with and addiction to opium. De Quincey emphasises the transformation of his experiences into symbolic and revealing visionary forms under the influence of the drug, although the euphoric start to the book shades into nightmare.

Flaubert, Gustave (1821–80), French novelist. Born into a medical family in Rouen, Flaubert was forced to abandon public life because of a series of epileptic fits in 1844. Retreating to his family's home in Le Croisset, Flaubert became the most gifted stylist in French writing of the nineteenth century. Flaubert did not live in seclusion, however, travelling twice to Egypt and the Middle East, regularly visiting Paris from the 1860s onwards to keep in touch with literary life and conducting an affair with female author Louise Colet during the 1840s. His letters to Colet are a lesson in passion and commitment to precision in style and imaginative literature.

Flaubert is best known for his tale of provincial adultery, *Madame Bovary* (1857), and *L'Éducation sentimentale* (1869), a partially autobiographical novel of a young student's experience in Paris. The last work he published during his lifetime, *Trois contes* (1877), is a collection of exquisitely written short stories.

Free verse – see **vers libre**.

Gautier, Théophile (1811–72), French poet, novelist and critic at the heart of the literary and journalistic scene in Paris during the mid-nineteenth century. Friend and contemporary to **Baudelaire** and Nerval, the preface to his novel *Mademoiselle de Maupin*, with its rejection of political and didactic writing in favour of aesthetic formal values, supplied the **Parnassian** movement with its slogan of 'L'Art pour l'art' ('art for art's sake'). The novel itself contains a story of cross-dressing desire and sexual passion that challenged contemporary morals. Gautier also achieved popularity in France with *Le Capitaine Fracasse* (1863), a historical adventure story set in the seventeenth century.

His collection of exquisitely sculpted quatrains, *Émaux et camées* (1852), would later inspire T.S. Eliot and Ezra Pound to experiment with the constraints of the same form.

Goethe, Johann Wolfgang von (1749–1832), foremost German Romantic writer, best known for his epic drama *Faust*, but also known throughout Europe for novels such as *The Sorrows of Young Werther* (1774) – the book which made him a celebrity at the age of 25. Other works include his travel narrative *Italian Journeys* (1816), the novel *Elective Affinities* (1809), and a confessional work, *Dichtung und Wahrheit* ('Poetry and Truth'), published in the year of his death.

Goncourt, Jules de (1830–70) **and Edmond de** (1822–96), French novelists and men of letters, most famous for their *Journal* (1887–96), recording in biographical and anecdotal form their view of contemporary artistic and literary life in Paris between 1851 and 1896. During the Second Empire they attended the salon of Princess Mathilde regularly, as well as the 'dîners Magny' where they met with **Flaubert**, **Gautier** and **Taine**, among others.

Towards the end of his life (after his brother's death) Edmond de Goncourt held his own literary salons and left money towards the founding of the Académie Goncourt and the prestigious literary prize, le prix Goncourt.

Together the brothers wrote a series of novels, *Germinie Lacerteux* (1864), *Manette Salomon* (1867) and *Madame Gervaisais* (1869); and Edmond authored his own novels, including *La Fille Élisa* (1877), *La Faustin* (1882) and *Chérie* (1884). Their works are characterised by an emphasis on psychological and sexual realism, associated with the **Naturalism** of **Émile Zola**.

Symons refers to the Goncourts in 'The Decadent Movement in Literature' and advertisements for the book that was to become *The*

Symbolist Movement indicate that he planned to include them in the volume, but this did not happen until the expanded edition of 1919 (see Section II).

Heine, Heinrich (1797–1856), German poet best known for the short lyrics set to music by Robert Schumann and Franz Schubert as *Lieder*. Heine spent much of his life exiled in Paris, where his works were translated by Gerard de Nerval, amongst others. His essay 'The Romantic School' (1836) helped define our current understanding of that movement.

Heredia, José-María de (1842–1905), Cuban-born French poet on the editorial board of *Le Parnasse contemporain*. He was strongly influenced by **Leconte de Lisle** and attempted the systematic application of **Parnassian** principles to his poetry, working in the sonnet form from the 1860s. His best known work is the collection of sonnets *Les Trophées* (1893), published shortly before his election to the Académie française.

Hugo, Victor (1802–85), French poet, dramatist and novelist. One of the most famous writers in the nineteenth century and leader of the Romantic movement in French literature, he is probably best known today for two novels, *The Hunchback of Notre Dame* (1831) and *Les Misérables* (1862). However, collections of poems such as *Feuilles d'Automne* (1831), *Les Châtiments* (1856) and *Les Contemplations* (1856) have also received widespread acclaim.

Ibsen, Henrik (1828–1906), Norwegian dramatist, renowned for his 'problem plays' that present key social and sexual topics in explicit, realistic terms. His plays are sometimes discussed in terms of **Naturalism**. These include *A Doll's House* (1880) which addresses marriage and the roles imposed upon men and women within it by social convention, and *The Wild Duck* (1884), which deals with social morals, sexual guilt and inheritance. Ibsen's work was espoused in England (where it caused controversy) by George Bernard Shaw, especially in his pamphlet *The Quintessence of Ibsenism* (1891).

The Kabbalah is a Jewish mystic theosophy, medieval in origins, which lays claim to open up scriptures using secret forms of knowledge, derived from a magical understanding of the cosmos. This is arrived at largely through numeric values and mathematical combinations derived from the Hebrew alphabet. For a history of its expansion into a global phenomenon, see Dan Joseph, *Kabbalah: A Very Short History* (Oxford: Oxford University Press, 2006).

Kahn, Gustave (1859–1936), French poet and editor who played a crucial role in *le Symbolisme* in France, publishing work by Rimbaud and Laforgue (with whom he was friends) in the magazine *Vogue*. He was a keen exponent of **vers libre** and even claimed to have invented the term, including a preface defending it in his first collection of poems in 1897.

Leconte de Lisle, Charles Marie René (1818–94), French poet and a leading figure in the **Parnassian** movement in Paris, which found his commitment to impersonal aesthetic values exemplary. Leconte de Lisle's major works are *Poèmes antiques* (1852), *Poèmes barbares* (1862) and *Poèmes tragiques* (1884).

Mendès, Catulle (1841–1919), French poet and critic, central figure in the **Parnassian** movement and co-founder of *Le Parnasse Contemporain*. Mendès married the historical novelist and poet Judith Gautier, daughter of **Théophile Gautier**, with whom he was friends.

Moreau, Gustave (1826–98), French painter closely associated with both **Decadence** and Symbolism. His works tend to combine mythic or classical topics with a style that mixed precise details and closely worked colours with nebulous, suggestive passages. J.-K. Huysmans singled out his work for praise in *À Rebours*, he was awarded the Légion d'Honneur in 1883 and became a professor at the École des Beaux-Arts in Paris in 1892.

Naturalism. The literary movement most closely associated with the work of **Émile Zola**, who used the term in the 1860s to describe his own attempts to surpass the literature of **Realism**. Naturalist texts draw on **Positivism** in their emphasis on the determining importance of science and fact. Zola conceived of fiction as a form of experiment intended to expose the workings of nature. Huysmans was also closely associated with Naturalism before rejecting it in favour of **Decadence**; he was one contributor (along with Zola, Guy de Maupassant, and others) to *Les Soirées de Medan* (1880), a collection of short stories, intended as a manifesto for the movement.

Parnasse. The Parnassians were a group of poets and writers largely organised by the efforts of **Catulle Mendès**, and taking inspiration from the poetic example of **Leconte de Lisle**. They rejected Romantic theories of inspiration and didactic poetry in favour of an emphasis on formal values, adopting **Théophile Gautie**r's 'art for art's sake' as their rallying cry. Members included **José-Maria de Heredia** and Théodore de Banville, whose treatise on French verse gave voice to their views on rhyme. They published three volumes of verse, *Le Parnasse contemporain*, in 1866, 1871 and 1876, which included work by Verlaine, Mallarmé, Rimbaud and **Baudelaire**. Many of the poets associated with 'Le Parnasse' would later become associated with Symbolism.

Pater, Walter (1839–94), fellow of Brasenose College, Oxford and foremost writer of Decadent critical prose. Pater is best known for the highly crafted essays on art and culture in *The Renaissance* and his carefully wrought historical novel, *Marius the Epicurean* (1885). His critical writings drew accusations of scandal for their hedonistic celebration of fleeting moments of appreciation. His writings were a sustained influence upon Symons from early in his career (see Introduction).

Poe, Edgar Allan (1809–49), American author, best known for his gothic and macabre short stories. Translated into French and popularised by **Baudelaire**, Poe's works became highly influential upon French literature in the second half of the nineteenth century, inspiring the short stories of Villiers de l'Isle Adam and prompting Mallarmé to write his elegy 'Le tombeau d'Edgar Poe' in 1876.

Positivism. System of thought most strongly associated with the work of French philosopher and social theorist Auguste Comte (1798–1857). In *Cours de philosophie positive* (1830–42), Comte outlined a history of human thought, beginning with an emphasis on the role of supernatural forces, progressing to the development of metaphysical or abstract concepts, before culminating in scientific or positive methods, where knowledge is derived from material, observable phenomena. His confidence in the triumph of rationalism and experimental scientific methods was highly influential for thinkers such as John Stuart Mill and **Hippolyte Taine**.

Rabelais, François (d. 1553), medieval French writer and humanist scholar, most famous for the satirical, bawdy and fantastic sequence of comic novels known as *Pantagruel* and *Gargantua* (1534–64).

Realism. The Realist movement in France is strongly associated with the painter Gustave Courbet (1819–77), who chose to exhibit his paintings (particularly *The Burial at Ornans* (1850)) under the title of 'Le Réalisme' when they were rejected by the official salons in 1855. Art critic and novelist 'Champfleury' (Jules Husson, 1821–89) wrote a catalogue for this exhibition, followed by a collection of articles, *Le Réalisme* (1857). The debate provoked Louis Duranty to establish a journal of the same title, which produced six issues in 1856–57.

In literary terms, realism has become associated with an emphasis on the working class, on sexual frankness and on the material circumstances of characters. It has been closely linked with the novels of **Honoré de Balzac**, **Stendhal**, **Gustave Flaubert** and **Émile Zola**, although the latter evolved his own species of realism, **Naturalism**.

Redon, Odilon (1840–1916), French painter and print-maker, known for his mysterious and fantastic charcoal drawings and lithographs. During the 1880s the dreamy evocative forms in Redon's works became associated with the Symbolist movement in France. Symons met Redon in 1890 and compared him to the self-taught British artist and mystic William Blake (1757–1827) in his article 'A French Blake: Odilon Redon' for the short-lived journal *Art Review* (July 1890).

Rossetti, Dante Gabriel (1828–82), English poet and painter, son of Italian parents and brother to the poet Christina. Rossetti is most famous as a member of the Pre-Raphaelite Brotherhood (PRB). His best known poems include the sonnet sequence *The House of Life* (1868) and his best known paintings include *The Blessed Damozel* (1875–78).

Rossetti and the other members of the PRB came under attack from Robert Buchanan for their sensual values in an article titled 'The Fleshly School of Poetry', published under the pseudonym 'Thomas Maitland' in the *Contemporary Review* in 1871. Although Rossetti proclaimed his indifference, his response to these criticisms has been linked to a period of mental breakdown. Symons' essay 'The Decadent Movement in Literature' has been construed as a defence of literature in the face of similar criticisms.

Stendhal, pseudonym of Henri Beyle (1783–1842), French novelist, journalist and autobiographer. Stendhal is best known for *Le Rouge et le noir* (1830), depicting the rise of Julien Sorel, a carpenter's son from the provinces, through the echelons of French society (until his fall), and *La Chartreuse de Parme* (1839), a novel of contemporary historical events. His works combine a realistic style with social and political satire. *La Vie de Henry Brulard* (wr. 1835) turns his piquant wit upon his own early life and experiences in the Napoleonic wars in Italy.

Swedenborg, Emanuel (1688–1772), Swedish scientist turned philosopher and mystic. Inspired by dreams and visions, in *Heaven and Hell* (1758) and other works he developed a theory of correspondences, according to which the physical world, including the body, is a symbol of the spiritual world and spiritual values. Swedenborg travelled extensively in England and died in London. A group of his followers there formed the New Church (poet William Blake was a member for a while) and in 1810 formed the Swedenborg Society to translate and propagate his works. As well as Nerval and Blake, Swedenborg's writings were an important influence on **W.B. Yeats**, **Charles Baudelaire** and **Honoré de Balzac**, amongst others.

Swift, Jonathan (1667–1745), Irish-born clergyman and writer, best known for his satirical fantasy in the form of a travel narrative, *Gulliver's Travels* (1726).

Taine, Hippolyte (1823–93), French critic and historian, strongly interested in English writers and philosophers and closely associated with the philosophy of positivism. His *Histoire de la littérature anglaise* (1864) sets out his belief in the determining influence of material contexts upon society (defined as 'race, milieu, moment') and outlines his method of identifying the dominant characteristic (or 'faculté maîtresse') in works of art. He was a leading critic of his generation, who boldly championed **Balzac** and **Stendhal** and influenced the **Naturalism** of **Émile Zola**.

Tennyson, Alfred (1802–92), English poet, most famous for his celebration of English defeat during the Crimean War in 'The Charge of the Light Brigade' (1854). In 1833, following the death of his close friend Arthur Hallam, Tennyson began the long confessional elegy *In Memoriam*, although it was not published until 1850. He acquired fame and popularity with his allegorical study *The Princess* (1847) and his re-workings of Arthurian stories from Malory in verse form, *Idylls of the King* (1859); in 1850 he was appointed poet laureate. Although he has a reputation for conservatism, Tennyson's output includes challenging works, such as his dramatic monologue *Maud* (1855), with its tale of erotic obsession and madness.

Vers libre (or free verse) breaks with key conventions of French versification, such as the use of a medial caesura or the alternation of masculine and feminine end-rhymes. Its development is closely associated with the poetry of Rimbaud, who experimented with abandoning rhyme in favour of assonance, although Verlaine also experimented with the use of lines containing an odd number of syllables (*vers impairs*), breaking with French traditions of symmetrical rhythmic patterning. Their Symbolist successors, such as Laforgue and Mallarmé, are credited with taking these innovations and freedoms even further.

Wagner, Richard (1813–83), German composer, known for his operatic re-tellings of Old German and Norse myths, most notably in *Tristan und Isolde* (wr. 1857–59; perf. 1865) and his *Ring* cycle of four operas: *Das Rheingold* (1869), *Die Walküre* (1870), *Siegfried* (1876) and *Götterdämmerung* (1876). Wagner's emphasis upon the symbolic and narrative value of recurring musical themes, or *leitmotifs*, was a strong influence on nineteenth-century French poets and writers. One of the earliest Symbolist journals in France was the *Revue wagnérienne* founded by Téodor de Wyzewa and Édouard Dujardin in 1885.

Whistler, James McNeill (1834–1901), American painter and writer associated with Impressionism, aestheticism and the Decadent movement. He worked and travelled through Europe, but spent a considerable part of his life in London where he moved in the same literary circles as Oscar Wilde. He is most famous for *Arrangement in Grey and Black: Portrait of the Painter's Mother* (1872).

Yeats, William Butler (1865–1939), Irish poet, dramatist and politician. As founder of the Abbey Theatre in Dublin he was a key figure in the Literary Revival in Ireland at the end of the nineteenth century. Symons and Yeats met through the Rhymers' Club in London during 1890; they later travelled to Paris together in 1896 and even shared lodgings at Fountaincourt together. As editor of the *Savoy* magazine (1896), Symons was instrumental in publishing work by Yeats. The two men corresponded closely during the period in which Symons edited *The Symbolist Movement in Literature*. For a discussion of the mutual channels of influence between Symons and Yeats see the Introduction. Yeats' conduct during the period of Symons' mental breakdown in 1908–10 was, however, a source of discord between the men and they never met after that period.

Yeats' disillusionment with the politics and personnel of Irish culture is linked to the emergence in his work of a direct and confrontational voice. While he never abandoned Irish themes, he became known during the twentieth century as a mythopoeic poet of modernism and influenced almost every poet after him.

Following Irish independence in 1922, he became a senator and founder of the Irish academy.

Zola, Émile (1840–1902), French novelist, best known for the Rougon-Macquart series of novels, which attempts to depict French life in the nineteenth century across classes and material conditions. Zola was very much influenced by **Positivism** and theorised his practice as a novelist in *Le Roman Experimental* (1880), arguing that the novel should start from facts and material data. This essay became the ground of French **Naturalism**. His most famous novels are *Germinal* (1885), about a French mining community, and *Thérèse Raquin* (1867), about the guilty experiences of a dressmaker and her lover after the murder of her husband.

Zola's novels became controversial in England when Henry Vizetelly was successfully prosecuted for obscenity in 1888 for his translation of Zola's *La Terre*. Symons translated *L'Assommoir* by Zola in 1894, published Havelock Ellis's defence of Zola in the first issue of the *Savoy* in 1896 and added 'A Note on the Method of Zola' to the second American edition of *The Symbolist Movement* in 1919 (see Appendix 2).

Bibliography and Further Reading

General

Anna Balakian, ed., *The Symbolist Movement in the Literature of Europe* (Budapest: Akademia Kiado, 1984)

Karl Beckson, *Arthur Symons: A Life* (Oxford: Clarendon Press, 1987)

—, *London in the 1890s: A Cultural History* (New York: W.W. Norton, 1992)

Karl Beckson, Ian Fletcher, Lawrence W. Markert and John Stokes, *Arthur Symons: A Bibliography* (Greensboro: ELT Press, 1990)

Margaret Beetham, 'Towards a Theory of the Periodical as a Publishing Genre', in *Investigating Victorian Journalism*, ed. Laurel Brake, Aled Jones and Lionel Madden (London: Macmillan, 1990), pp. 19–32

Laurel Brake, *Subjugated Knowledges: Journalism, Gender and Literature in the Nineteenth Century* (New York: New York University Press, 1994)

—, *Print in Transition, 1850–1910: Studies in Media and Book History* (Basingstoke: Palgrave, 2001)

J.W. Burrow, *The Crisis of Reason: European Thought 1848–1914* (New Haven: Yale University Press, 2000)

Jason Camlot, *Style and the Nineteenth-Century British Critic: Sincere Mannerisms* (Aldershot: Ashgate, 2008)

G.A. Cevasco, *The Breviary of the Decadence: J.-K. Huysmans' À Rebours and English Literature* (New York: AMS Press, 2001)

Charles Chadwick, *Symbolism* (London: Methuen, 1971)

Olive Classe, ed., *Encyclopaedia of Literary Translation in English*, 2 vols. (London: Fitzroy Dearborn, 2000)

Patricia Clements, *Baudelaire and the English Tradition* (Princeton: Princeton University Press, 1985)

Anne Margaret Daniel, 'Arthur Symons and *The Savoy*', *The Literary Imagination* 7:2 (2005): 165–93

Linda Dowling, *Language and Decadence in the Victorian Fin de Siècle* (Princeton: Princeton University Press, 1986)

Richard Ellmann, 'Discovering Symbolism', in *Golden Codgers: Biographical Speculations* (Oxford: Oxford University Press, 1960), pp. 101–12

Ian Fletcher, ed., *Decadence and the 1890s* (London: Edward Arnold, 1979)

C. Jay Fox, Carol Simpson Stern and Robert S. Means, eds., *Arthur*

Symons, Critic among Critics: An Annotated Bibliography (Greensboro: ELT, 2007)

Tom Gibbons, *Rooms in the Darwin Hotel: Studies in English Literary Criticism and Ideas, 1880–1920* (Nedlands: University of Western Australia Press, 1973)

Sebastian Hayes, *Arthur Symons: Leading Poet of the English Decadence* (Shaftesbury: Brimstone Press, 2007)

Jennifer Higgins, *English Responses to French Poetry 1880–1940: Translation and Mediation* (London: Legenda, 2011)

Graham Hough, *The Last Romantics* (London: Duckworth, 1949)

Holbrook Jackson, *The Eighteen Nineties: A Review of Art and Ideas at the Close of the Nineteenth Century* (1913; repr. New York: Knopf, 1922)

Frank Kermode, *Romantic Image* (London: Routledge and Kegan Paul, 1957)

A.G. Lehmann, *The Symbolist Aesthetic in France 1885–1895* (Oxford: Basil Blackwell, 1950)

Gail Marshall, ed., *The Cambridge Companion to the Fin de Siècle* (Cambridge: Cambridge University Press, 2002)

Patrick McGuinness, ed., *Symbolism, Decadence and the Fin de Siècle* (Exeter: University of Exeter Press, 2000)

Bruce Morris, 'Mallarmé's Letters to Arthur Symons: Origins of the Symbolist Movement', *English Literature in Transition, 1880–1920*, 28:4 (1985): 346–53

—, 'Elaborate Form: Symons, Yeats and Mallarmé', *Yeats: An Annual of Critical Studies* 4 (1986): 99–120

Murray Pittock, *Spectrum of Decadence: The Literature of the 1890s* (London: Routledge, 1993)

Mario Praz, *The Romantic Agony* (Oxford: Oxford University Press, 1951)

Lynn Pykett, 'Reading the Periodical Press: Text and Context', *Victorian Periodicals Review* 22 (1989): 100–108

Peter Quennel, *Baudelaire and the Symbolists: Five Essays* (London: Chatto & Windus, 1929)

Andrew Radford and Victoria Reid, eds., *Channel Packets: Franco-British Cultural Exchanges 1880–1940* (Basingstoke: Palgrave Macmillan, 2012)

Clive Scott, *Channel Crossings: French and English Poetry in Dialogue 1550–2000* (Oxford: Legenda, 2002)

Enid Starkie, *From Gautier to Eliot: The Influence of France on English Literature 1851–1939* (London: Hutchinson, 1960)

Ruth Temple, *The Critic's Alchemy: A Study of the Introduction of French Symbolism into England* (New York: Twayne, 1953)

R.K.R. Thornton, *The Decadent Dilemma* (London: Edward Arnold, 1983)

Robert and Isabelle Tombs, *That Sweet Enemy: The French and the British from the Sun King to the Present* (London: Heinemann, 2006)

David Weir, *Decadence and the Making of Modernism* (Amherst: University of Massachusetts Press, 1995)

Edmund Wilson, *Axel's Castle* (New York: Scribner, 1931)

Villiers de l'Isle Adam (1838–89)

English translations

Robert Martin Adams, *Tomorrow's Eve* (Urbana: University of Illinois Press, 1982)

Robert Baldick, *Cruel Tales,* intr. & ed. by A.W. Raitt (Oxford: Oxford University Press, 1985)

H.P.R. Finberg, *Axel*, pref. by W.B. Yeats (London: Jarrolds, 1925)

Marilyn Gaddis Rose, *Axel* (Dublin: Dolmen Press, 1970)

—, *Eve of the Future Eden* (Lawrence, Kansas: Coronado Press, 1981)

June Guicharnard, *Axel* (Englewood Cliffs, NJ: Prentice Hall, 1970)

Hamish Miles, *Sardonic Tales* (London: Knopf, 1927)

Brian Stableford, *The Scaffold and Other Cruel Tales* (Encino: Black Coat, 2004)

—, *The Vampire Soul and Other Sardonic Tales* (Encino: Black Coat, 2004)

Arthur Symons, *Queen Ysabeau* (Chicago: Pembroke Press, 1925)

—, *Clare Lenoir* (New York: Boni, 1925)

Suggestions for further reading

Jean-Paul Bourre, *Villiers de L'Isle-Adam: Splendeur et misère* (Paris: Les Belles Lettres, 2002)

A.W. Raitt, *The Life of Villiers de L'Isle-Adam* (Oxford: Clarendon Press, 1981)

Edmund Wilson, *Axel's Castle: A Study in the Imaginative Literature of 1870–1930* (New York: Scribner, 1931)

Honoré de Balzac (1799–1850)

English translations

Donald Adamson, *The Black Sheep* (Harmondsworth: Penguin, 1970)

Anon., *Daddy Goriot; or Unrequited Affection* (London: Ward and Lock, 1860)

Anon., *Eugénie Grandet* (London: Routledge, 1859)

Helen Constantine, *The Wild Ass's Skin* [Le Peau de Chagrin] (Oxford: Oxford University Press, 2012)

Marion Ayton Crawford, *Old Goriot* (Harmondsworth: Penguin, 1951)

—, *Eugenie Grandet* (Harmondsworth: Penguin, 1955)

—, *Cousin Bette* (Harmondsworth: Penguin, 1965)

Ernest Dowson, *La Fille aux yeux d'or* (London: Leonard Smithers, 1896)

John Hawkins, *History of the Grandeur and Downfall of César Birotteau* (London: Saunders, Otley & Co., 1860)

Rayner Heppenstall, *A Harlot High and Low* [Splendeurs et misères d'une courtisane] (Harmondsworth: Penguin, 1970)

Herbert J. Hunt, *Cousin Pons* (Harmondsworth: Penguin, 1968)

—, *Lost Illusions* (Harmondsworth: Penguin, 1971)

—, *The Wild Ass's Skin* [Le Peau de Chagrin] (Harmondsworth: Penguin, 1977)

G.B. Ives, et al., *The Human Comedy, Now for the First Time Completely Translated into English*, 53 vols. (London: Caxton Press, 1895–1900)

A.J. Krailsheimer, *Père Goriot* (Oxford: Oxford University Press, 1991)

Burton Raffel, *Père Goriot* (New York: Norton, 1997)

Kathleen Raine, *Cousin Bette* (London: Hamish Hamilton, 1948)

—, *Lost Illusions* (London: Hamish Hamilton, 1951)

Sylvia Raphael, *Cousin Bette* (Oxford: Oxford University Press, 1992)

—, *Eugénie Grandet* (Oxford: Oxford University Press, 1990)

William Robson, *Balthazar, or Science and Love* (London: Routledge, 1859)

George Saintsbury, ed., *The Human Comedy*, trans. Clara Bell, Ellen Marriage, James Waring and R.S. Scott, 40 vols. (London: Dent, 1895–99)

Wormeley, Katharine Prescott, *Balzac's Novels in English* (London: Routledge, 1886–91)

Suggestions for further reading

M.R. Axelrod, *The Politics of Style in the Fiction of Balzac, Beckett and Cortàzar* (London: Macmillan, 1992)

Michel Butor, 'Balzac and Reality', in *Inventory*, trans. Richard Howard (London: Jonathan Cape, 1970)

Christopher Prendergast, *Balzac: Fiction and Melodrama* (London: Edward Arnold, 1978)

Graham Robb, *Balzac* (London: Picador, 1994)

Michael Tilby, ed., *Balzac* (London: Longman, 1995)

Charles Baudelaire (1821–67)

English translations

Norman Cameron, *My Heart Laid Bare and Other Prose Writings* (London: Weidenfeld and Nicolson, 1950)

Roy Campbell, *Poems of Baudelaire* (London: Harvill, 1952)

P.E. Carret, *Selected Writings on Art and Artists* (Harmondsworth: Penguin,

1972)

Henry Carrington, *Some Translations from Charles Baudelaire* (London: Digby Long, 1894)

George Dillon and Edna St Vincent Millay, *Flowers of Evil* (New York: Harper, 1936)

Christopher Isherwood, *Intimate Journals* (London: Blackamore Press, 1949)

Edward Kaplan, *The Parisian Prowler* (Athens: University of Georgia Press, 1997)

Rosemary Lloyd, *The Prose Poems and La Fanfarlo* (Oxford: Oxford University Press, 1991)

—, *Selected Letters of Charles Baudelaire: The Conquest of Solitude* (Chicago: University of Chicago Press, 1986)

C.F. MacIntyre, *One Hundred Poems from 'Les Fleurs du Mal'* (Berkeley: University of California Press, 1947)

Walter Martin, *The Complete Poems* (Manchester: Carcanet, 1997)

Jonathan Mayne, *The Painter of Modern Life and Other Essays* (London: Phaidon, 1955)

James McGowan, *The Flowers of Evil* (Oxford: Oxford University Press, 1993)

Peter Quennell, *'The Essence of Laughter' and Other Essays* (New York: Meridian Books, 1956)

Joanna Richardson, *Selected Poems: Baudelaire* (Harmondsworth: Penguin, 1975)

Francis Scarfe, *The Poems in Prose, with La Fanfarlo* (London: Anvil Press, 1989)

Lewis Piaget Shanks, *Les Fleurs du Mal* (New York: Holt, 1926)

Richard Herne Shepherd, *Translations from Charles Baudelaire* (London: John Camden Hotten, 1869)

J.C. Squire, *Poems and Baudelaire Flowers* (London: New Age Press, 1909)

Martin Sorrell, *Paris Spleen* (Richmond: Alma Classics, 2010)

F.P. Sturm, *The Poems of Charles Baudelaire* (London: Walter Scott, 1906)

Arthur Symons, *Poems in Prose* (London: Elkin Mathews, 1905)

—, *Les Fleurs du mal, Petits poèmes en prose, Les paradis artificiels* (London: Casanova, 1925)

—, *Charles Baudelaire: Letters to his Mother* (London: John Rodker, 1928)

Suggestions for further reading

Walter Benjamin, *The Writer of Modern Life: Essays on Charles Baudelaire*, trans. Michael Jennings (Cambridge, MA: Harvard University Press, 2006)

Leo Bersani, *Baudelaire and Freud* (Berkeley: University of California Press, 1978)

Richard Burton, *Baudelaire and the Second Republic: Writing and Revolution* (Oxford: Clarendon Press, 1991)

Patricia Clements, *Baudelaire and the English Tradition* (Princeton: Princeton University Press, 1985)

Alison Fairlie, *Baudelaire: 'Les Fleurs du Mal'* (London: Edward Arnold, 1960)

J.A. Hiddleston, *Baudelaire and the Art of Memory* (Oxford: Clarendon Press, 1999)

Rosemary Lloyd, ed., *Cambridge Companion to Baudelaire* (Cambridge: Cambridge University Press, 2006)

Claude Pichois and Jean Ziegler, *Baudelaire*, trans. Graham Robb (London: Hamish Hamilton, 1989)

Christopher Prendergast, *Paris and the Nineteenth Century* (Oxford: Blackwell,1992)

Joanna Richardson, *Baudelaire* (London: John Murray, 1994)

Clive Scott, *Translating Baudelaire* (Exeter: University of Exeter Press, 2000)

Sonya Stephens, *Baudelaire's Prose Poems: The Practice and Politics of Irony* (Oxford: Oxford University Press, 1999)

Gustave Flaubert (1821–80)

English translations

Anon., *Complete Works of Gustave Flaubert*, intr. Ferdinand Brunetière, 10 vols. (London: M. Walter Dunne, 1904)

Robert Baldick, *Sentimental Education* (Harmondsworth: Penguin, 1964)

W. Blaydes, *Madame Bovary*, intr. Henry James (New York: Collier, 1902)

J.S. Chartres, *Salambo* (London and Edinburgh: Vizetelly, 1886)

Paul de Man, *Madame Bovary* (New York: Norton, 1965)

D.F. Hannigan, *The Temptation of Saint Anthony* (London: Nichols, 1895)

—, *Bouvard and Pécuchet* (London: Nichols, 1896)

—, *A Sentimental Education: A Young Man's History*, 2 vols. (London: Nichols, 1898)

Gerard Hopkins, *Madame Bovary: Life in a Country Town* (Oxford: Oxford University Press, 1949)

George Burnham Ives, *Gustave Flaubert: A Simple Heart; The Legend of St Julian the Hospitalier; Herodias*, intr. Frank Thomas Marzials (London: Putnam, 1903)

A.J. Krailsheimer, *Bouvard and Pécuchet* (Harmondsworth: Penguin, 1976)

—, *Salammbo* (Harmondsworth: Penguin, 1977)

—, *Three Tales* (Oxford: Oxford University Press, 1991)

Aimée L. MacKenzie, *The George Sand – Gustave Flaubert Letters* (Chicago:

Academy Chicago, 1979)

Eleanor Marx-Aveling, *Madame Bovary: Provincial Manners* (London and Edinburgh: Vitzetelly, 1886)

E. Powys Mathers, *Salambo* (New York: Rarity Press, 1932)

J.W. Matthews, *Salammbô*, intr. Arthur Symons (New York: Doubleday Page, 1901)

Margaret Mauldon, *Madame Bovary: Provincial Manners* (Oxford: Oxford University Press, 2004)

J. Lewis May, *Madame Bovary: A Story of Provincial Life* (London: Bodley Head, 1928)

Kitty Mrosovsky, *The Temptation of Saint Anthony* (Harmondsworth: Penguin, 1983)

Douglas Parmée, *A Sentimental Education: The Story of a Young Man* (Oxford: Oxford University Press, 1989)

Alan Russell, *Madame Bovary* (Harmondsworth: Penguin, 1950)

M.F. Sheldon, *Salammbô* (New York: United States Book Co., 1885)

Francis Steegmuller, *Madame Bovary: Patterns of Provincial Life* (New York: Random House, 1957)

—, *The Letters of Gustave Flaubert, 1830–1857* (London: Faber, 1981)

—, *The Letters of Gustave Flaubert, 1857–1880* (London: Faber, 1984)

—, *Flaubert in Egypt* (Harmondsworth: Penguin, 1996)

Geoffrey Wall, *Madame Bovary: Provincial Lives* (Harmondsworth: Penguin, 1992)

—, *Selected Letters* (London: Penguin, 1997)

Roger Whitehouse, *Three Tales* (London: Penguin, 2005)

Suggestions for further reading

Jonathan Culler, *Flaubert: The Uses of Uncertainty* (Ithaca: Cornell University Press, 1985)

Anne Green, *Flaubert and the Historical Novel: Salammbô Reassessed* (Cambridge: Cambridge University Press, 1982)

Stephen Heath, *Madame Bovary* (Cambridge: Cambridge University Press, 1992)

Herbert Lottman, *Flaubert: A Biography* (London: Methuen, 1989)

Jean-Paul Sartre, *The Family Idiot*, trans. Carol Cosman, 5 vols. (Chicago: University of Chicago Press, 1981–93)

Enid Starkie, *Flaubert the Master* (London: Weidenfeld, 1971)

Timothy Unwin, ed., *Cambridge Companion to Flaubert* (Cambridge: Cambridge University Press, 2005)

Geoffrey Wall, *Flaubert: A Life* (London: Faber, 2001)

Théophile Gautier (1811–72)

English translations

Anon., *Mademoiselle de Maupin: A Romance of Love and Passion* (London: Vizetelly, 1887)

Helen Constantine, *Mademoiselle de Maupin* (London: Penguin, 2005)

Brian Hill, *The Gentle Enchanter: Thirty-Four Poems* (London: Rupert Hart-Davis, 1960)

George Burnham Ives, *The Romances of Théophile Gautier*, 10 vols. (Boston: Little Brown, 1903)

R. and E. Powys Mathers, *Mademoiselle de Maupin* (London: Cassell, 1948)

Joanna Richardson, *Mademoiselle de Maupin* (Harmondsworth: Penguin, 1981)

Brian Stableford, *Clarimond and Other Stories* (Leyburn: Tartarus, 2011)

F.C. Sumichrast, *The Complete Works of Théophile Gautier*, 24 vols. (New York: George D. Sprout, 1900–1901)

M. Young, *The Romance of a Mummy* (London: J. & R. Maxwell, 1886)

Suggestions for further reading

Maxime Du Camp, *Théophile Gautier*, trans. J.E. Gordon (Freeport, NY: Books for Libraries, 19710)

Christopher Prendergast, ed., *Nineteenth-Century French Poetry* (Cambridge: Cambridge University Press, 1990)

Joanna Richardson, *Théophile Gautier: His Life and Times* (London: Max Reinhardt, 1958)

Constance Gosselin Schick, *Seductive Resistance: The Poetry of Théophile Gautier* (Amsterdam: Rodopi, 1994)

Enid Starkie, *From Gautier to Eliot: The Influence of France on English Literature 1851–1939* (London: Hutchinson, 1960)

Jules de Goncourt (1830–70) and Edmond de Goncourt (1822–96)

English translations

Anon., *Germinie Lacerteux: A Realistic Novel* (London: Vizetelly, 1887)

Anon., *Renée Mauperin* (London: Vizetelly, 1888)

Robert Baldick, *Pages from the Goncourt Journals* (London: Oxford University Press, 1962)

George Becker and Edith Philips, *Paris and the Arts, 1851–1896: From the Goncourt Journal* (Ithaca: Cornell University Press, 1971)

Ernest Boyd, *Germinie Lacerteux* (New York: Knopf, 1922)

John Chestershire, *Germinie Lacerteux* (Philadelphia: G. Barrie, 1897)

Lewis Galantière, *The Goncourt Journals, 1851–1870* (New York: Doubleday, 1937)

Robin Ironside, *French Eighteenth Century Painters* (New York: Phaidon, 1948)

Leonard Tancock, *Germinie Lacerteux* (New York: Penguin Viking, 1984)

Suggestions for further reading

Katherine Ashley, *Edmond de Goncourt and the Novel: Naturalism and Decadence* (Amsterdam: Rodopi, 2005)

Robert Baldick, *The Goncourts* (London: Bowes & Bowes, 1960)

Richard B. Grant, *The Goncourt Brothers* (New York: Twayne, 1972)

Joris-Karl Huysmans (1848–1907)

English translations

Alfred Allison, *Down There* [Là-bas] (Paris: Groves and Michaux, 1928)

Anon., *Against the Grain* [À Rebours] (Paris: Groves and Michaux, 1926)

James Babcock, *The Vatard Sisters* (Lexington: University Press of Kentucky, 1983)

Robert Baldick, *Against Nature* [À Rebours] (Harmondsworth: Penguin, 1959)

Clara Bell, *The Cathedral* (London: Kegan Paul & Co., 1898)

Terry Hale, *The Damned* [Là-bas] (Harmondsworth: Penguin, 2001)

John Howard, *Against the Grain* [À Rebours] (New York: Lieber and Lewis, 1922)

Wallis Keene, *Down There* [Là-bas] (New York: Boni, 1924)

Brendan King, *The Vatard Sisters* (Sawtry: Dedalus, 2012)

—, *Marthe, the Story of a Whore* (Sawtry: Dedalus, 2006)

—, *Against Nature* [À Rebours] (Sawtry: Dedalus, 2008)

Margaret Mauldon, *Against Nature*, intr. Nicholas White (Oxford: Oxford University Press, 1998)

Charles Kegan Paul, *En Route* (London: Kegan Paul, Trench, Trübner & Co., 1897)

Edward Percival, *The Oblat* (London: Kegan Paul Trench Trübner, 1924)

W. Fleming, *En Route* (Sawtry: Dedalus, 2002)

Suggestions for further reading

Robert Baldick, *The Life of J.-K. Huysmans* (1955: new edition revised by Brendan King, Sawtry: Dedalus Books, 2006)

Brian R. Banks, *The Image of Huysmans* (New York: AMS Press, 1990)

Barbara Beaumont, ed., *The Road from Decadence* (London: Athlone Press, 1989)

Jennifer Birkett, *The Sins of the Fathers: Decadence in France, 1870–1914* (New York: Quartet, 1984)

Christopher Lloyd, *J.-K. Huysmans and the Fin-de-siècle Novel* (Edinburgh: Edinburgh University Press, 1990)

Patrice Locmant, *J.-K. Huysmans, le forçat de la vie* (Paris: Bartillat, 2007)

Jules Laforgue (1860–87)

English translations

Peter Dale, *Poems of Jules Laforgue* (London: Anvil Press, 1986)

Graham Dunstan Martin, *Selected Poems* (Harmondsworth: Penguin, 1998)

Frances Newman, *Six Moral Tales from Jules Laforgue* (New York: Liveright, 1928)

Wiliam Jay Smith, *Selected Writings of Jules Laforgue* (Westport, CT: Greenwood Press, 1956)

Patricia Terry, *Poems of Jules Laforgue* (Berkeley: University of California Press, 1958)

Suggestions for further reading

David Arkell, *Looking for Laforgue: An Informal Biography* (Manchester: Carcanet, 1979)

Michael Collie, *Laforgue* (Edinburgh: Oliver and Boyd, 1963)

Warren Ramsey, *Jules Laforgue and the Ironic Inheritance* (Oxford: Oxford University Press, 1953)

Warren Ramsey, ed., *Jules Laforgue: Essays on a Poet's Life and Works* (Carbondale: South Illinois University Press, 1969)

Maurice Maeterlinck (1862–1949)

English translations

Laurence Alma-Tadema, *Pelleas and Melisanda and The Sightless* (London: Scott, 1892)

William Archer, *Interior* (London: Gowan's International Library, 1908)

Francis Booth, *Five Marionette Plays* (n.p.: Lulu.com, 2010)

Gerard Harry, *The Princess Maleine* ([London]: Heinemann, 1892)

Richard Hovey, *The Plays of Maurice Maeterlinck (Princess Maleine, The Intruder, The Blind, Seven Princesses)* (Chicago: Herbert Stone, 1904)

J.T. Stoddart, *Ruysbroeck and the Mystics* (London: Hodder & Stoughton, 1894)

Alfred Sutro, *The Treasure of the Humble* (London: George Allen, 1897)

—, *Aglavaine and Selysette* (London: Grant Richards, 1897)

—, *Wisdom and Destiny* (London: George Allen, 1899)

—, *The Death of Tintagiles* (London: Gowans and Gray, 1899)

—, *Alladine and Palomides* (Glasgow: Gowan, 1907)

Alexander Teixeira de Mattos, *Life and Flowers* (London: George Allen, 1907)

E. Winslow, *Pélleas and Mélisande* (New York: Crowell, 1894)

Suggestions for further reading

May Daniels, *The French Drama of the Unspoken* (Edinburgh: Edinburgh University Press, 1953)

W.D. Halls, *Maurice Maeterlinck: A Study of His Life and Thought* (Oxford: Oxford University Press, 1960)

Bettina Knapp, *Maurice Maeterlinck* (Boston: Twayne, 1975)

Patrick McGuinness, *Maurice Maeterlinck and the Making of Modern Theatre* (Oxford: Oxford University Press, 2000)

Arnaud Rykner, *Maurice Maeterlinck* (Paris and Rome: Memini, 1998)

Stéphane Mallarmé (1842–98)

English translations

A.M. Blackmore, *Collected Poems and Other Verse*, intr. Elizabeth McCombie (Oxford: Oxford University Press, 2008)

Brian Coffey, *Poems of Mallarmé* (Dublin: New Writers' Press, 1990)

Bradford Cook, *Selected Prose Poems, Essays and Letters* (Baltimore: Johns Hopkins University Press, 1956)

Arthur Ellis, *Stéphane Mallarmé in English Verse* (London: Jonathan Cape, 1927)

Roger Fry, *Poems* (London: Chatto and Windus, 1936)

Anthony Hartley, *Mallarmé* (Harmondsworth: Penguin, 1965)

Barbara Johnson, *Divagations* (Cambridge, MA: Belknap, 2007)

Rosemary Lloyd, ed., *Selected Letters of Stéphane Mallarmé* (Chicago: University of Chicago Press, 1988)

C.F. MacIntyre, *Selected Poems* (Berkeley: University of California Press, 1957)

Peter Manson, *Stéphane Mallarmé: The Poems in Verse* (Oxford, OH: Miami University Press, 2012)

Patrick McGuinness, *For Anatole's Tomb* (Manchester: Carcanet, 2003)

Henry Weinfield, *Collected Poems* (Berkeley: University of California Press, 1994)

Suggestions for further reading

Leo Bersani, *The Death of Stéphane Mallarmé* (Cambridge: Cambridge University Press, 1982)

Harold Bloom, ed., *Stéphane Mallarmé* (New York: Chelsea House, 1987)

Malcolm Bowie, *Mallarmé and the Art of Being Difficult* (Cambridge: Cambridge University Press, 1978)

Heath Lees, *Mallarmé and Wagner: Music and Poetic Language* (Aldershot: Ashgate, 2007)

Rosemary Lloyd, *Mallarmé: The Poet and his Circle* (Ithaca, NY: Cornell University Press, 1999)

Elizabeth McCombie, *Mallarmé and Debussy: Unheard Music, Unseen Text* (Oxford: Oxford University Press, 2003)

Roger Pearson, *Stéphane Mallarmé (Critical Lives)* (London: Reaktion Books, 2010)

Graham Robb, *Unlocking Mallarmé* (New Haven: Yale University Press, 1996)

Prosper Mérimée (1803–70)

English translations

W.J. Cobb, *Carmen, Colomba and Selected Stories* (New York: Signet, 1963)

Jean Kimber, *The Venus of Ille and other Stories* (Oxford: Oxford University Press, 1966)

Lady Mary Loyd, *Columbia and Carmen* (London: William Heinemann, 1901)

Nicholas Jotcham, *Carmen and Other Stories* (Oxford: Oxford University Press, 1989)

Edward Marielle, *Carmen and Colomba* (Harmondsworth: Penguin, 1965)

Douglas Parmée, *A Slight Misunderstanding* [Une Double Méprise] (London: John Calder, 1959)

—, *The Etruscan Vase and Other Stories* (Richmond: Alma Classics, 2012)

Nadine S. Peppard, *The Venus of Ille and the Blue Room* (London: George G. Harrap & Co., 1948)

Suggestions for further reading

F.P. Bowman, *Prosper Mérimée: Heroism, Pessimism and Irony* (Berkeley: University of California Press, 1962)

R.C. Dale, *The Poetics of Prosper Mérimée* (The Hague and Paris: Mouton, 1966)

A.J. George, *Short Fiction in France 1800–50* (New York: Syracuse University Press, 1964)

A.W. Raitt, *Prosper Mérimée* (London: Eyre & Spottiswoode, 1970)

Gérard de Nerval (1808–55)

English translations

Richard Aldington, *Aurelia* (London: Chatto and Windus, 1932)

Norman Glass, *Journey to the Orient* (London: Peter Owen, 1972)

Brian Hill, *Fortune's Fool: Thirty-Five Poems by Gérard de Nerval* (London: Rupert Hart-Davis, 1959)

Vyvyan Holland, *Dreams and Life / La Rève et la vie* (London: First Edition Club, 1933)

Peter Jay, *Les Chimères: The Chimeras* (London: Anvil Press, 1984)

Derek Mahon, *The Chimeras* (Dublin: Gallery Press, 1982)

Richard Sieburth, *Selected Writings of Gérard de Nerval* (Harmondsworth: Penguin, 1999)

Geoffrey Wagner, *Selected Writings of Gérard de Nerval* (London: Peter Owen, 1958)

James Whitall, *Daughters of Fire: Sylvie-Emilie-Octavie* (London: Heinemann, 1923)

Suggestions for further reading

Jacques Bony, *Le Récit nervalien* (Paris: Corti, 1990)

Claire Gilbert, *Nerval's Double: A Structural Study* (Missouri: Romance Monographs, 1979)

Bettina Knapp, *Gérard de Nerval: The Mystic's Dilemma* (Tuscaloosa: University of Alabama Press, 1980)

Kari Lokke, *Gérard de Nerval: The Poet as Social Visionary* (Lexington: French Forum, 1987)

David Miller, *There and Here: A Meditation on Gérard de Nerval* (Frome: Bran's Head, 1982)

Claude Pichois and Michel Brix, *Gérard de Nerval* (Paris: Fayard, 1995)

Norma Rinsler, *Gérard de Nerval* (London: Athlone Press, 1973)

Arthur Rimbaud (1854–91)

English translations

John Ashbery, *Illuminations* (Manchester: Carcanet, 2011)

Oliver Bernard, *Rimbaud: Collected Poems* (London: Penguin, 1962)

Norman Cameron, *Selected Verse Poems of Arthur Rimbaud* (London: Hogarth Press, 1942)

Jeremy Harding, *Arthur Rimbaud: Selected Poems and Letters*, intr. John Sturrock (London: Penguin, 2004)

Wyatt Mason, *Rimbaud Complete*, 2 vols. (London: Scribner, 2002)

Ezra Pound, *The Translations of Ezra Pound* (London: Faber, 1953)

Edith Rhodes Peschel, *A Season in Hell with Illuminations* (Oxford:

Oxford University Press, 1973)

Edgell Rickword, *Rimbaud: The Boy and the Poet* (London: Heinemann, 1924)

Paul Schmidt, *Arthur Rimbaud: Complete Works* (New York: Harper and Row, 1975)

Mark Treharne, *A Season in Hell, with Illuminations* (London: Dent, 1998)

Louise Varèse, *Prose Poems from 'The Illuminations'* (New York: New Directions, 1946)

Suggestions for further reading

R.G. Cohn, *The Poetry of Rimbaud* (Columbia: University of South Carolina Press, 1973)

Karin J. Dillman, *The Subject in Rimbaud: From Self to 'Je'* (New York: Peter Lang, 1984)

James Lawler, *Rimbaud's Theatre of the Self* (Cambridge, MA: Harvard University Press, 1992)

Graham Robb, *Rimbaud: A Biography* (London: Picador, 2000)

Edmund White, *Rimbaud: The Double Life of a Rebel* (London: Grove, 2008)

Paul Verlaine (1844–96)

English translations

Gertrude Hall, *Poems of Paul Verlaine* (Chicago: Stone and Kimball, 1895)

Jacques Le Clercq, *Poems* (Westport, CT: Greenwood Press, 1977)

C.F. MacIntyre, *Selected Poems* (Berkeley: University of California Press, 1948)

Joanna Richardson, *Selected Poems* (Harmondsworth: Penguin, 1974)

Norman Shapiro, *One Hundred and One Poems by Paul Verlaine* (Chicago: University of Chicago Press, 1999)

Martin Sorrell, *Selected Poems* (Oxford: Oxford University Press, 1999)

A. Wrigate, *Paul-Marie Verlaine, Poems Selected and Translated by A. Wrigate* (London: Canterbury Poets, 1904)

Suggestions for further reading

A.E. Carter, *Paul Verlaine* (New York: Twayne, 1971)

David Hillery, *Verlaine: Fixing an Image* (Durham: University of Durham Press, 1988)

James R. Lawler, *The Language of French Symbolism* (Princeton: Princeton University Press, 1969)

Joanna Richardson, *Verlaine* (London: Weidenfeld and Nicolson, 1971)

V.P. Underwood, *Verlaine et l'Angleterre* (Paris: Librairie Nizet, 1956)

Émile Zola (1840–1902)

English translations

Anon., *The 'Assommoir': A Realistic Novel* (London: Vizetelly, 1884)

Anon., *Nana* (London: Vizetelly, 1884)

Anon., *Germinal, or Master and Man: A Realistic Novel* (London: Vizetelly, 1885)

Anon., *Piping Hot!* [Pot-Bouille] (London: Vizetelly, 1885)

Anon., *The Fortune of the Rougeons: A Realistic Novel* (London: Vizetelly, 1886)

Anon., *The Rush for the Spoil* [La Curée] (London: Vizetelly, 1886)

Anon., *Thérèse Raquin: A Realistic Novel* (London: Vizetelly, 1887)

Anon., *The Fat and the Thin* [Le Ventre de Paris] (London: Vizetelly, 1888)

Anon., *The Soil* [La Terre] (London: Vizetelly, 1888)

Frank Belmont, *The Ladies' Paradise* [Au Bonheur des dames] (London: Tinsley Bros., 1883)

Andrew Brown, *The Dream* (London: Hesperus, 2005)

Robin Buss, *Thérèse Raquin* (Harmondsworth: Penguin, 2004)

—, *The Ladies' Delight* [Au Bonheur des dames] (Harmondsworth: Penguin, 2001)

—, *The Dram Shop* [L'Assommoir] (Harmondsworth: Penguin, 2000)

Peter Collier, *Germinal* (Oxford: Oxford World's Classics, 1993)

G.D. Cox, *The Soil* [La Terre] (Philadelphia: T.B. Peterson & Bros., c.1888)

—, *The Human Beast* [La Bête Humaine] (Philadelphia: T.B. Peterson & Bros., 1891)

Elinor Dorday, *La Débâcle* (Oxford: Oxford University Press, 2000)

Ernest Dowson, *La Terre* (London: Lutetian Society, 1895)

Havelock Ellis, *Germinal* (London: Lutetian Society, 1894)

S.J. Adair Fitzgerald, *Drink: Adapted from the 'L'Assommoir' of E. Zola* (London: Greening & Co., 1903)

April Fitzlyon, *The Ladies' Delight* [Au Bonheur des dames] (London: John Calder, 1957)

Michael Glencross, *The Dream* [Le Rêve] (London: Peter Owen, 2005)

Gerard Hopkins, *The Dram Shop* [L'Assommoir] (London: Hamish Hamilton, 1951)

David Hughes and Marie-Jacqueline Mason, *Savage Paris* [Le Ventre de Paris] (London: Elek Books, 1955)

Joseph Keating, *Nana* (London: Cecil Palmer, 1926)

Margaret Mauldon, *L'Assommoir* (Oxford: Oxford University Press, 1995)

Brian Nelson, *The Ladies' Paradise* [Au Bonheur des dames] (Oxford:

Oxford University Press, 1995)

—, *Pot Luck* [Pot-Bouille] (Oxford: Oxford University Press, 1999)

—, *The Kill* [La Curée] (Oxford: Oxford University Press, 2004)

—, *The Belly of Paris* (Oxford: Oxford University Press, 2007)

—, *The Fortune of the Rougons* (Oxford: Oxford University Press, 2012)

Douglas Parmée, *The Earth* [La Terre] (Harmondsworth: Penguin, 1980)

—, *The Attack on the Mill and Other Stories* (Oxford: Oxford University Press, 1984)

—, *Nana* (Oxford: Oxford University Press, 1992)

Roger Pearson, *La Bête humaine* (Oxford: Oxford University Press, 1996)

—, *Germinal* (London: Penguin, 2004)

Percy Pinkerton, *Pot-Bouille* (London: Lutetian Society, 1895)

Victor Plarr, *Nana* (London: Lutetian Society, 1894)

Andrew Rothwell, *Thérèse Raquin* (Oxford: Oxford University Press, 1992)

Mary Neal Sherwood, *L'assommoir* (Philadelphia: T.B. Peterson & Bros., 1879)

—, *La Belle Lisa: or, the Paris Market Girls* [Le Ventre de Paris] (Philadelphia: T.B. Peterson & Bros., 1882)

—, *Shop Girls of Paris* [Au Bonheur des dames] (Philadelphia: T.B. Peterson & Bros., 1883)

Arthur Symons, *The Drunkard* [L'Assommoir] (London: Walter Scott, 1884)

Leonard Tancock, *Germinal* (Harmondsworth: Penguin, 1954

—, *L'Assommoir* (Harmondsworth: Penguin, 1970)

A. Teixeira de Mattos, *The Kill* [La Curée] (London: Lutetian Society, 1895)

Albert Vandam, *Germinal* (London: Vizetelly, 1886)

Edward Vizetelly, *Thérèse Raquin* (London: Vizetelly, 1887)

—, *The Monomaniac* [La Bête Humaine] (London: Hutchinson, 1901)

Thomas Watson and Roger Pearson, *The Masterpiece* (Oxford: Oxford University Press, 1993)

Suggestions for further reading

David Baguley, *Naturalist Fiction: The Entropic Vision* (Cambridge: Cambridge University Press, 1990)

Frederick Brown, *Zola, A Life* (London: Macmillan, 1996)

Anthony Cummins, 'Émile Zola's Cheap English Dress: The Vizetelly Translations, Late Victorian Print Culture and the Crisis of Literary Value', *Review of English Studies* 60 (2008): 108–32

Graham King, *Garden of Zola: Emile Zola and his Novels for English Readers* (London: Barrie and Jenkins, 1978)

Harry Levin, *The Gates of Horn: A Study of Five French Realists* (New

York: Oxford University Press, 1963)

Brian Nelson, *Zola and the Bourgeoisie* (London: Macmillan, 1983)

Brian Nelson, ed., *Cambridge Companion to Zola* (Cambridge: Cambridge University Press, 2007)

R. Lethbridge and T. Keefe, eds., *Zola and the Craft of Fiction* (Leicester: Leicester University Press, 1990)

Henri Mitterand, *Le Discours du roman* (Paris: Presses Universitaires de France, 1980)

Naomi Schor, *Zola's Crowds* (Baltimore: Johns Hopkins University Press, 1978)

Angus Wilson, *Zola: An Introductory Study of his Novels* (London: William Morrow, 1952)